GREYHOUND BUSES
1914 THROUGH 2000 PHOTO ARCHIVE

William A. Luke

Iconografix
Photo Archive Series

Iconografix
PO Box 446
Hudson, Wisconsin 54016 USA

© 2000 William A. Luke

All rights reserved. No part of this work may be reproduced or used in any form by any means... graphic, electronic, or mechanical, including photocopying, recording, taping, or any other information storage and retrieval system... without written permission of the publisher.

The information in this book is true and complete to the best of our knowledge. All recommendations are made without any guarantee on the part of the author or Publisher, who also disclaim any liability incurred in connection with the use of this data or specific details.

We acknowledge that certain words, such as model names and designations, mentioned herein are the property of the trademark holder. We use them for purposes of identification only. This is not an official publication.

Iconografix books are offered at a discount when sold in quantity for promotional use. Businesses or organizations seeking details should write to the Marketing Department, Iconografix, at the above address.

Library of Congress Card Number: 00-132397

ISBN 1-58388-027-5

00 01 02 03 04 05 06 5 4 3 2 1

Printed in the United States of America

Cover and book design by Shawn Glidden

Copy editing by Dylan Frautschi

Book Proposals

Iconografix is a publishing company specializing in books for transportation enthusiasts. We publish in a number of different areas, including Automobiles, Auto Racing, Buses, Construction Equipment, Emergency Equipment, Farming Equipment, Railroads & Trucks. The Iconografix imprint is constantly growing and expanding into new subject areas.

Authors, editors, and knowledgeable enthusiasts in the field of transportation history are invited to contact the Editorial Department at Iconografix, Inc., PO Box 446, Hudson, WI 54016.

Table of Contents

Acknowledgments 4
Foreword by Greyhound President 5
Introduction 6-7
Pioneer Greyhound Buses 8-15
Early Greyhound-named Buses 16-27
Greyhound Buses of the 1930s and 1940s.. 28-44
Greyhound Buses in the Movies 45-48
Small Greyhound Buses 49-56
World's Fair Buses 57-61
Greyhound Bus Stations 62-65
Buses of Companies Acquired by Greyhound and Affiliated Companies 66-75
Transit-type Greyhound Buses 76-79
Mid-20th Century Greyhound Buses 80-86
Experimental Greyhound Buses 87-89
Scenicruisers 90-94
Greyhound Buses Overseas 95-96
Final Greyhound General Motors Buses.. 97-98
Greyhound Motor Coach Industries Buses 99-109
Greyhound Buses in the 1980s and 1990s 110-111
Modern Greyhound Buses 112-119
Miscellaneous.. 120-125
    Greyhound Bus Origin Museum 120
    Restored Greyhound Buses 121-122
    Travel Brochures 123
    Timetables 124-125
A Word from the author 126

ACKNOWLEDGMENTS

Photographs in this book are from the bus history library of the author, William A. Luke, unless noted as photo credits from other individuals and organizations.

The following persons and organizations were very helpful in providing information that has made this book possible.

Donald Coffin, Greyhound Lines historian, Hawley, Pennsylvania

Gene Nicolelli, Curator, Greyhound Bus Origin Museum, Hibbing, Minnesota

Tom Jones, Librarian, Motor Bus Society, Clark, New Jersey

Paul Leger, President, Bus History Association, Halifax, Nova Scotia

Greyhound Lines, Dallas, Texas

Special mention should also be made to acknowledge the late Tom Van De Grift, who, for a number of years, presented many photographs (some of which are used in this book) to the library of William A. Luke and others.

FOREWORD

Greyhound Lines built a national network by making connections between cities and small towns all across America. We trace our roots to northern Minnesota in 1914, where an entrepreneur with a Hupmobile connected the town of Hibbing with the mines in nearby Alice.

Over the decades that followed, our company spread across 48 states, connecting thousands of urban and rural locations. We were the industry's first consolidator, growing in the period between World Wars I and II through acquisitions and mergers that involved hundreds of small local and regional carriers.

After the national network was completed, the company continued to expand for the rest of the 20th century. Revenues, for example, grew from $55 million in 1940 to $683 million in 1999. Passenger miles more than doubled in that time, to nearly eight billion annually.

We are particularly proud of two operating statistics from the same period. The average number of passengers per bus rose to 26.9, from 17.6, reflecting efficiencies throughout the system. And the modern bus travels 130,000 miles a year, 70 percent more than pre-war models.

At the turn of the new century, 86 years after the first trip, we were still growing and adding new destinations. After years of separation, the Greyhound Lines companies in the United States and Canada were once again under common ownership. The Greyhound networks of the two countries are being integrated to make it easier for the people of the two countries to visit each other.

At the same time, we have formed joint ventures to provide passenger service between the United States and Mexico.

In the process we are creating a true North American transportation network that will enable us to connect almost every city and town in Canada, the United States, and Mexico. Our goal is to provide the opportunity for anyone to travel between any two locations in these three countries with safety, dignity, and comfort.

This dynamic, growing bus operation known around the world as Greyhound with its famous running dog logo rests on a solid foundation. We treasure our heritage, which was built by thousands of dedicated Greyhound people over nearly a century.

Craig Lentzsch, President & CEO
Greyhound Lines, Inc.
Dallas, Texas

INTRODUCTION

Greyhound Lines, America's transcontinental bus line, serves 3,700 communities in the contiguous United States and in Canada. These communities include large metropolitan centers and many smaller communities.

The company's mission statement is: "Providing the opportunity for anyone to travel between any two cities in North America with safety, dignity, and convenience." Over the years, Greyhound has brought America together. It has given mobility to the country. Visiting friends and relatives in distant cities and rural areas has been made possible. Travelers, especially senior citizens, travel to see America's scenic and historic places. Young people find Greyhound convenient when attending colleges and universities, and Greyhound often has special weekend and holiday services direct to campuses. In recent years, Greyhound has provided important service to many airports.

Not only has the regular-route traveler benefited from Greyhound, but also groups wishing to charter buses to attend special events or tourist attractions are finding Greyhound a service fitting their needs. Greyhound's package express service is helpful to many businesses.

Greyhound Lines has had a rich, colorful history. The beginning goes back to 1914 when Carl Eric Wickman, Andrew Anderson, and several others began a "bus" service with a large Hupmobile touring car between Alice and Hibbing on Minnesota's Iron Range.

Commemorating Greyhound's 85th anniversary, the Greyhound Bus Origin Museum was opened in 1999 by the City of Hibbing and persons interested in preserving the history of this important company.

Many other bus lines began early in the century. California bus pioneers were especially active in the early days. In 1928, after a number of the pioneer bus companies had joined together, the Greyhound name was adopted with the running dog as the company logo. This running dog logo is one of the most recognized and enduring symbols anywhere.

Buses took on many forms in the industry's early days. At first large touring cars were used, and later the touring cars were lengthened to accommodate more passengers. Truck chassis were used with passenger bodies often built in the company workshops. Then came the enterprising Fageol brothers, who built the first purpose-built bus and called it the Safety Coach. Large bus building firms followed, and greater standardization resulted with Greyhound buses.

Greyhound helped develop buses. The goal to accommodate more passengers in one vehicle continues. However, in striving to achieve this goal, seating could not become crowded. That would discourage the public from riding. In the late 1920s, bus builders found that placing the engine over the front axle could increase passenger capacity. Law has always restricted the length of buses, although the length has been increased over the years. Today, the 45-foot length is the maximum.

During the depression years of the 1930s, Greyhound and bus manufacturers made a number of important developments in bus design and performance. The Super Coach was a special Greyhound design that heralded a new era in bus travel. The Super Coach had a high deck, which increased passenger capacity. It also had a rear engine and entrance door ahead of the front wheels. Before the end of the 1930s, diesel engines almost became a standard for Greyhound buses, along with air-conditioning. An equally innovative Silversides model followed the Super Coach.

Following World War II, Greyhound did some experimenting with bus design, including a double-deck version. However, a deck-and-a-half concept was eventually chosen. It was the Scenicruiser, and to many it was Greyhound's most famous bus. Today, Greyhound is introducing another, yet unnamed bus with an ultramodern design to begin the 21st Century.

Greyhound has done much to promote bus travel. Some of the first printed timetables with attractive covers were distributed in 1928. Travel brochures were published soon afterward. During the depression years, Greyhound made special efforts to promote travel by bus. When the Super Coach was introduced, it was presented with considerable publicity. The World's Fairs in Chicago in 1933 and New York in 1939 gave Greyhound some special opportunities. An attractive fare was introduced, and on the sides of many of the buses there was a colorful World's Fair decal by the front door. Greyhound also provided buses for transportation on World's Fair sites.

Greyhound's contribution during the war years was considered outstanding. Buses were used for troop movements throughout the country. In addition, Greyhound and other bus companies provided service to many defense plants and other important manufacturing sites. The war effort limited new-bus production, therefore maintaining the fleet was important. Stories of great efficiency of Greyhound employees and the buses during that time are numerous.

As bus transportation developed, buses required more maintenance. Garages were in many locations and service was required frequently. Today, because of the efficiency of the modern buses, as well as the skill of technicians and improved maintenance practices, buses don't require the attention that was necessary in years past. Today Greyhound has major maintenance garages in 14 strategic locations.

Greyhound has taken a leadership in establishing bus terminals. Some of the distinctive terminals of the 1930s in art deco style have been upgraded and continue to serve. New terminals offering more convenience and comfort for passengers have been built in recent years. With the modern growth in suburban locations, many Greyhound routes serve suburbs. At one time, Greyhound had a number of meal stop locations often in rural areas. These were known as Post Houses. Interstate highways and better scheduling have caused an elimination of a number of the Post House establishments in recent years.

Of the present 13,400 employees, more than 5,000 are drivers. The Greyhound driver, throughout the history of bus transportation, has been recognized for excellence in safety, driving ability, and courtesy. Each driver must fulfill the high standards Greyhound sets for its drivers. In addition, Greyhound drivers must comply with all the requirements set forth by government agencies.

Deregulation came in the 1980s and changed transportation. There were some difficult years for Greyhound, but after new ownership and management changes, Greyhound is moving forward in the 21st Century. The new owner of Greyhound is Laidlaw, Inc., a Canadian company that specializes in a number of transportation fields. It has been a positive move. There is a new and exciting future for Greyhound.

Pioneer Greyhound Buses

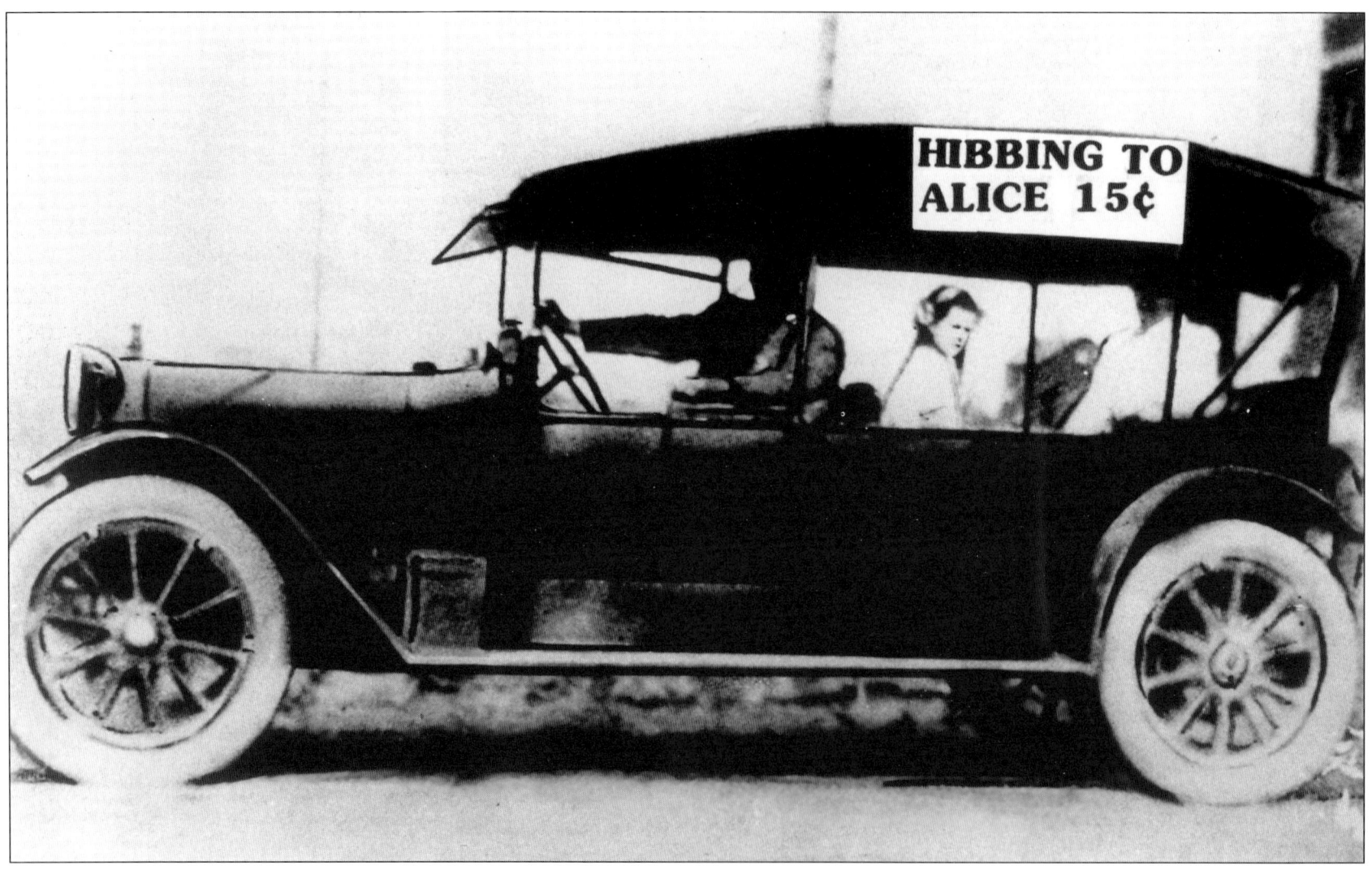

Carl Eric Wickman, the bus pioneer who went on to build the Greyhound empire and was its first president, operated this Hupmobile touring car as his first "bus." Partnering with Wickman when this bus service began in 1914 were Andy Anderson, Ralph Bogan, and Ed Ekstrom. The "bus" route was between Hibbing and Alice on Minnesota's Iron Range. The fare was 15 cents one way and 25 cents round trip. It quickly became a prosperous business. *Greyhound Bus Origin Museum*

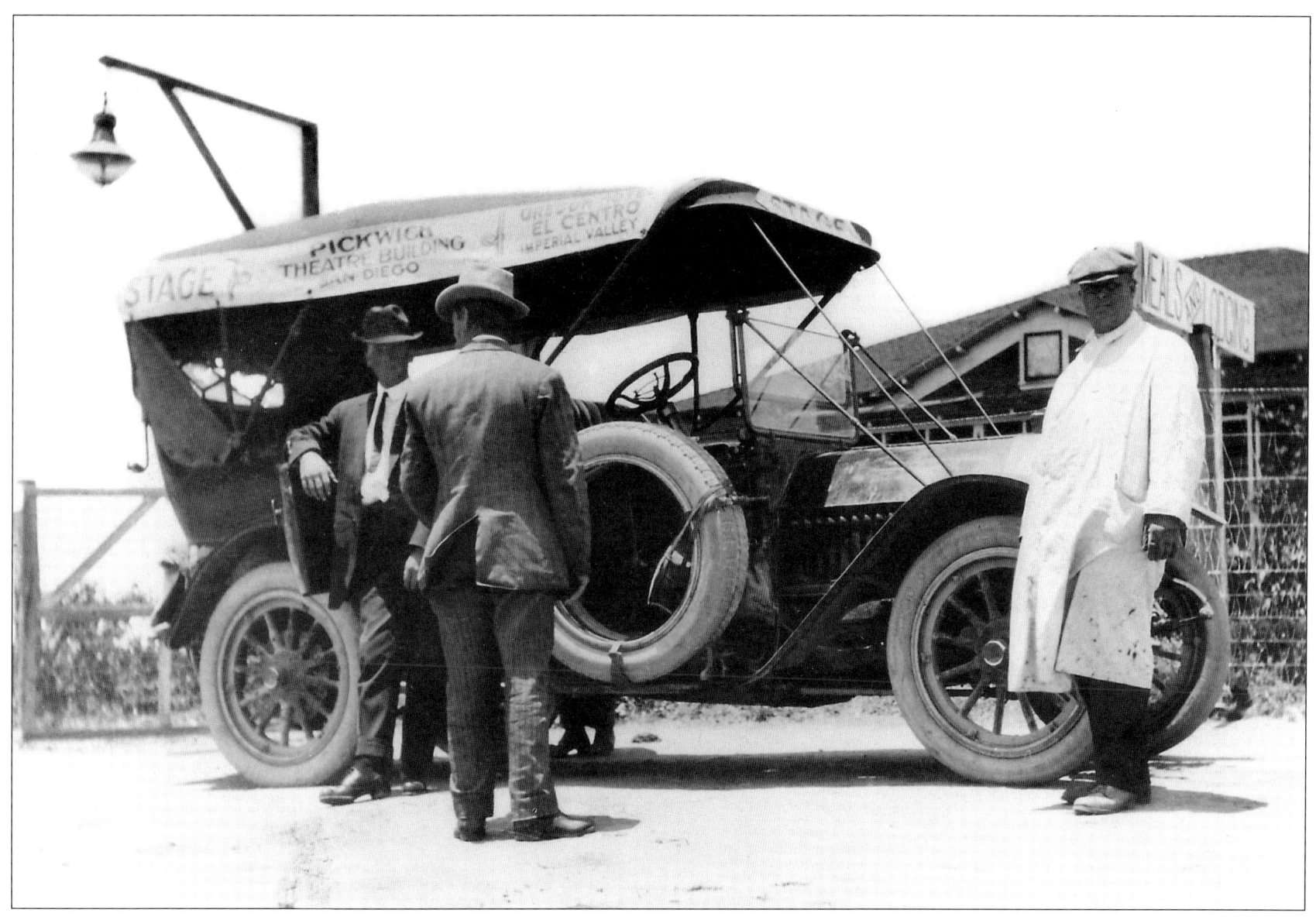

California was the center of early bus activities. Several companies merged to become Pickwick Stages, which eventually became Pickwick Greyhound Lines. An early California "bus" was this 1912 Locomobile touring car, pictured at the Warren Ranch rest stop in Campo, California. The "bus" carried nine passengers. The man on the right in this picture is Herbert B. Pattison, one of the bus pioneers in California.

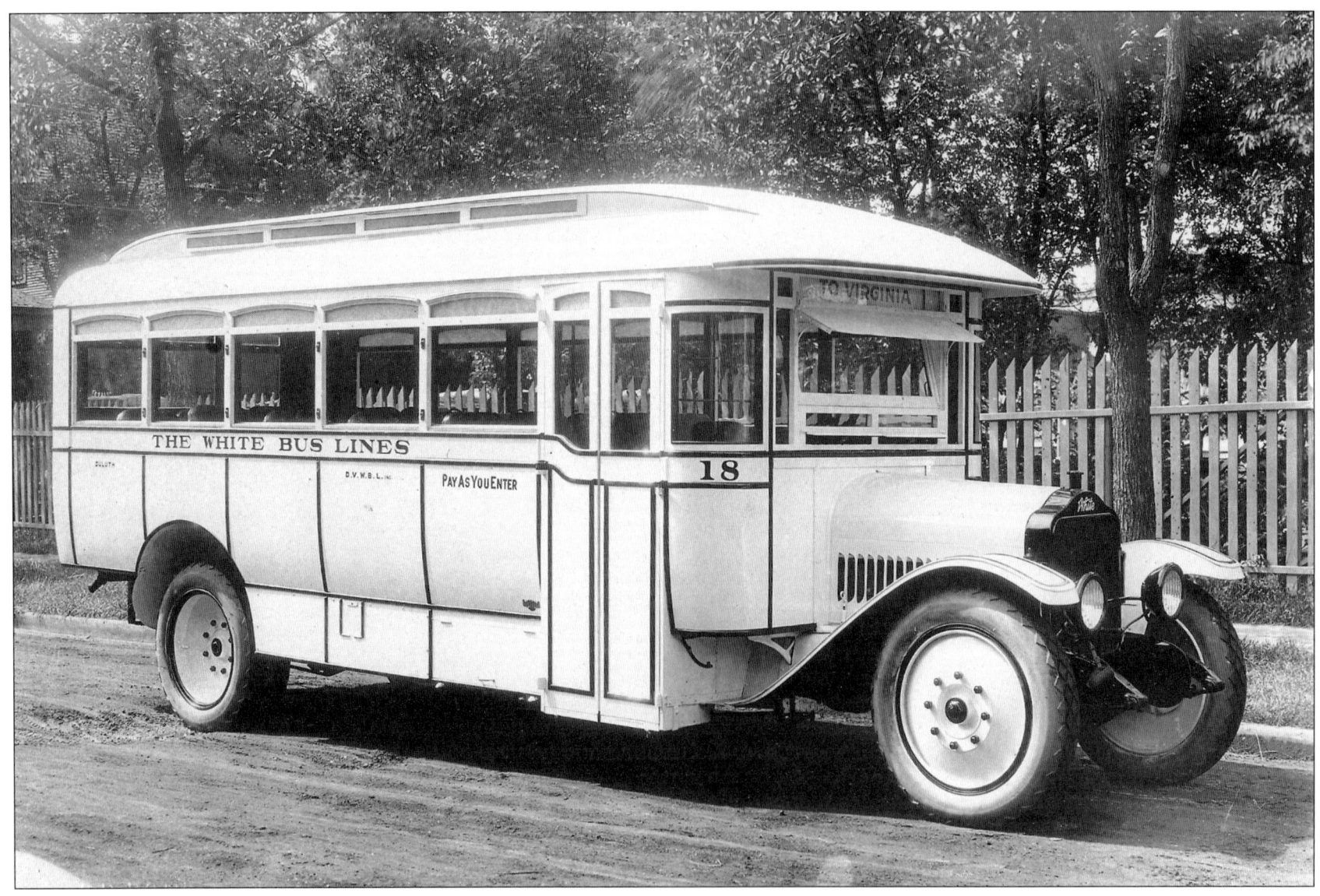

There was a scramble for 10 years or more after 1918 to start intercity bus lines. The White Bus Lines of Superior, Wisconsin, was one of the first. Heading the company was Orville Caesar. He later joined with Eric Wickman, who had begun a bus line in the Hibbing, Minnesota, area. The two were leaders in establishing Greyhound Lines. Also, bus manufacturers emerged. Eckland Brothers of Minneapolis began building buses, mainly on White truck chassis like number 18 shown here. Note the ventilation inlets at the roof, much like rail passenger cars of the day.

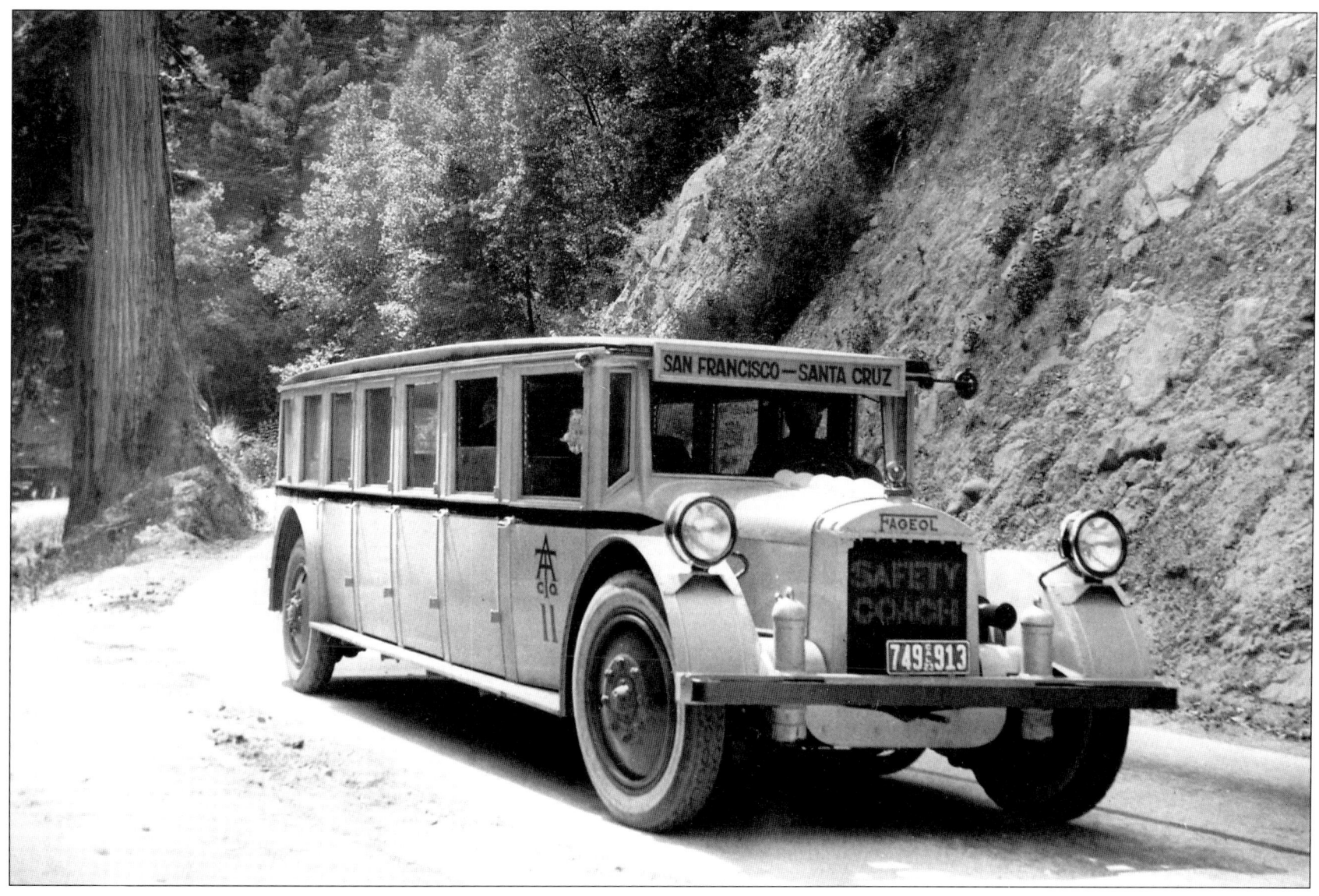

California bus operators were attracted to the Fageol Safety Coach. Auto Transit Company had this Safety Coach in 1923. It differed from the original Safety Coach design because it had an extended body. Four more passengers could be accommodated. Auto Transit Company's route became a part of Greyhound when a series of mergers and acquisitions took place.

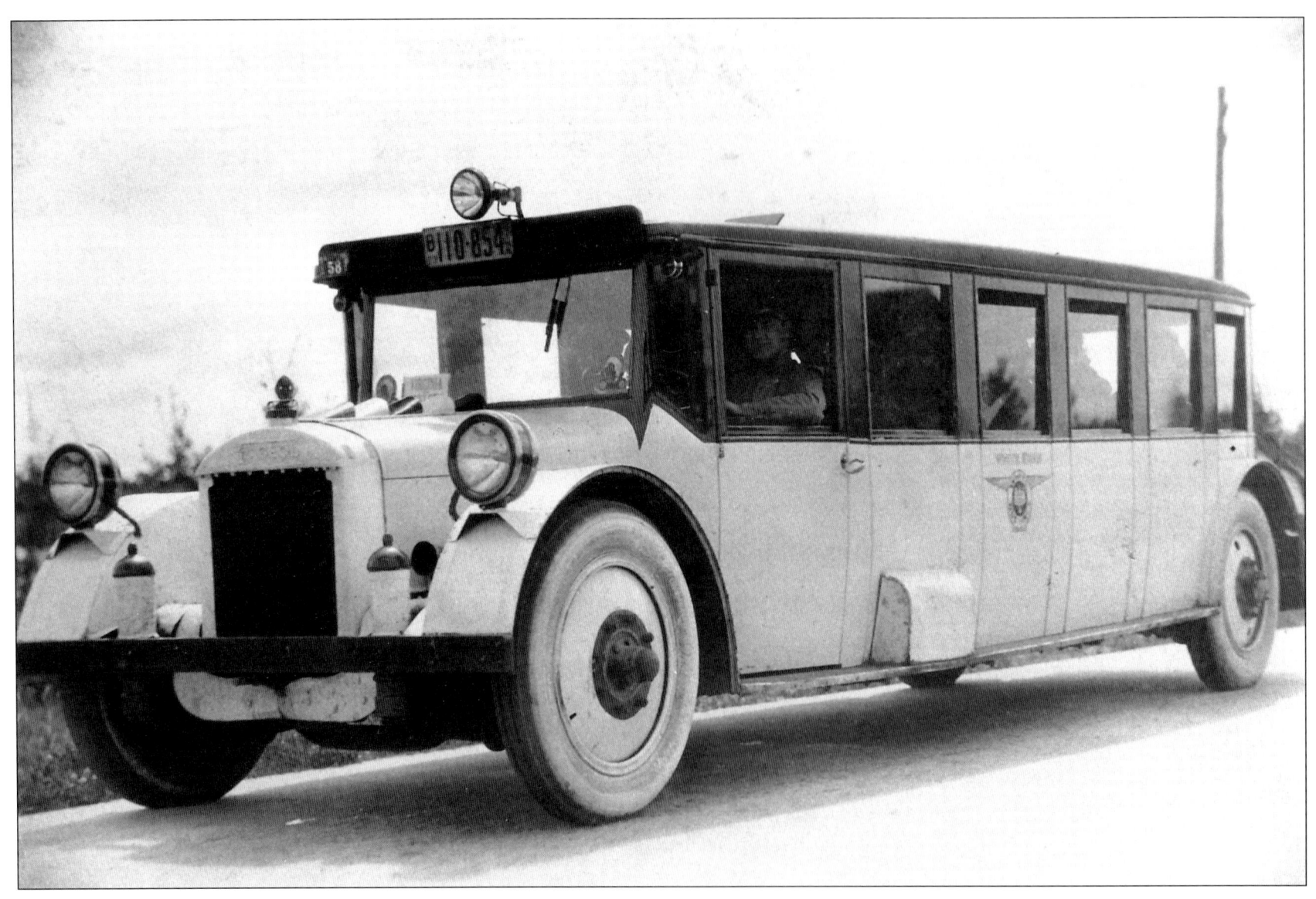

Frank R. and William B. Fageol had an idea for a purpose-built bus in the early 1920s. The result was the Fageol Safety Coach introduced in 1922. Orville Caesar, president of the White Bus Lines, saw the advantage of the Safety Coach and added several to the fleet. The new bus could seat 22 passengers. A Hall Scott four-cylinder engine was used. A truck chassis, popular with earlier buses, was not used. The louvers at the top of the hood were a distinct feature of the Fageol Safety Coach. The buses had a low center of gravity, thus the Safety Coach name.

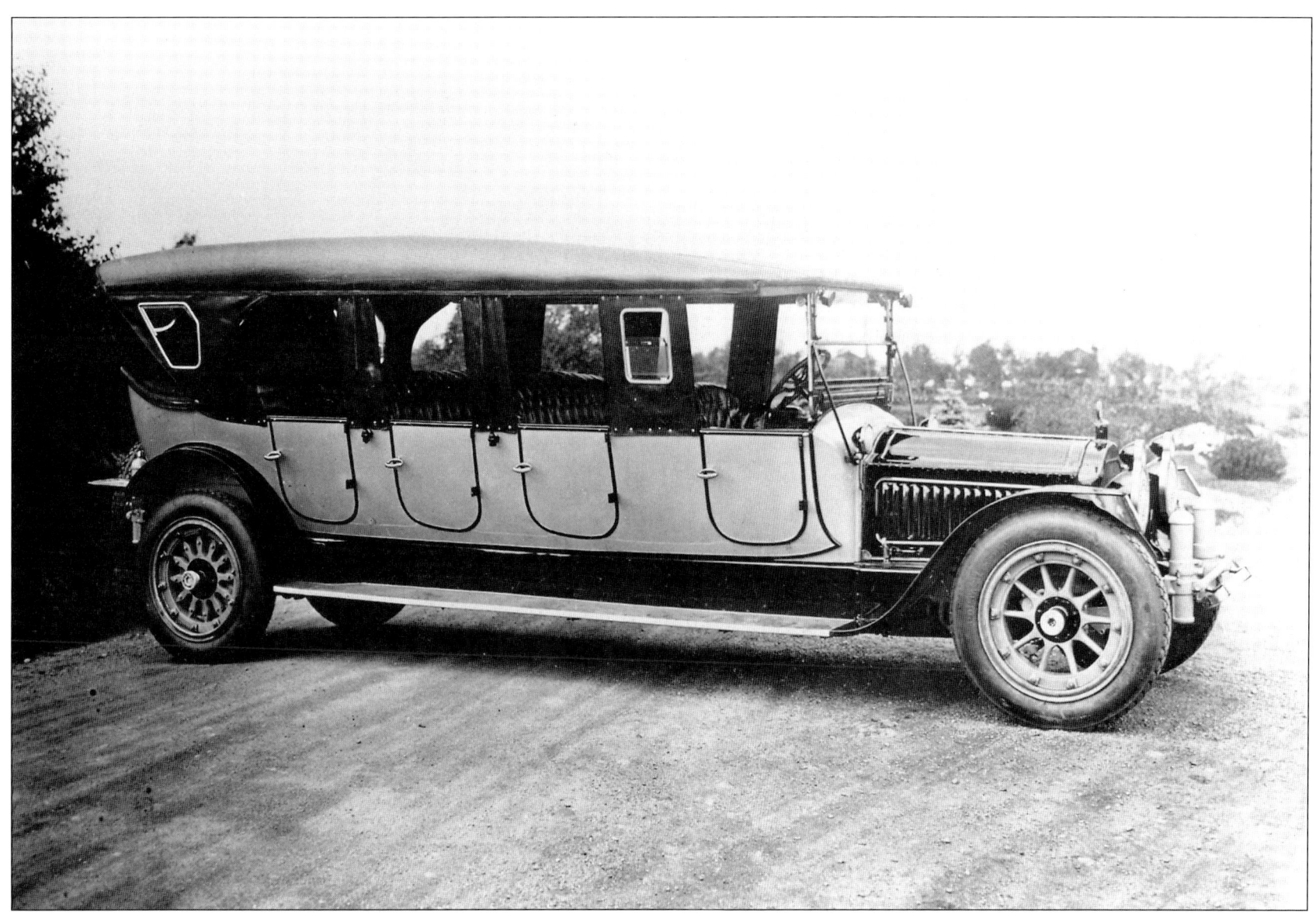

On a few occasions Packard touring cars were "stretched" to become buses. Heavy leather side curtains protected the passengers in the winter months. These side curtains could be removed. Motor Transit Lines operated this bus in the early 1920s between Hibbing and Duluth in northern Minnesota.

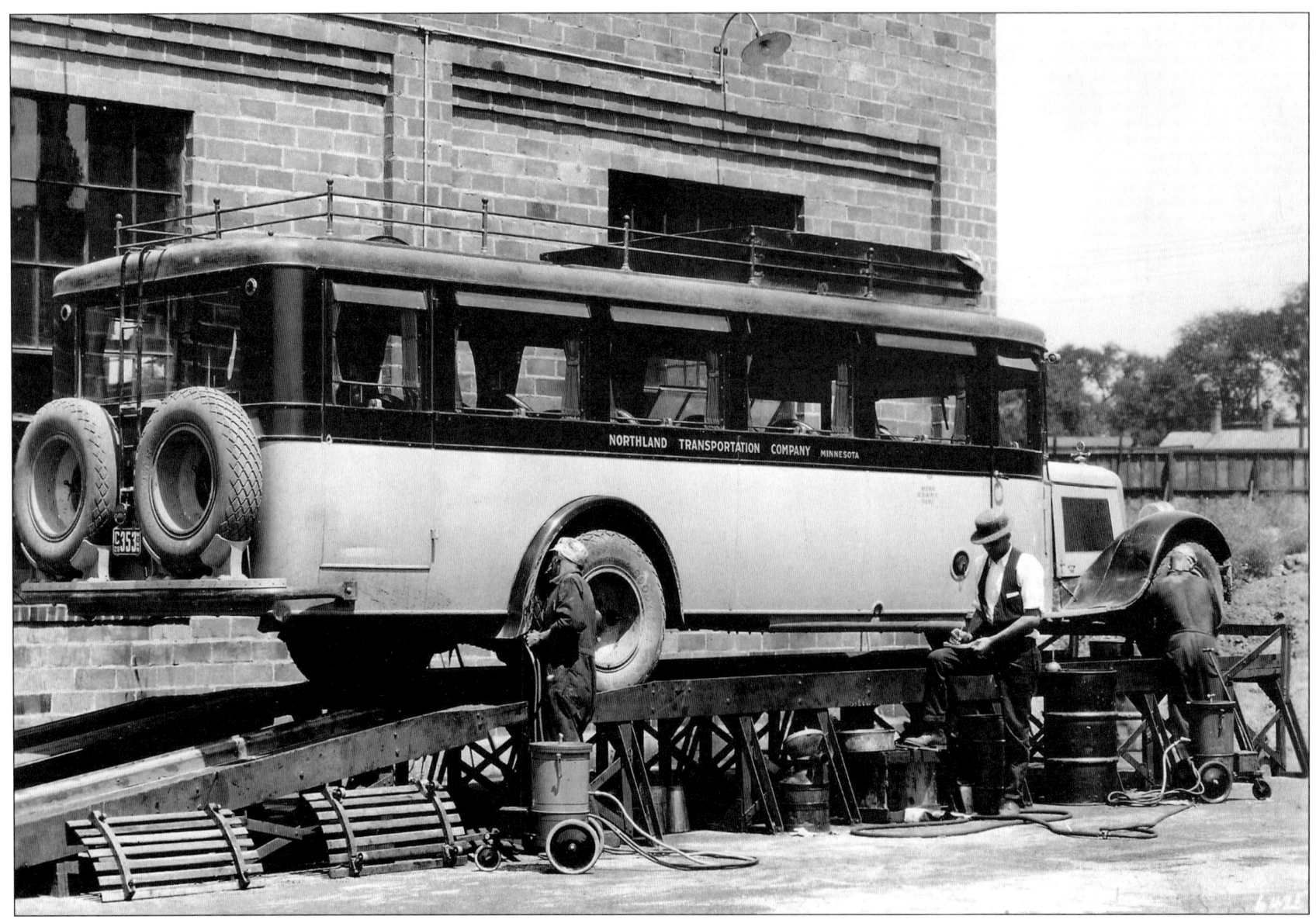

In this 1926 picture a Northland Transportation Company Will bus is shown being worked on by mechanics at one of the garages. Bus transportation grew rapidly in the 1920s and at some locations, maintenance was done outside in good weather. Note the two spare tires at the back of the bus, which was standard equipment on most buses of that day.

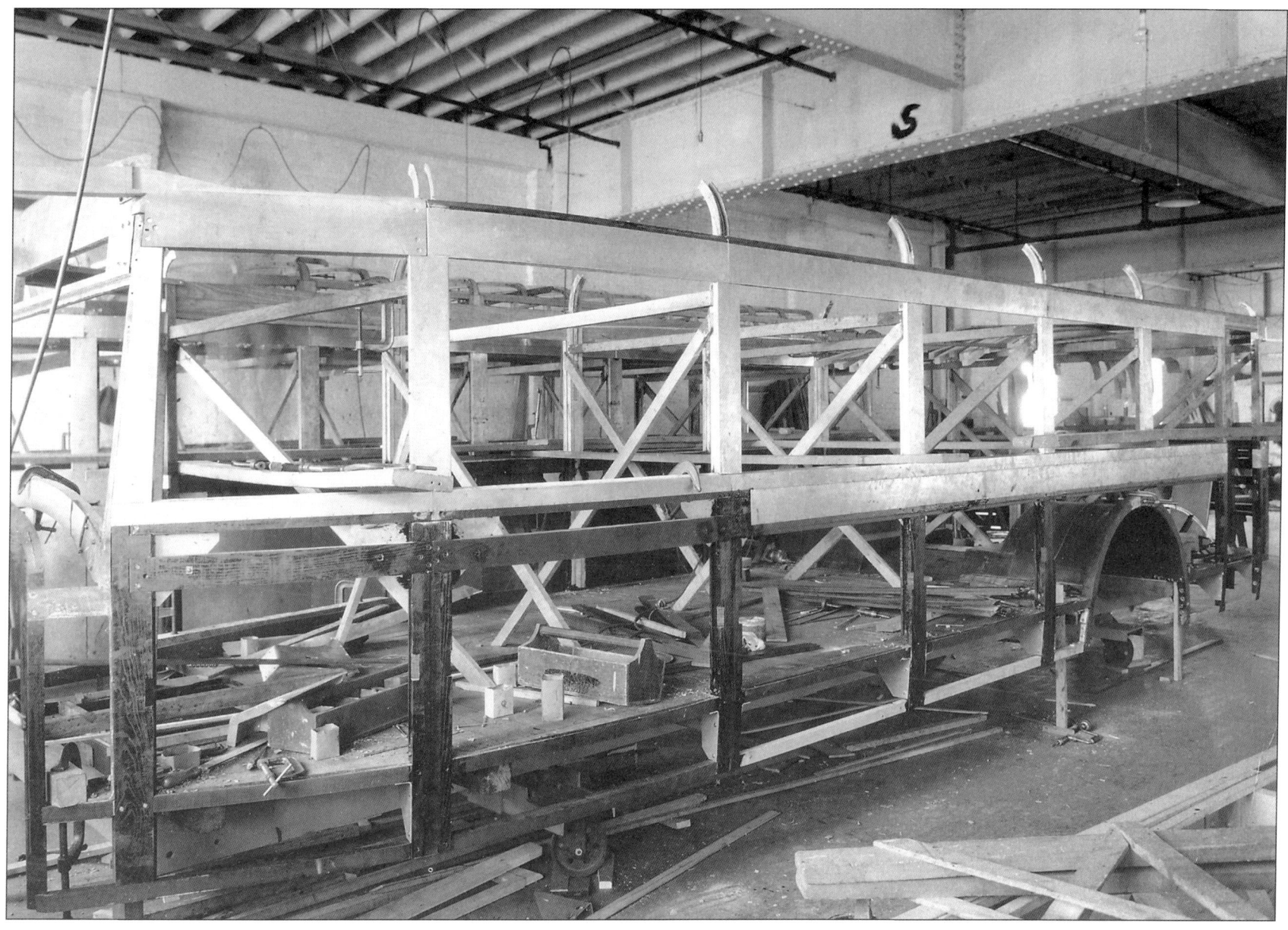

In the early days of bus building, wood was the basis of the framework for bus bodies. This picture shows the framework of one of the Greyhound buses under construction at the Eckland Brothers factory in Minneapolis, Minnesota.

Early Greyhound-named Buses

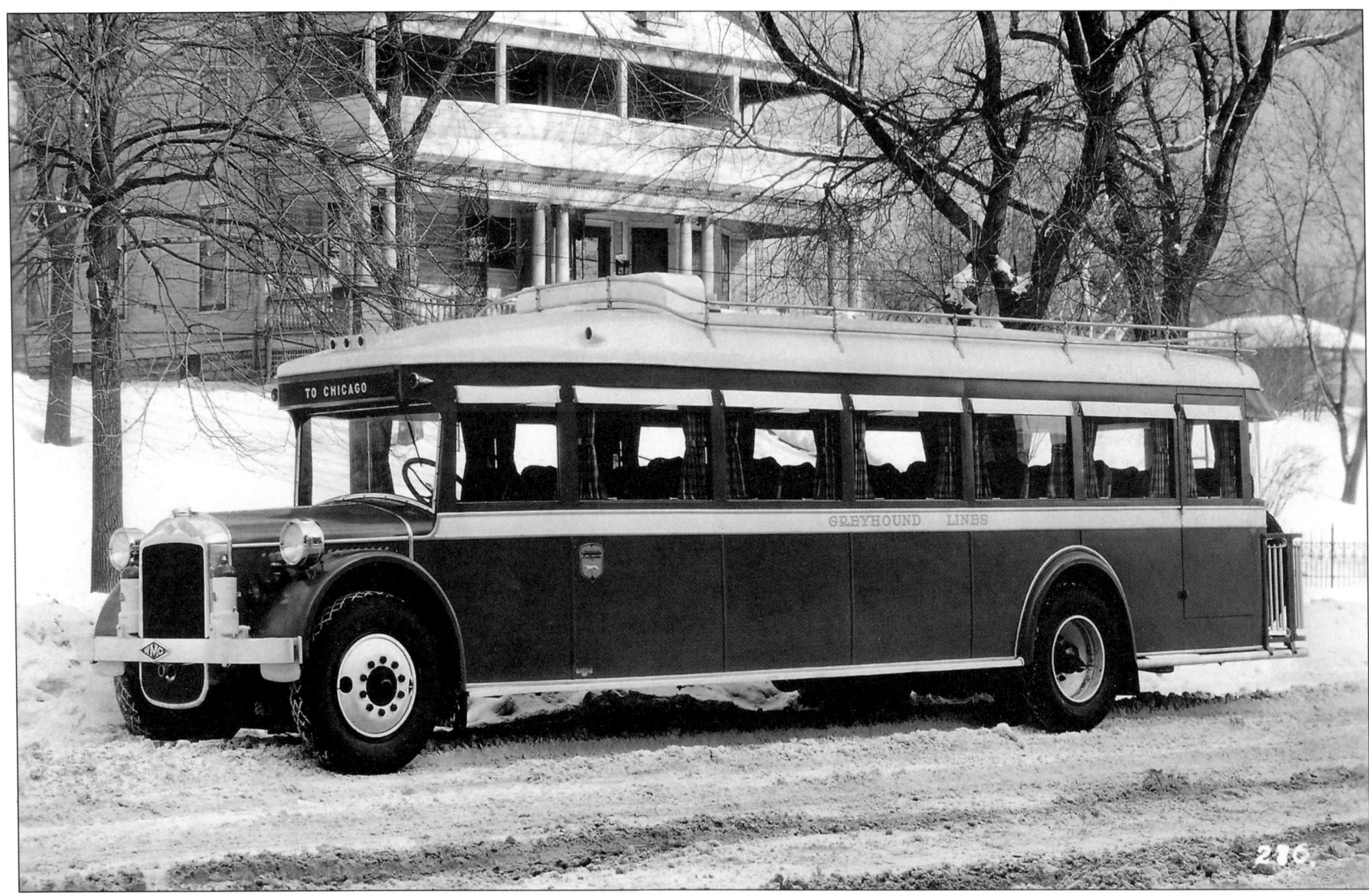

In 1929, Greyhound Lines took delivery of Model NTB Eckland-bodied Will buses. These buses were able to accommodate 33 passengers. The Waukesha engine was moved forward over the front axle, giving more space inside the bus. Large interior racks over the seats accommodated considerable baggage, although there was more baggage space on the roof.

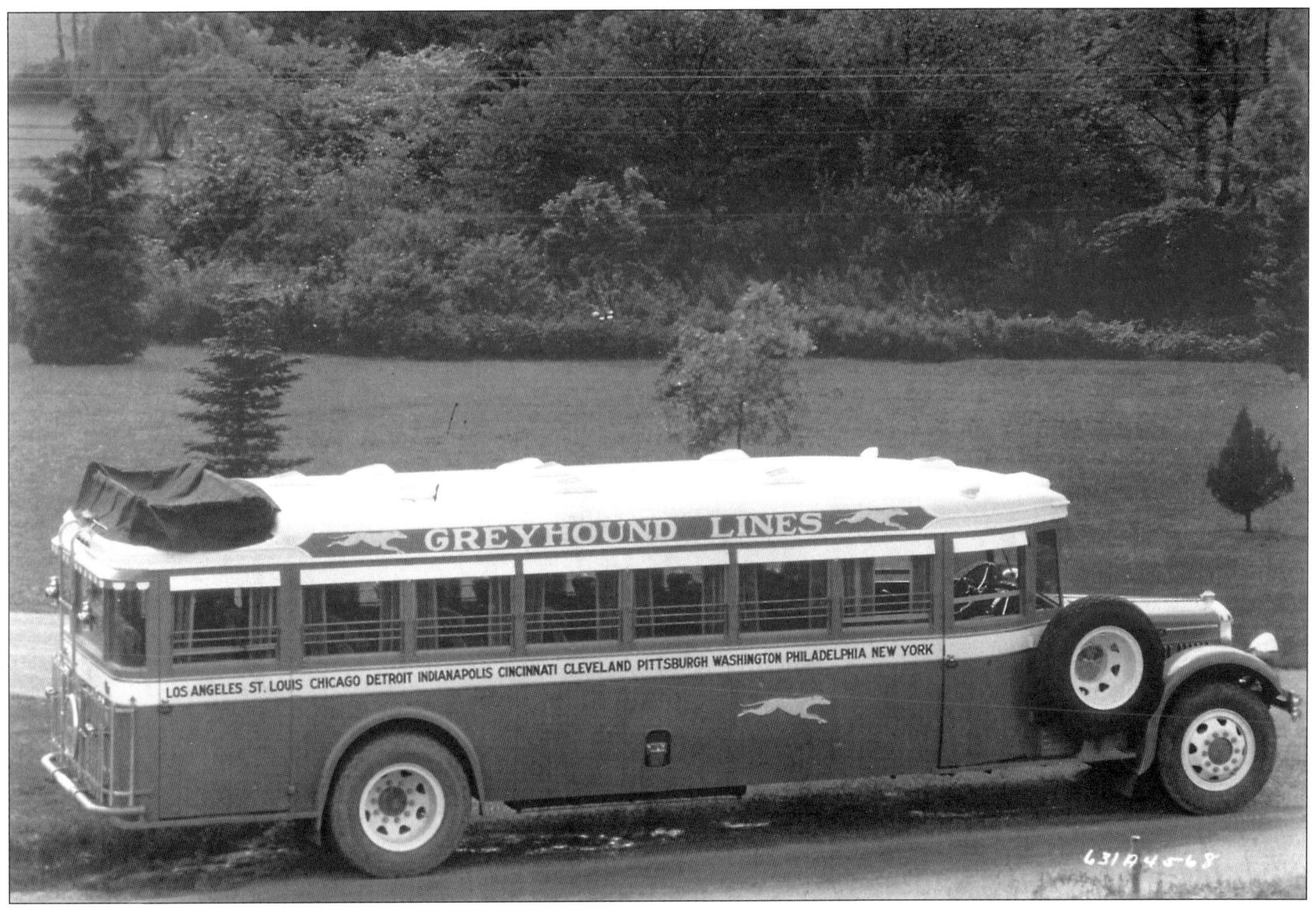

In 1930, Greyhound received 16 Mack Model 6BK 29-seat buses. The buses were originally lettered Greyhound Lines, but were later repainted by Eastern Greyhound Lines. The Mack 6BK buses had six-cylinder, 120-horsepower Mack gasoline engines. They carried spare tires up front behind each of the front fenders. *Don Coffin Collection*

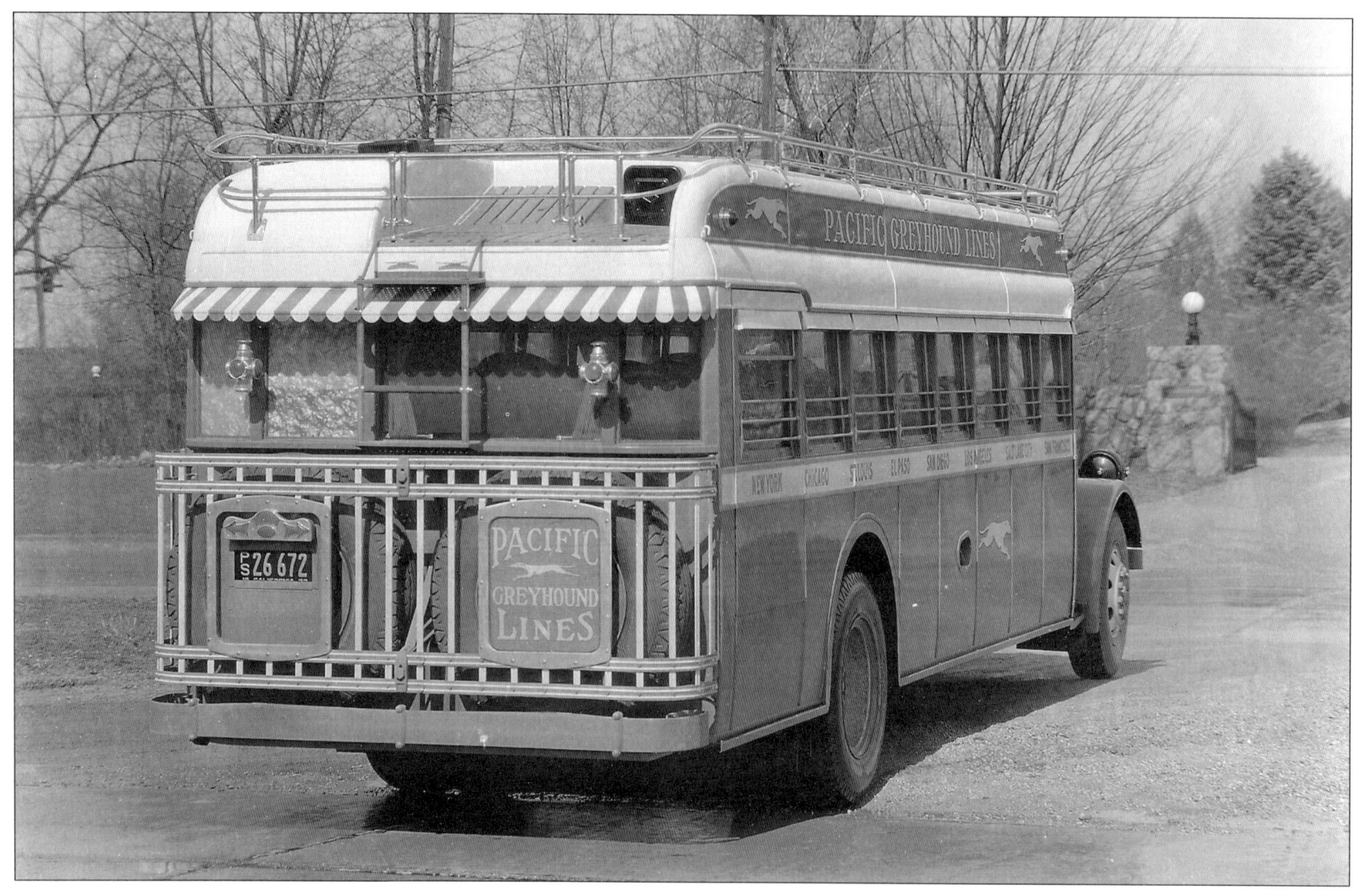

Pacific Greyhound Lines operated a number of Yellow Coach Z-250 Model 670 buses in the early 1930s. Many of the buses of that era had an interesting grillwork at the rear and an awning-like canopy. Two spare tires were mounted behind the grill as enroute tire failure happened frequently in those days. Also note the unusual tail lamps and the ladder to reach the roof baggage space. This special treatment given to the rear of buses gave them the appearance of luxury passenger-train observation cars.

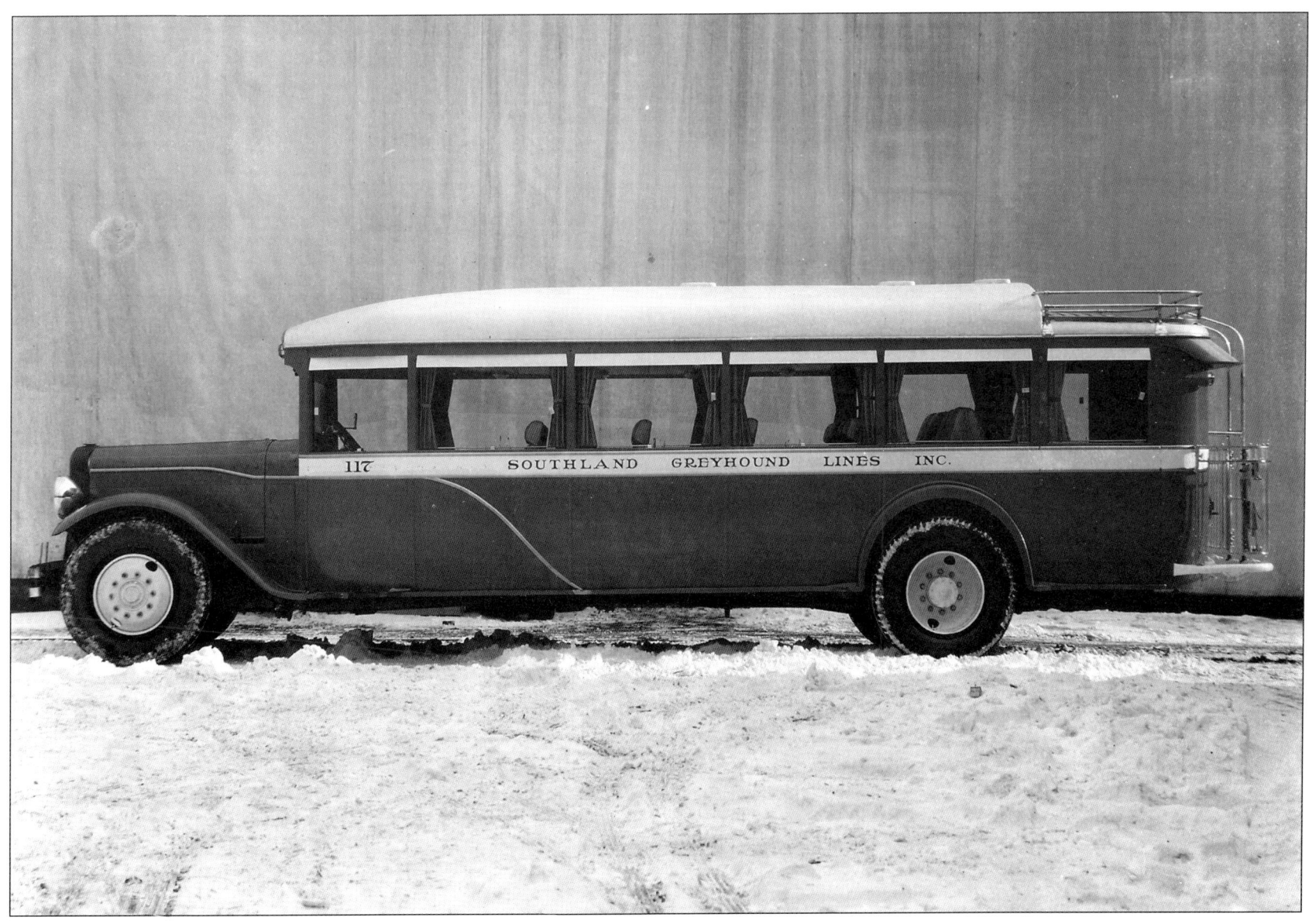

Southland Greyhound Lines acquired two 29-passenger Model P-30 ACF buses in 1929. The two buses operated in the company's West Texas division. Southland Greyhound was the result of the acquisition of several bus lines. Then in 1933, Southland Greyhound and Western Greyhound, a new name given to Pickwick Greyhound, merged to became Southwestern Greyhound Lines of Fort Worth, Texas.

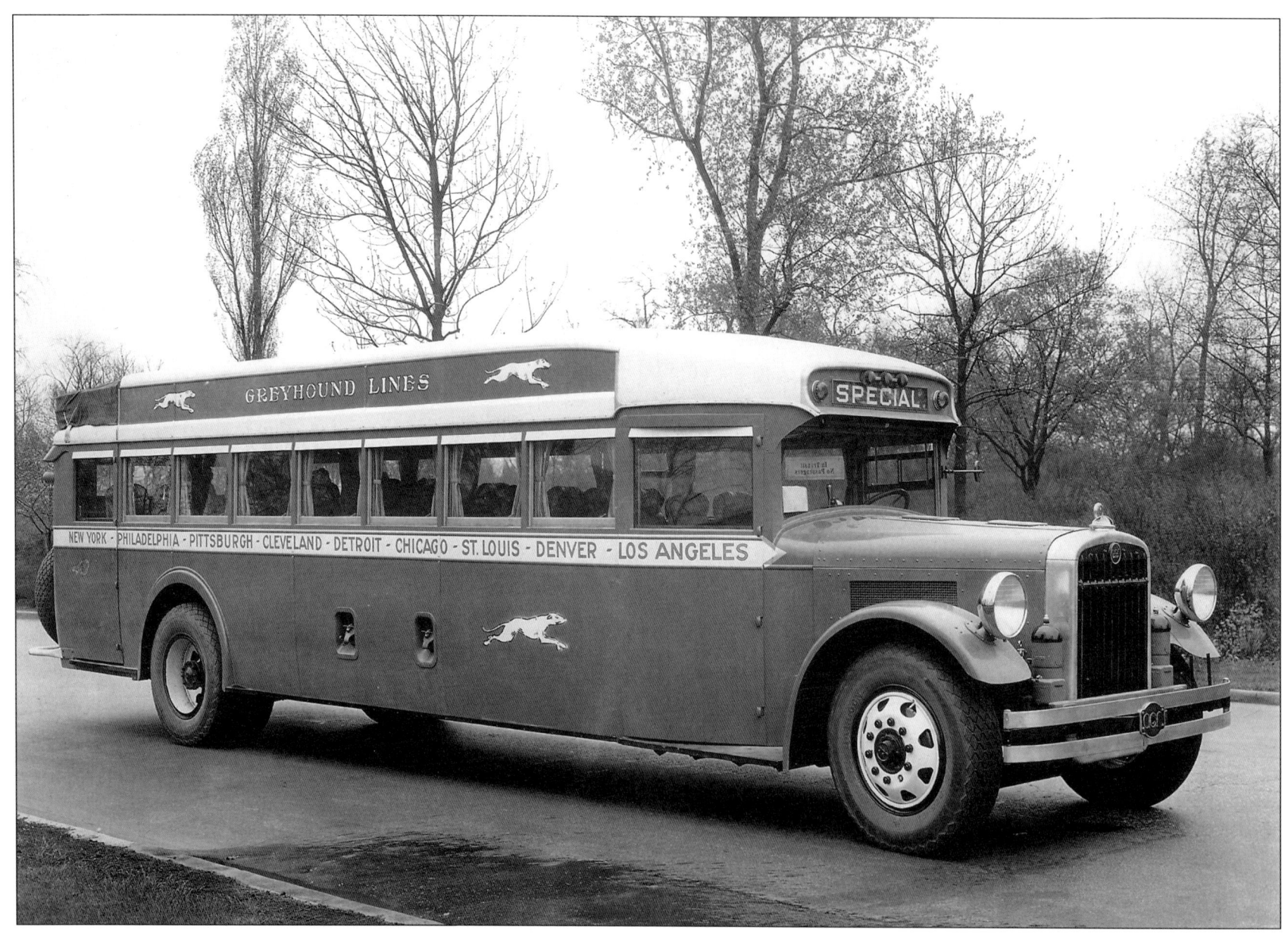

This 1930 ACF Model P-64 bus operated in the Pennsylvania Greyhound fleet for several years. American Car & Foundry Co. (ACF) entered the bus building business in 1925 when it acquired Fageol Motors Co. The P-64 had a 120-horsepower Hall Scott engine.

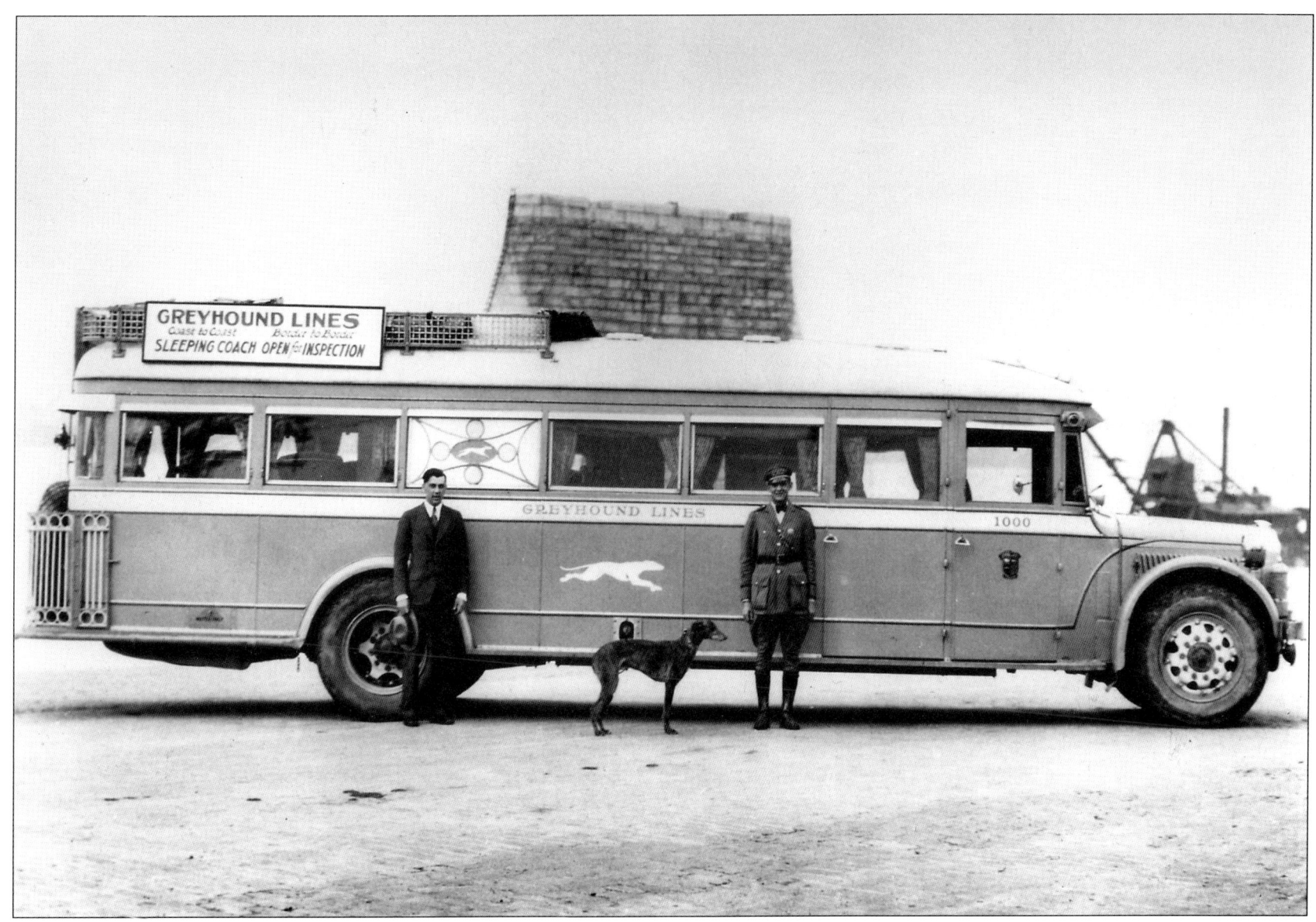

One of the first sleeper buses was this 1928 Will Executive Sleeping Coach. In addition to the berths, which were across the back and in back of the driver and along the sides, the bus had a lavatory and a small kitchen. In this publicity picture, note the driver in the typical Greyhound bus driver uniform of the day, featuring puttees and a Sam Brown belt. A Greyhound dog posed for this picture.

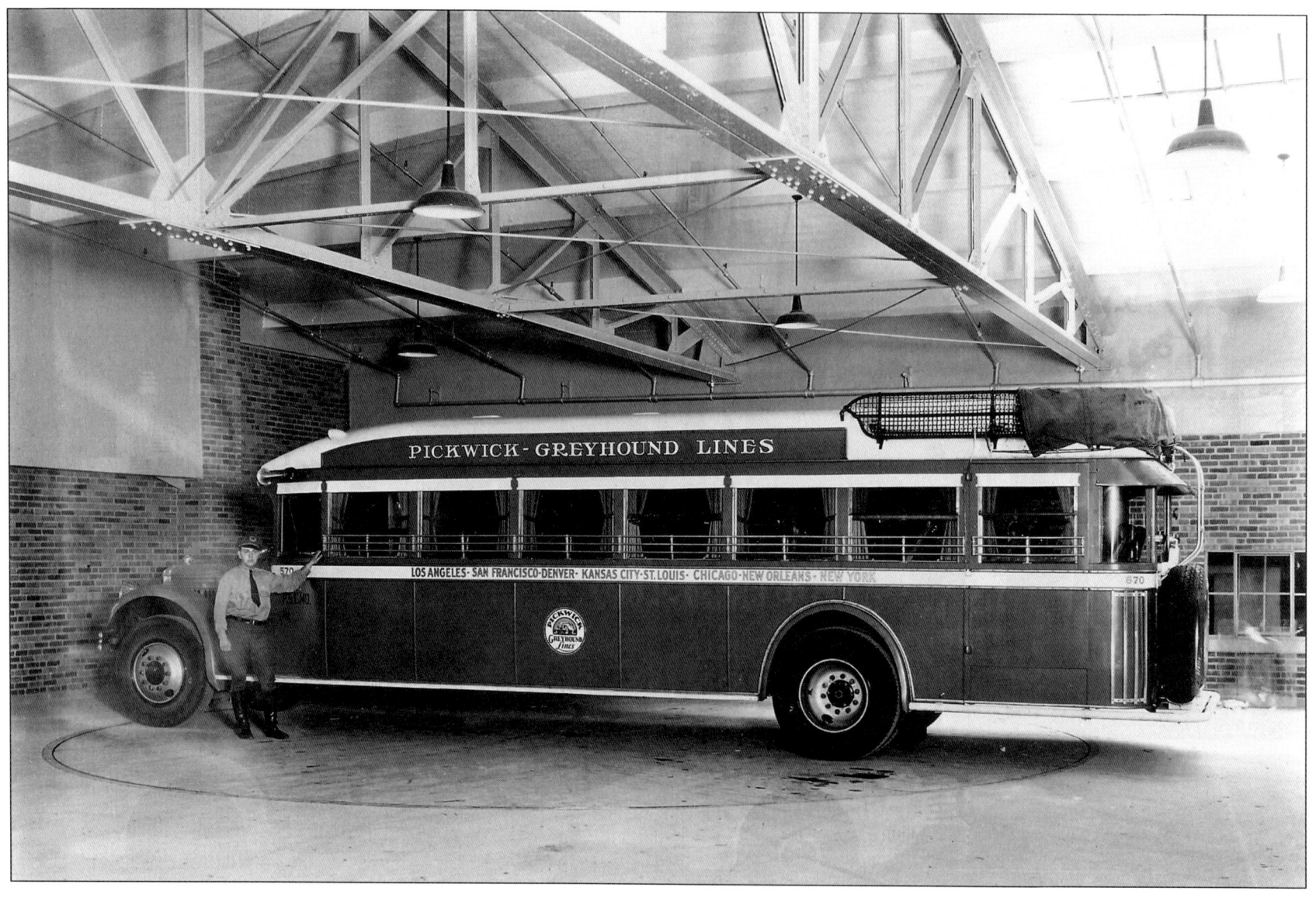

Pickwick Greyhound Lines was one of Greyhound's largest divisions in the early years. In addition to the bus system, Pickwick had a number of hotels and bus terminals. Kansas City had a Pickwick Hotel/Bus Terminal, which opened in 1930. In this picture a Pickwick Greyhound Model 6BK Mack is shown on a turntable inside the Kansas City terminal. Buses arrived on an upper level, and after being unloaded, they were turned around on the turntable for exiting. Incidentally, Mack buses were never common in Greyhound fleets.

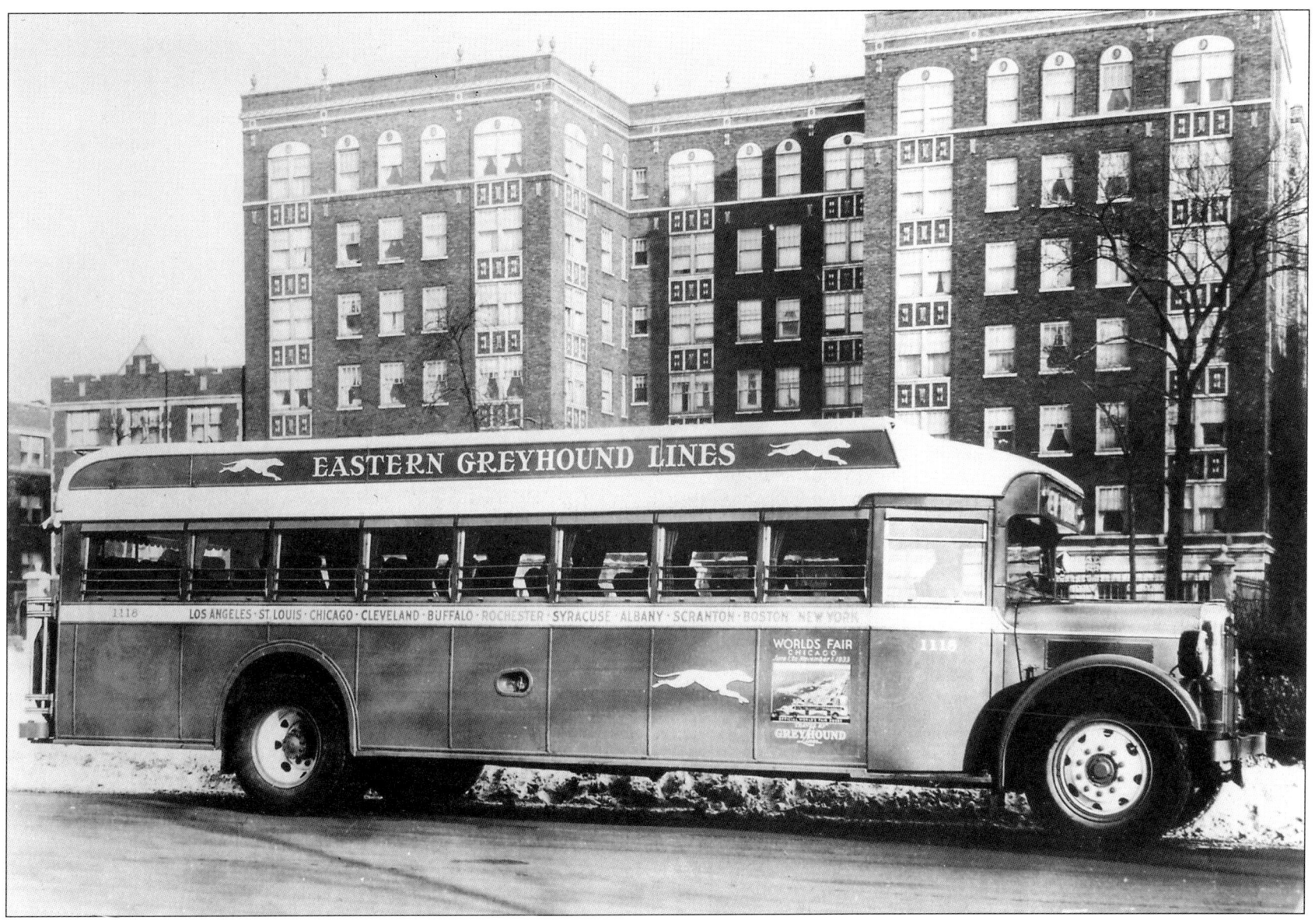

Eastern Greyhound Lines operated this Yellow Coach Z-250 Model 670 beginning in 1932. Note the advertisement next to the front door promoting the Chicago World's Fair of 1933. Many Greyhound buses at that time had this sign. The World's Fair brought many passengers to Greyhound and helped keep Greyhound in business during difficult depression years.

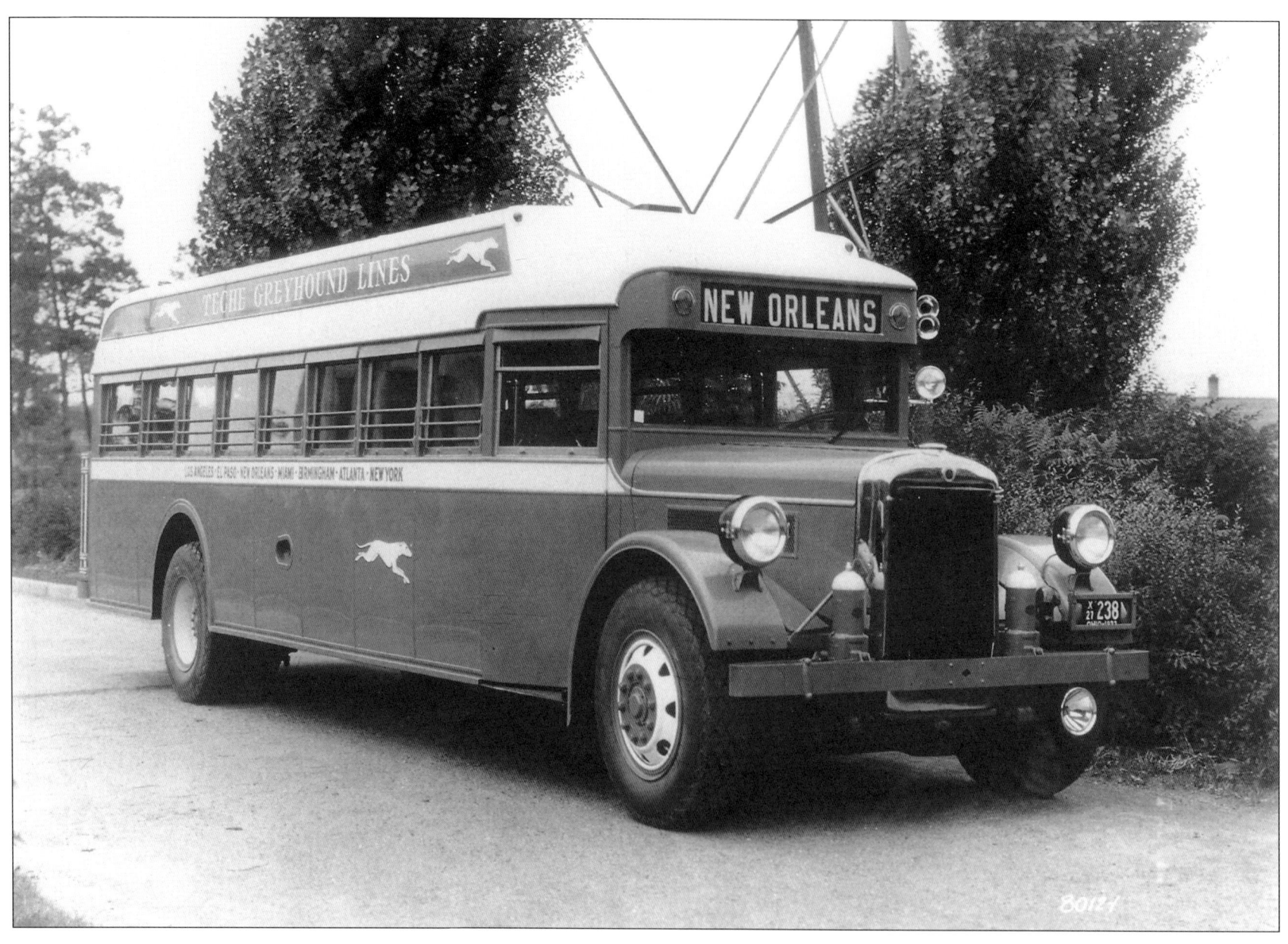

Teche Greyhound Lines purchased six Yellow Coach Model 670 33-passenger buses in 1932. Teche, headquartered in New Orleans, Louisiana, had routes that were linked to Greyhound services throughout the South. *Don Coffin Collection*

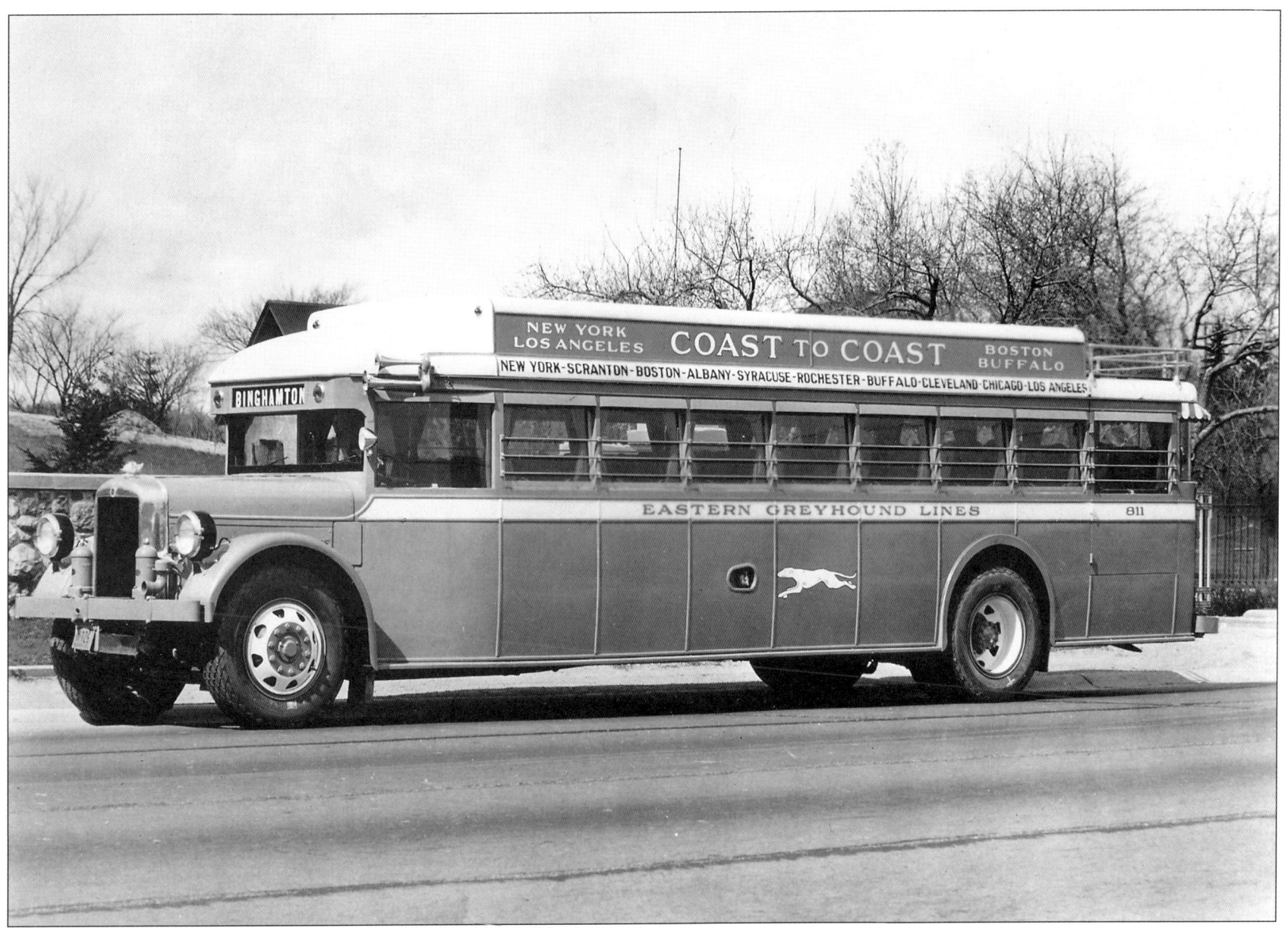

Greyhound companies began operating Yellow Coach Z-250 Model 376 buses in 1930. The Model 376 had seats for 33 passengers. Baggage was carried in overhead racks inside over the seats and on the roof. The buses had Yellow Coach Model 616 six-cylinder gasoline engines.

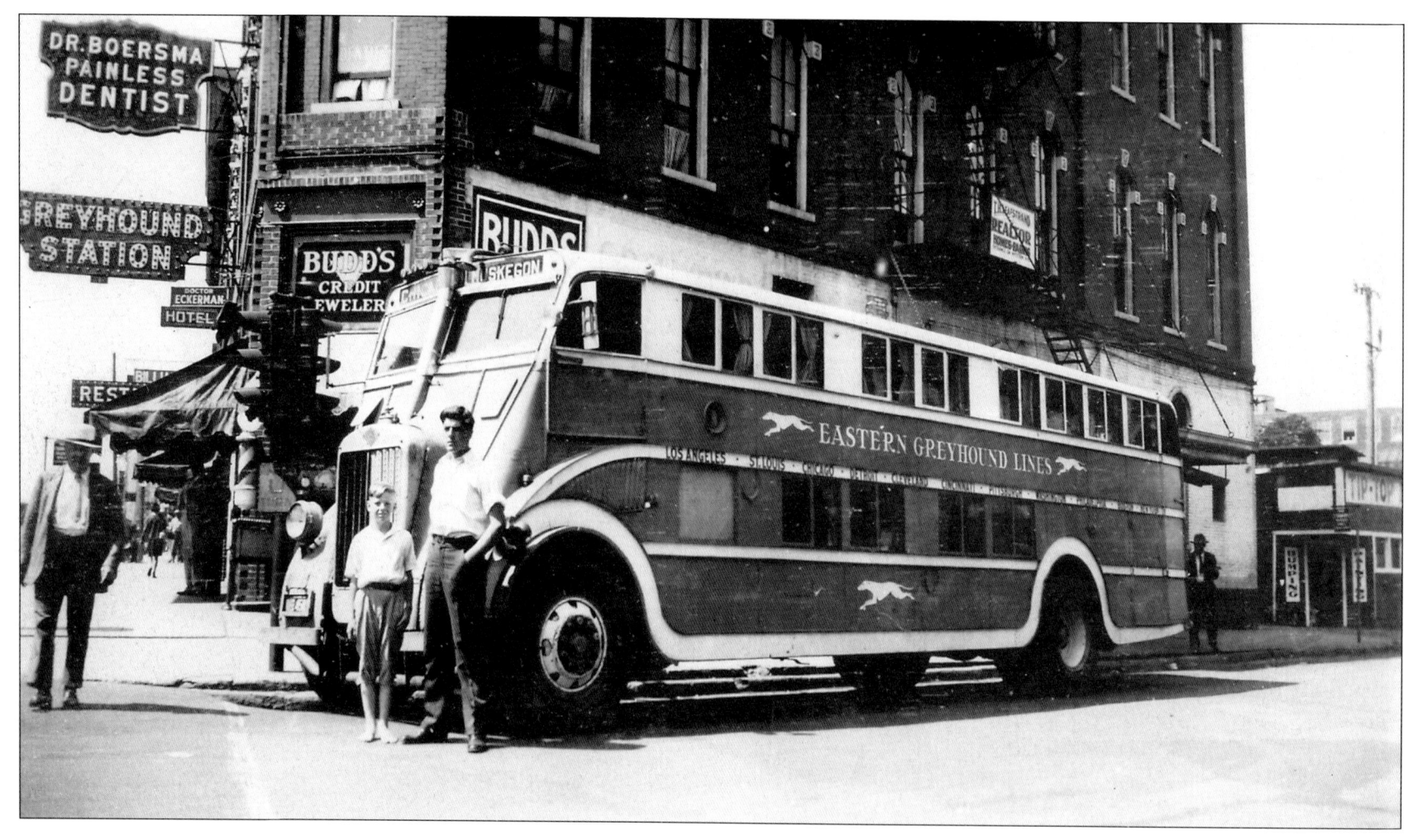

This Pickwick Duplex bus of Eastern Greyhound Lines was pictured in Muskegon, Michigan, in August 1933. These large buses would seat 50 passengers on the upper deck and 15 on the lower deck. These buses were similar to the Pickwick NiteCoaches, and were powered by Stirling gasoline engines.

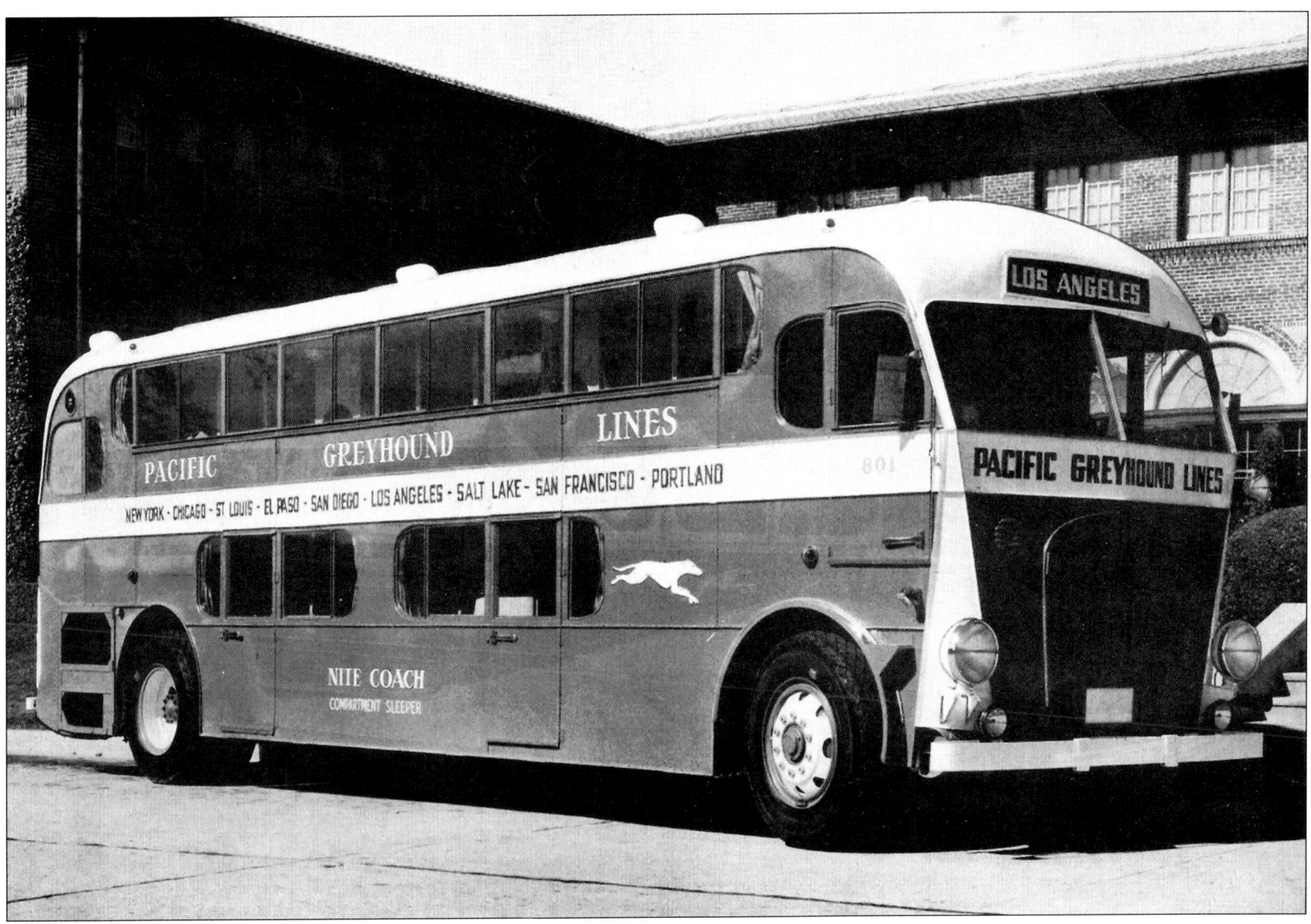

Pacific Greyhound Lines operated eight of these very large NiteCoaches beginning in 1932. They were used on the route between Los Angeles and San Francisco and Portland, and between Kansas City and Los Angeles via El Paso. The NiteCoaches featured a Hercules gasoline engine mounted transversally at the rear with a newly designed angle drive invented by Dwight Austin. The angle drive brought power from the rear engine to the drive axle.

Greyhound Buses of the 1930 and 1940s

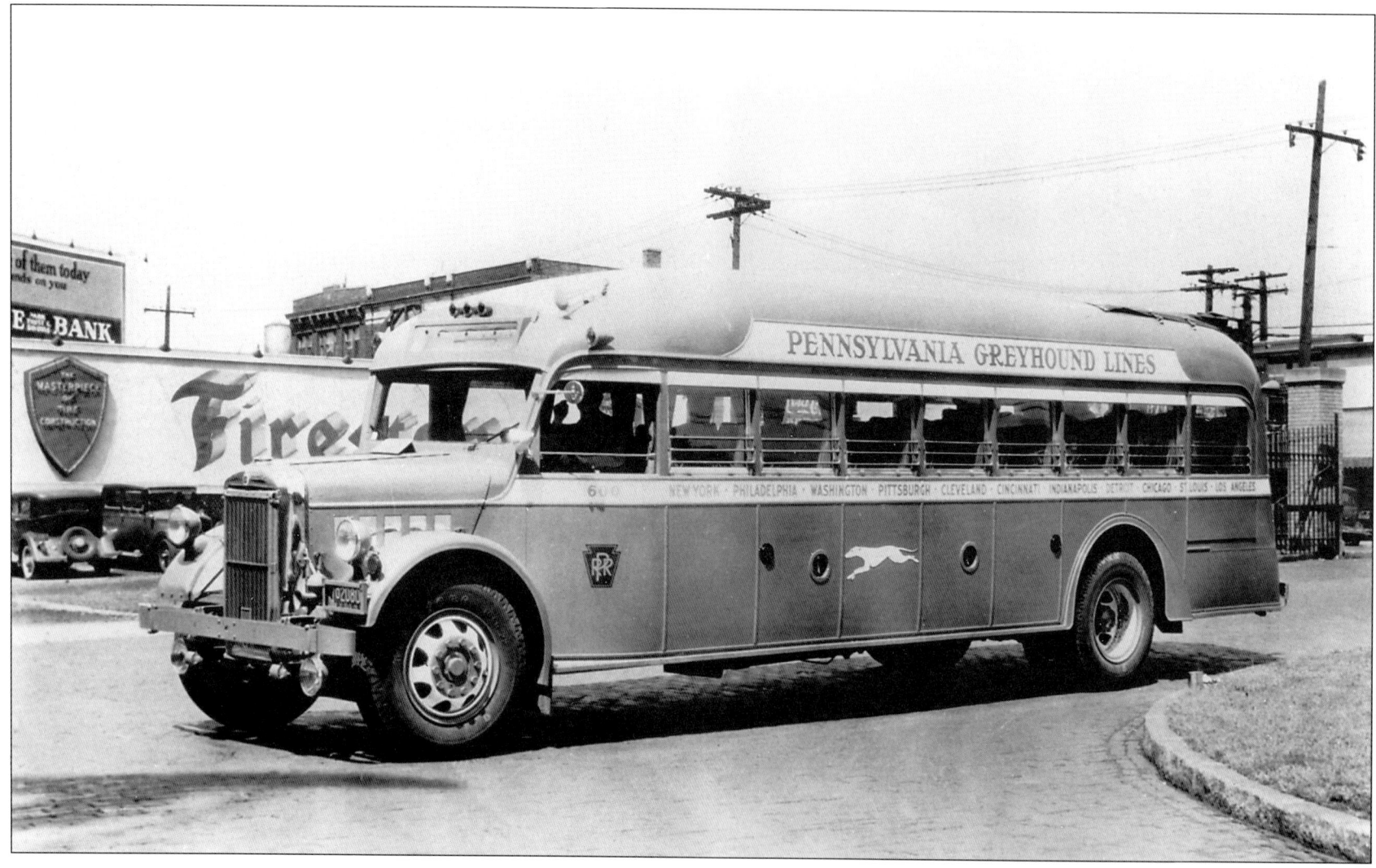

Pictured here is Pennsylvania Greyhound Lines' Yellow Coach Z-250, Model 843 bus at the Firestone Tire and Rubber Company plant in Akron, Ohio, in 1932. Interesting about this bus is that it has Trippe road lights in place of amber fog lights mounted below the front bumper. Also, the Pennsylvania Railroad keystone emblem is on the first panel below the front window. The Pennsylvania Railroad had a 50 percent non-voting interest in Pennsylvania Greyhound Lines.

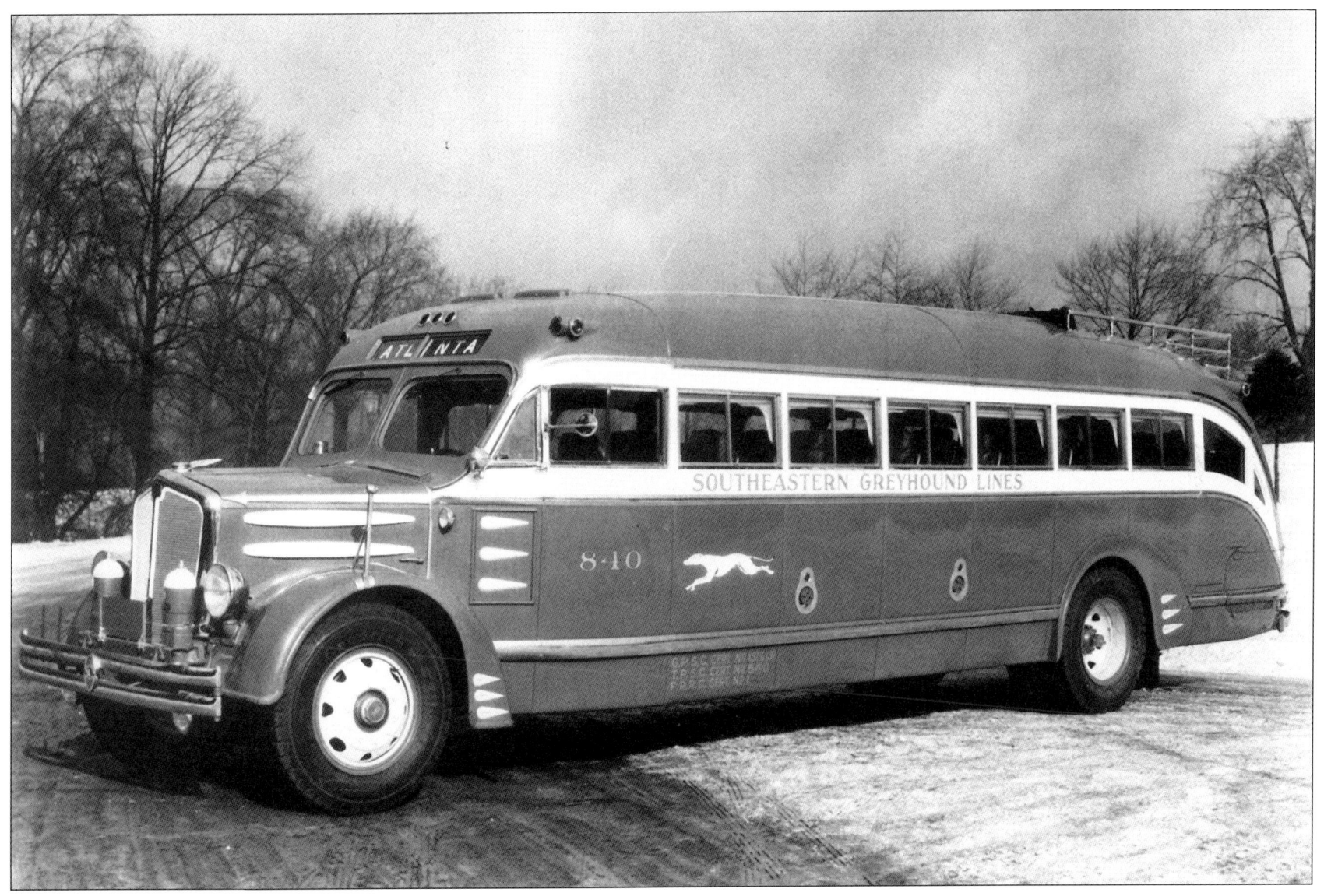

Southeastern Greyhound Lines operated buses built by White Motor Company in the early 1930s. In 1934, five 33-passenger Model 54-A White Palace Highway Coaches were delivered to Southeastern. These buses, which had a body built by Bender Body Company, featured streamlining. A White 130-horsepower, six-cylinder engine was mounted in the front. The streamlined White 54-A Palace Highway Coach had a short-lived popularity. *Don Coffin Collection*

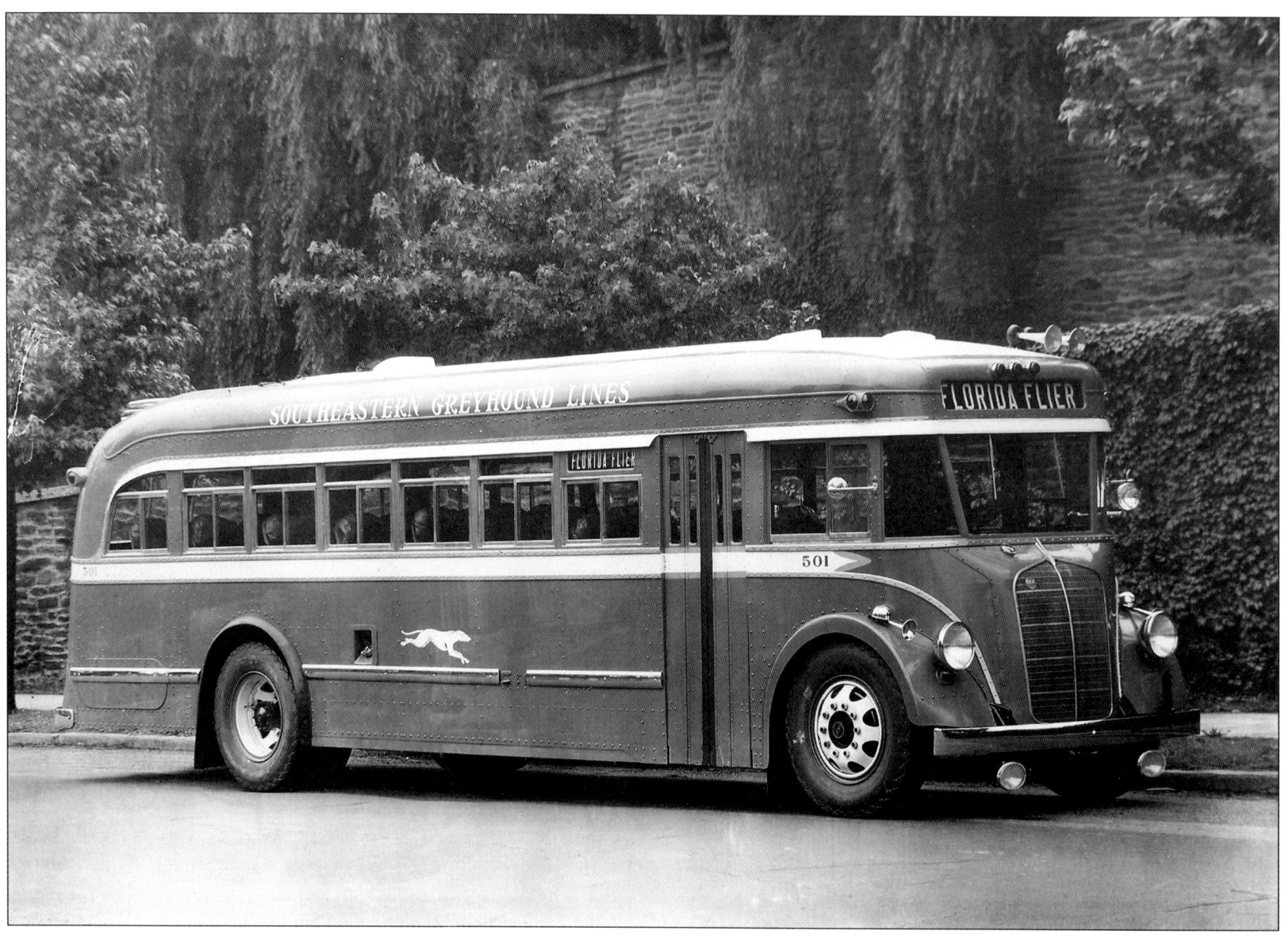

Southeastern Greyhound Lines began buying ACF buses in 1935. At that time, 10 of these ACF H-9-P buses entered service on Southeastern's popular Florida Flyer service. These ACF buses had 180-horsepower, six-cylinder Hall Scott gasoline engines mounted under the floor.

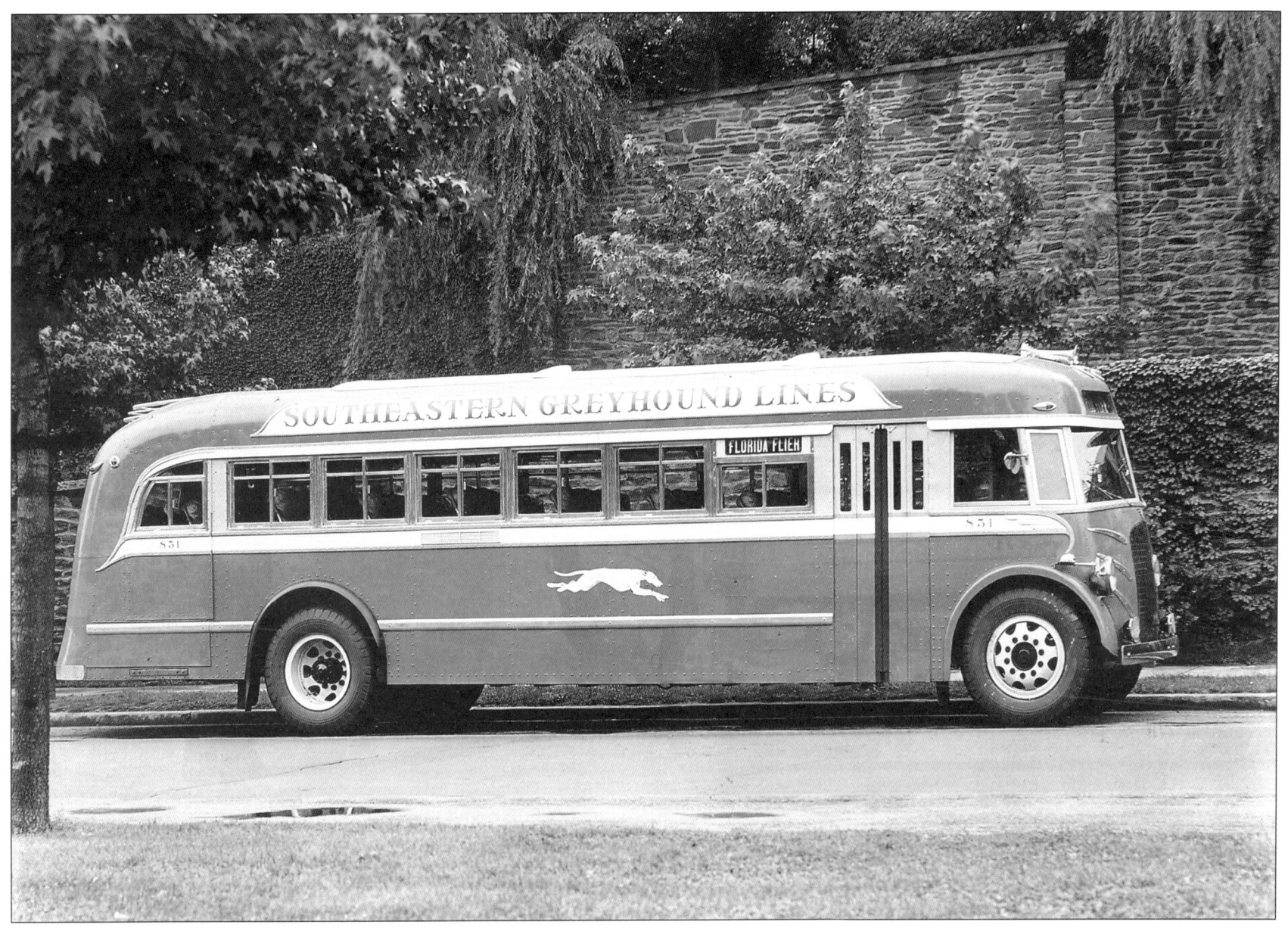

After an initial purchase of ACF buses in 1935, Southeastern Greyhound Lines ordered another 26 ACF H-9-P buses the following year. They had a front appearance different from those purchased the previous year. These new buses were assigned to Southeastern's services to and from Florida.

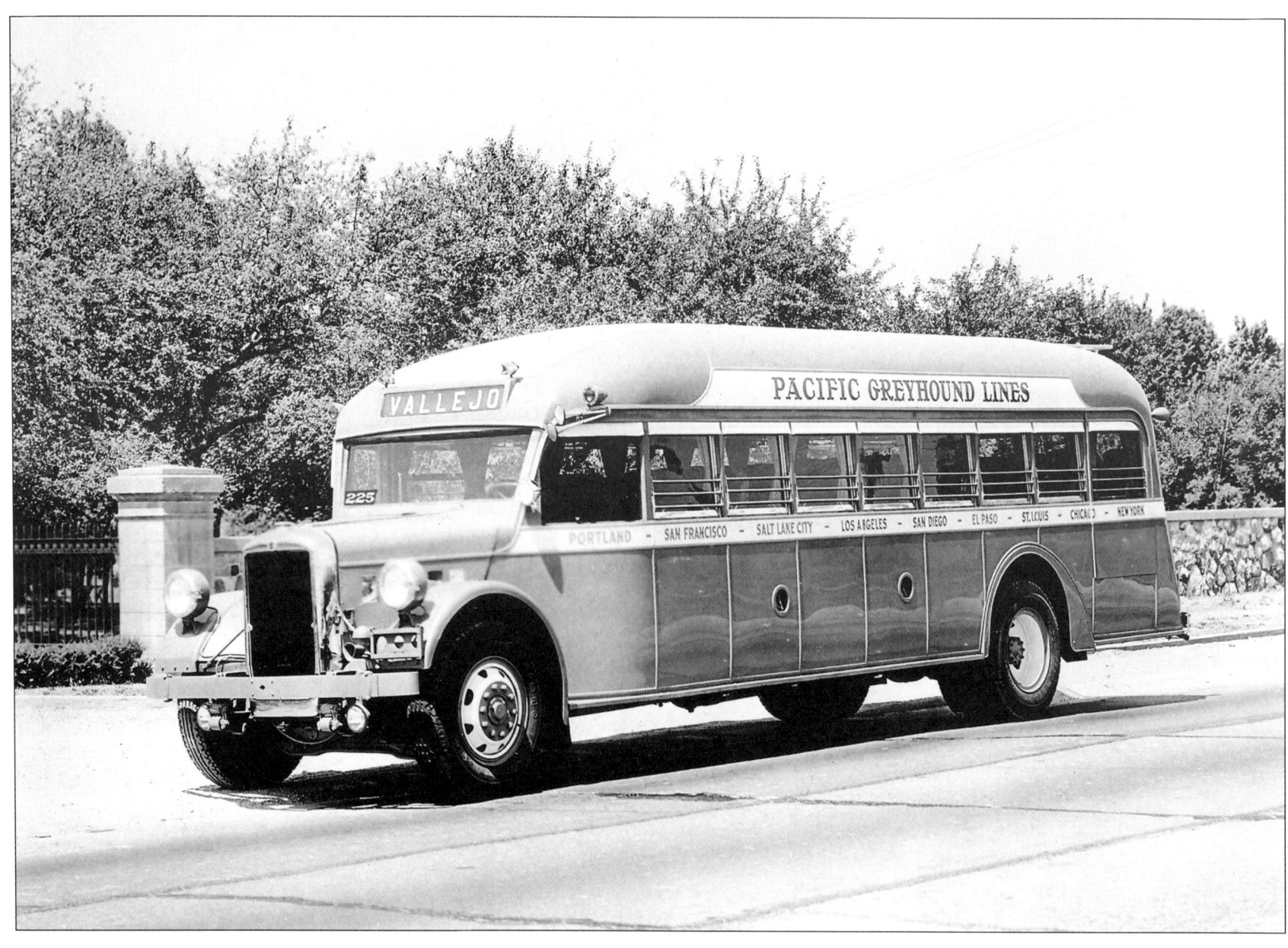

Pacific Greyhound Lines operated Yellow Coach Model 788 buses beginning in 1934. They were also referred to as Z-250s or Streamliners. The buses had large interior baggage racks, plus a recessed section on the roof at the rear for more baggage. These buses had seats for 33 passengers.

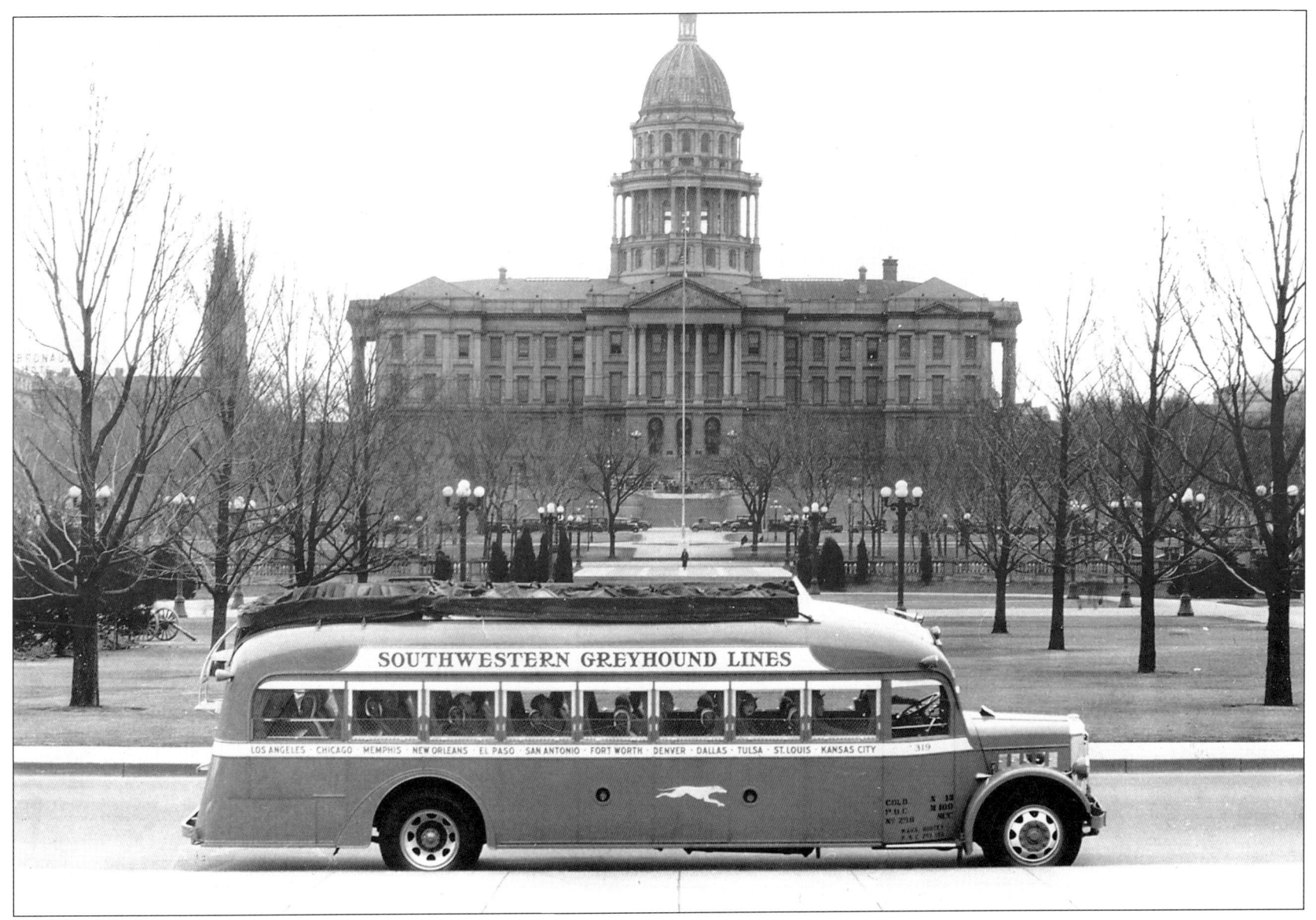

Southwestern Greyhound Lines' Yellow Coach Model 843 poses in front of the state Capitol Building in Denver, Colorado in 1934. These Model 843 buses were also referred to as Z-250 or Streamliner buses. Note that there was extra space on the roof of this bus for baggage with a tarpaulin for a cover. Also, there was a ladder in the back to access the baggage.

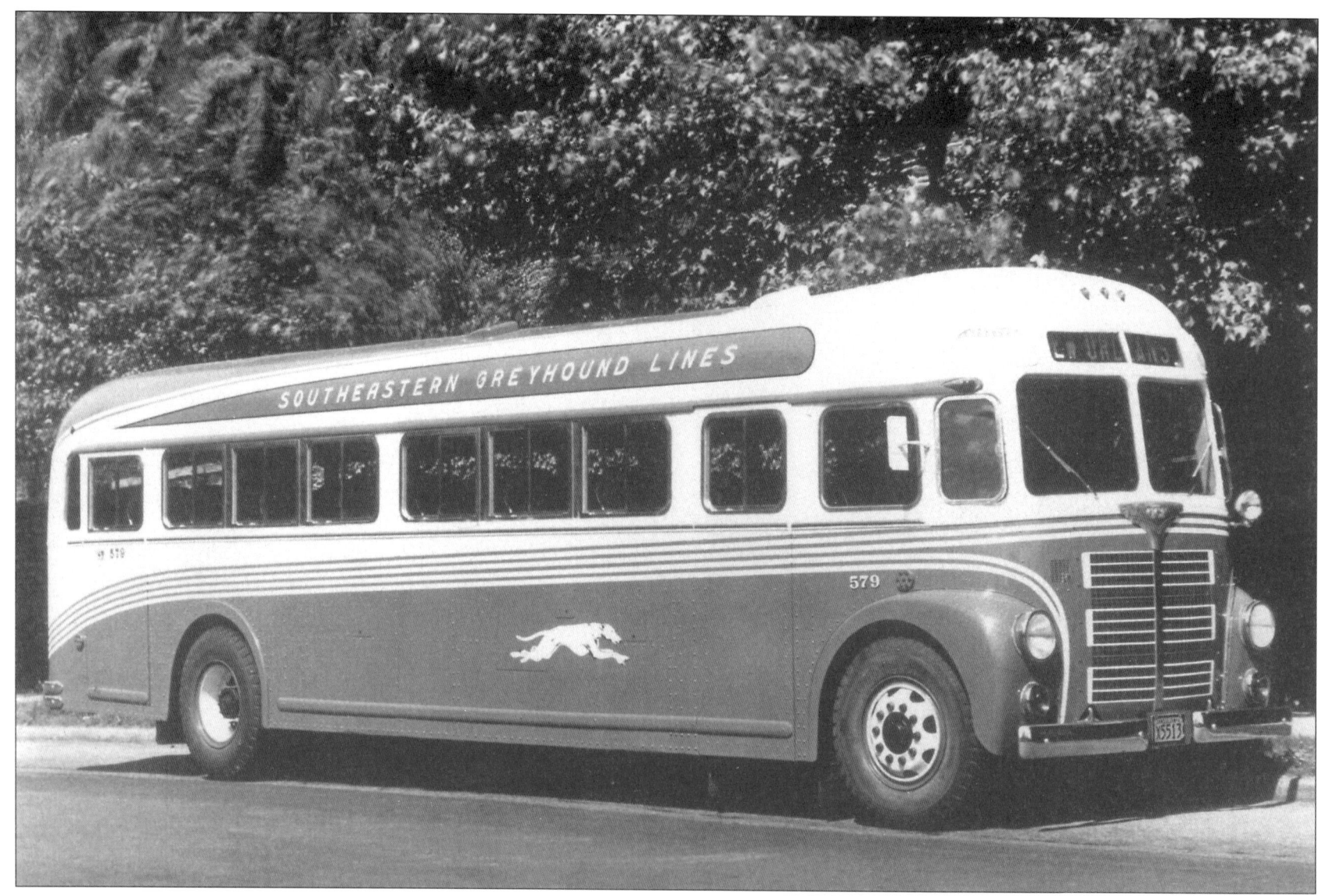

Southeastern Greyhound Lines added 21 ACF 37P buses to its fleet in 1938. These buses had 707-cubic-inch Hall Scott 180-horsepower gasoline engines. Southeastern Greyhound Lines was not wholly owned by the Greyhound Corporation until 1951, although Greyhound had acquired stock in 1947. Southeastern had been using the Greyhound name for a number of years through an agreement. The bus routes in the southeastern states were an important link between the east and Florida. *Don Coffin Collection*

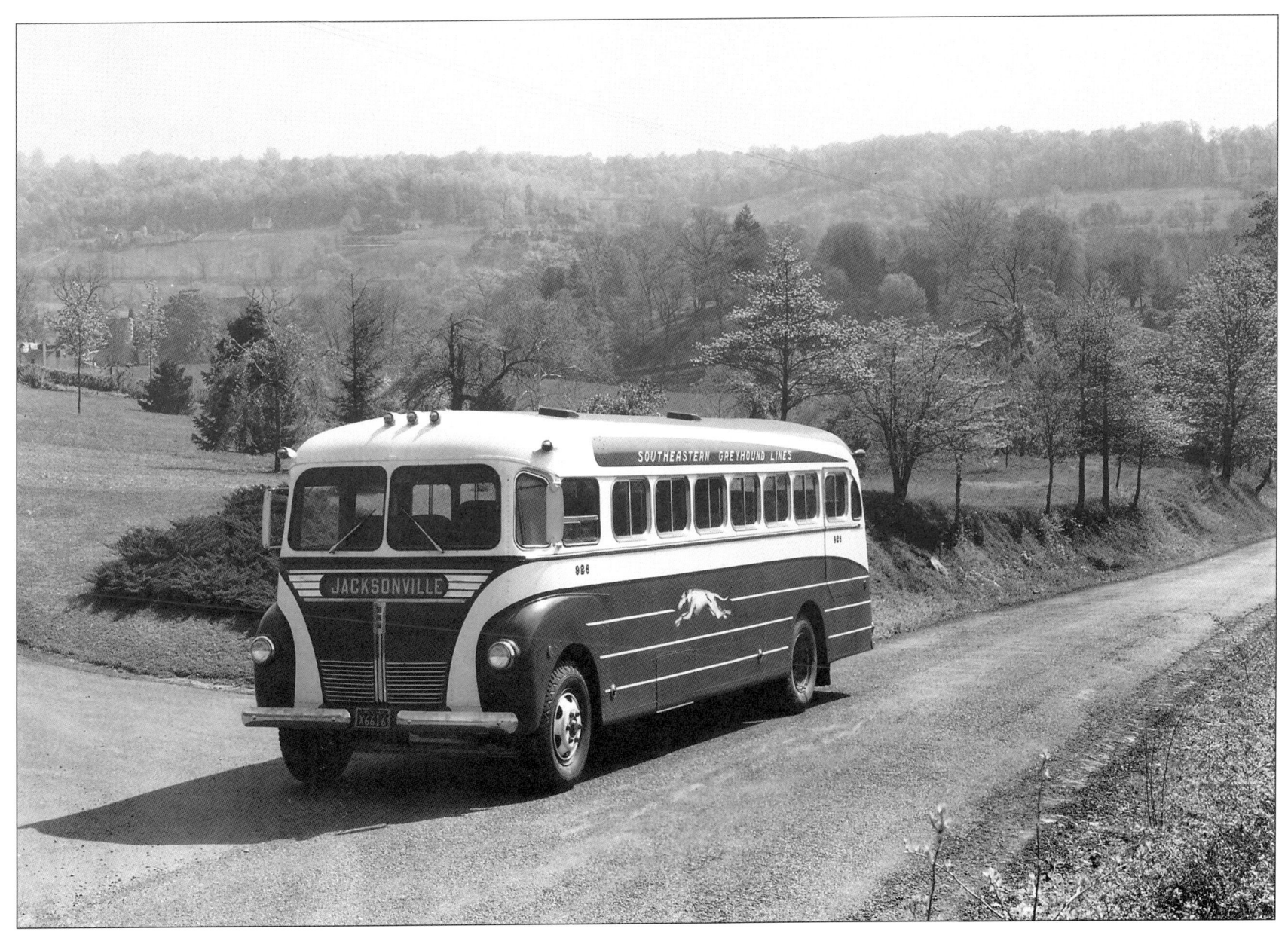

Southeastern Greyhound Lines standardized on ACF buses for its main line routes in the 1930s and 1940s. Southeastern ordered 25 ACF Model 29PBs like the one pictured here in 1941. These buses seated 29 passengers. Like most ACF buses they were powered by underfloor 124-horsepower Hall Scott engines.

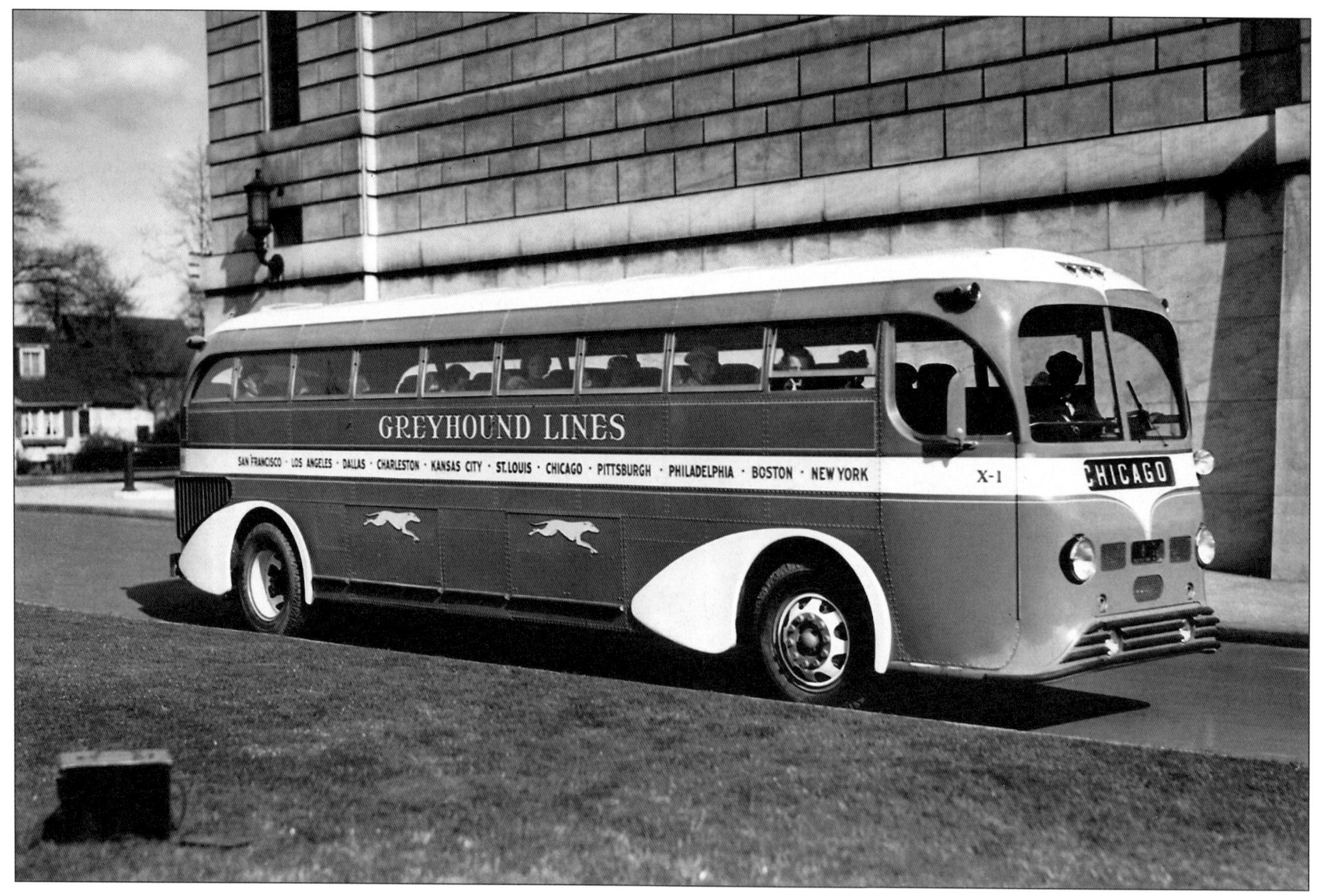

Greyhound and Yellow Coach developed a new intercity bus in 1935. It was first referred to as X-1. It and another experimental model were tested in service. The new Greyhound bus was called the Super Coach. It featured high level seating for 37 passengers, underfloor baggage compartments, and a number of other innovations. The experimental Super Coaches were followed by production models from Yellow Coach, first Model 719 and then Model 743. The gasoline engine was mounted longitudinally at the rear of the bus. It had Dwight Austin angle drive.

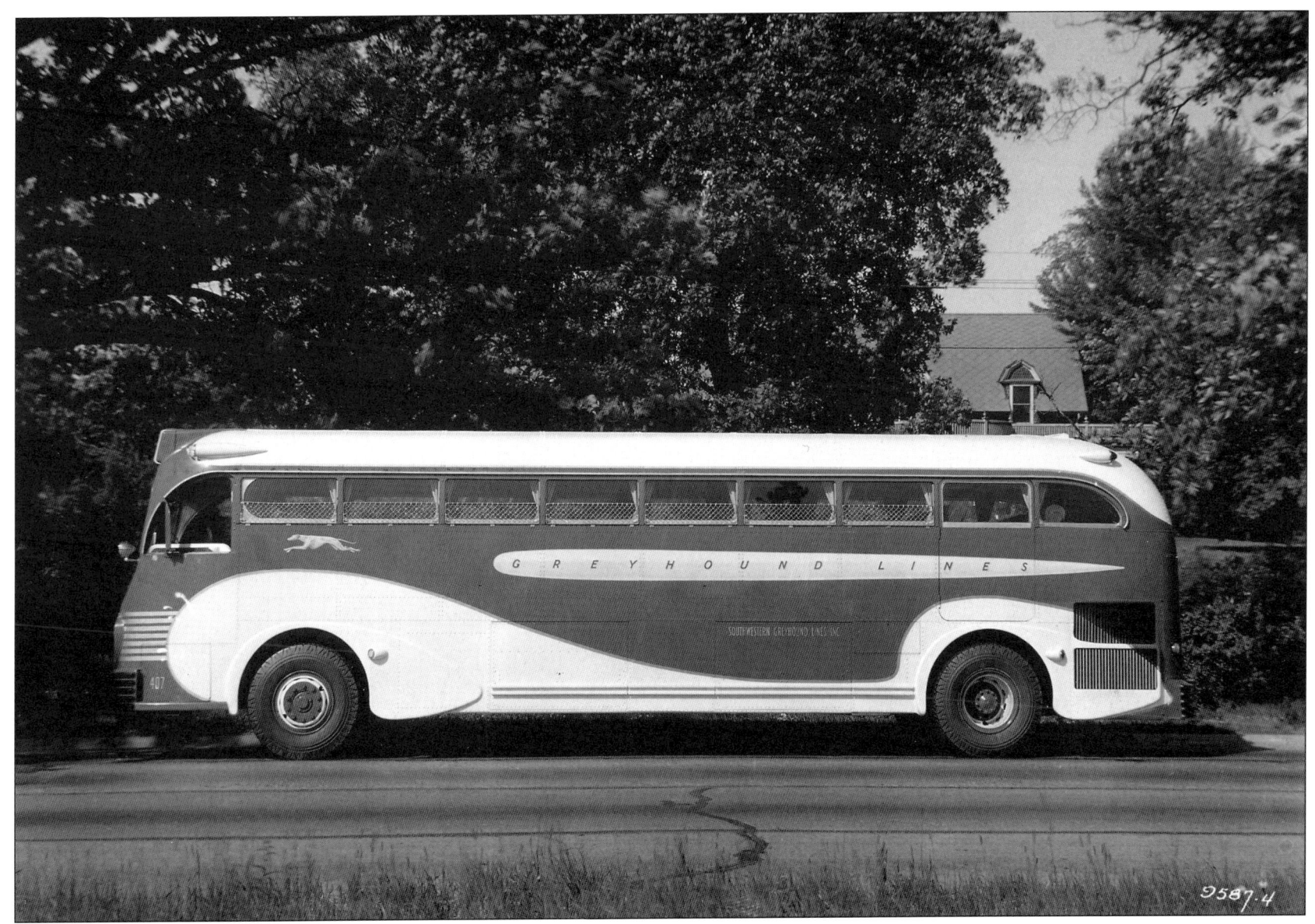

The Model 719 Yellow Coach, called the Greyhound Super Coach, first saw service in 1936. Yellow Coach and Manufacturing Company delivered 325 Model 719 buses. The new buses were presented to the public with a promotional campaign. It was reported passengers were very pleased with the new Super Coach. Southwestern Greyhound Lines operated this Model 719 Super Coach.

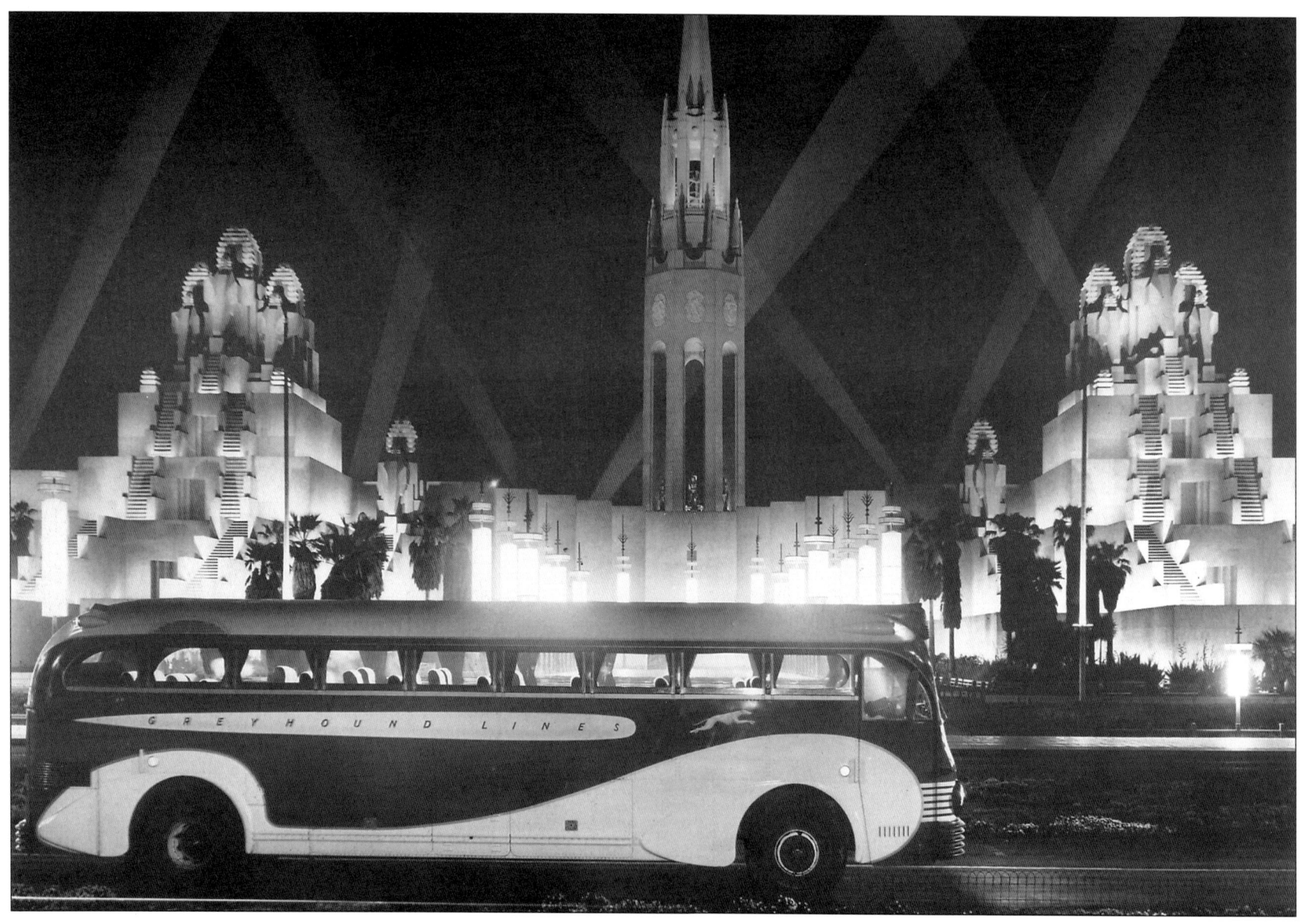

The first air-conditioned buses operated by Greyhound were the Yellow Coach Model 743 buses referred to as Super Coaches. A small half-moon vent over a window at the rear of the bus indicated that the bus was air-conditioned. This air-conditioned Pacific Greyhound Super Coach poses at the Golden Gate Exposition in San Francisco in 1939.

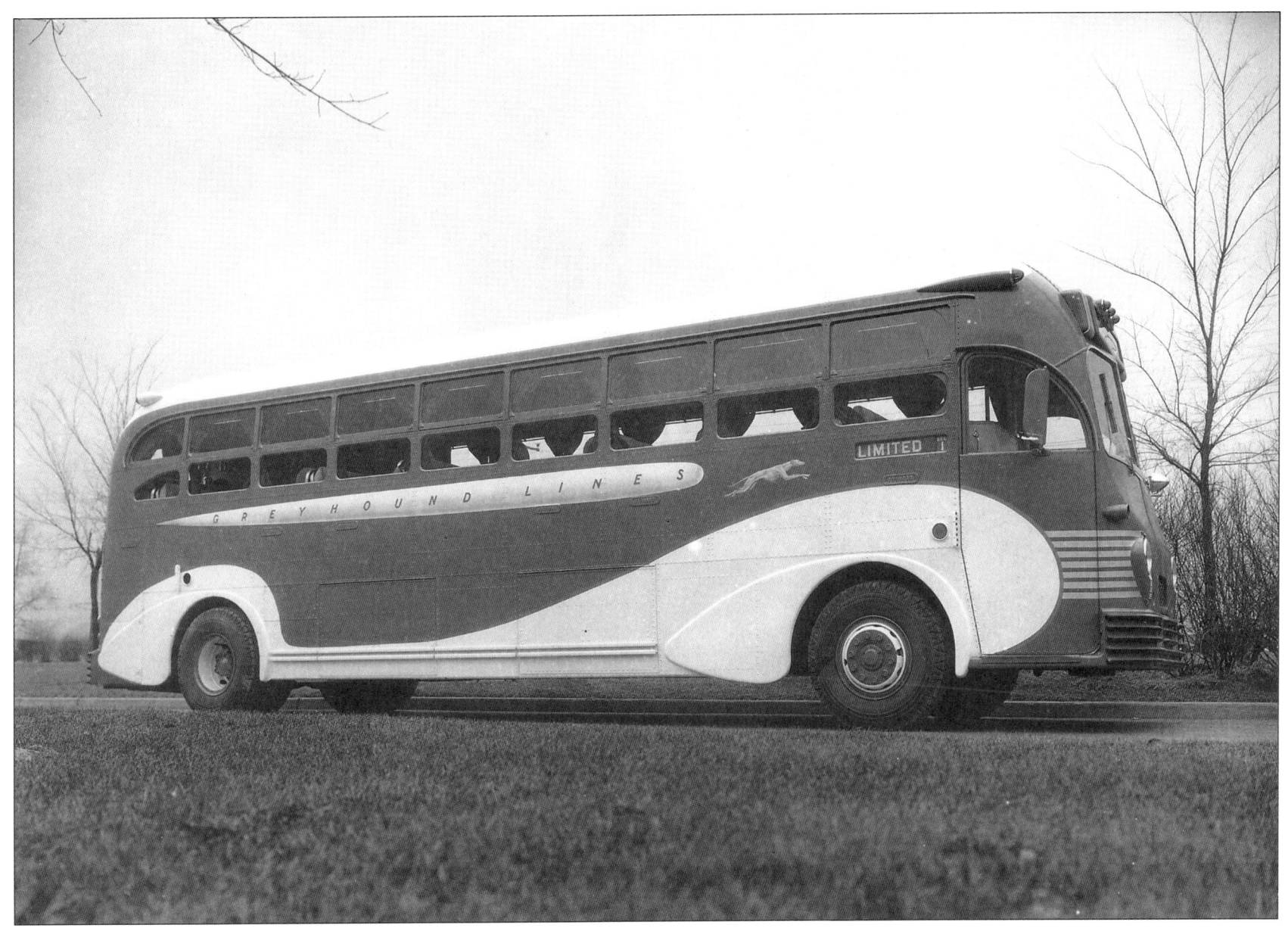

This Model 745 Yellow Coach was a Sleeper Bus. Only one was built, and was tested by Pacific Greyhound Lines. This Sleeper Bus was adapted from a Yellow Coach Model 719 bus, which had been owned by Greyhound. It could seat 30 passengers, and for night travel it could accommodate 20 passengers in berths.

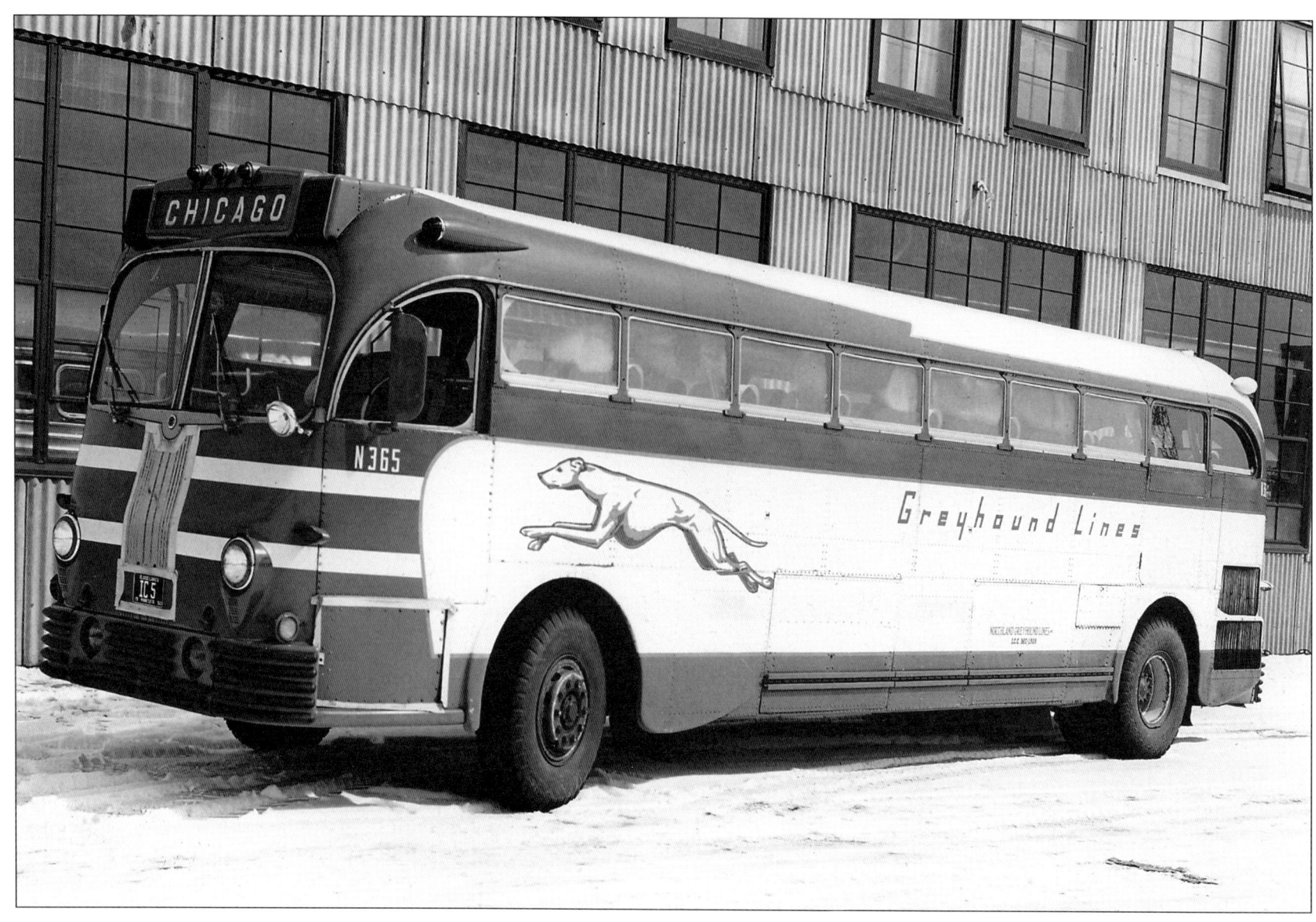

Northland Greyhound Lines' Yellow Coach Model 719 received a new paint scheme following the war, featuring a white midsection and a larger Greyhound dog logo. A number of the Model 719 Super Coaches were repainted in this manner. Note that storm windows were attached. This was common in cold climates. Also, a spotlight was standard on most buses in the 1930s and 1940s.

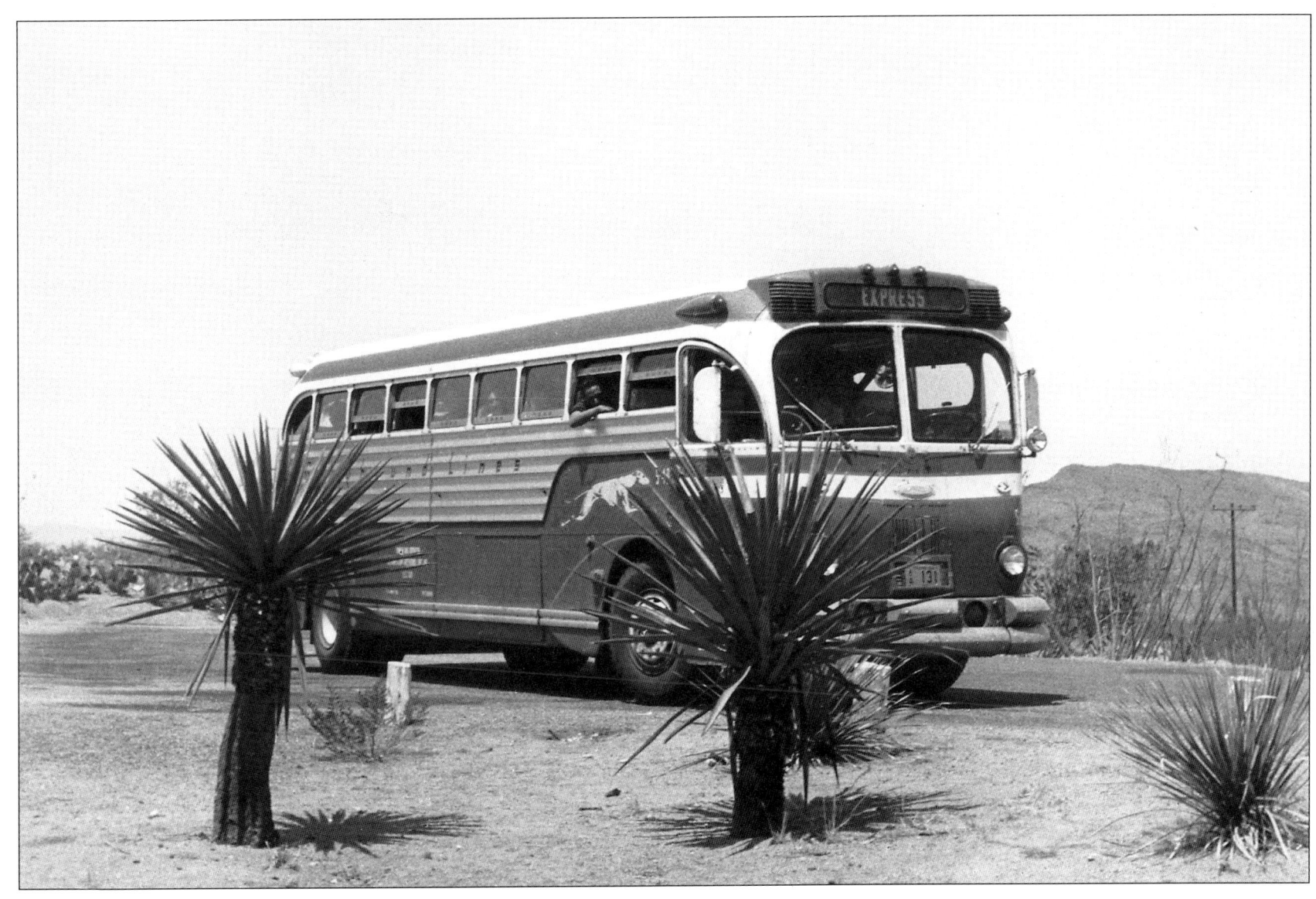

Greyhound Yellow Coach Model 743 buses had a second facelift beginning in 1948. This involved some 800 of these Super Coach buses. The partial silversiding gave the buses a different modern appearance. New drive trains were also added at the same time. The work was done at the General American Aerocoach plant in Chicago. The Southwestern Greyhound Super Coach with its new look was on a charter trip and pictured at a picnic stop on U.S. Highway 90 near Van Horn, Texas.

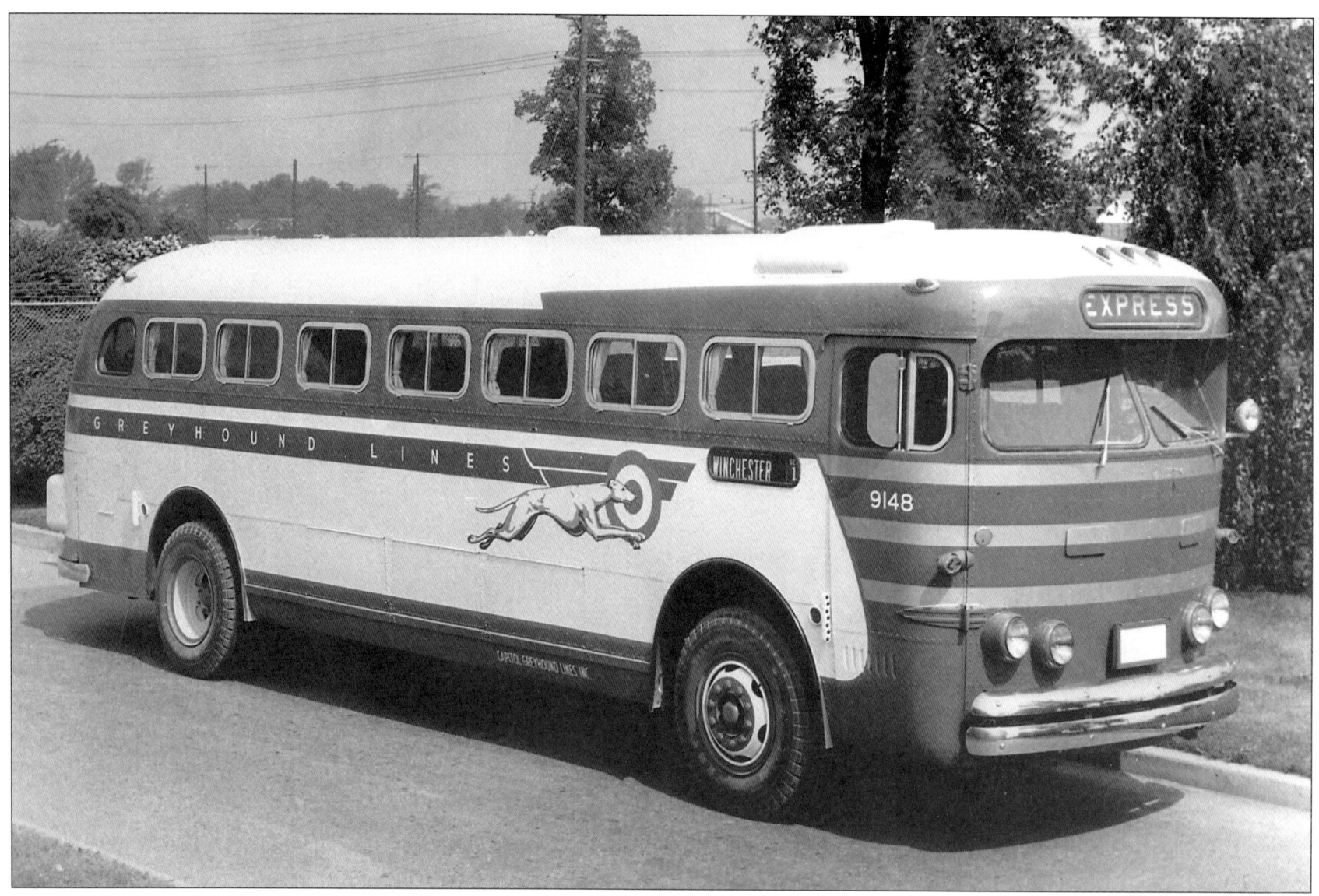

During the World War II years, only a limited number of buses were built. Most bus manufacturers were devoting their entire effort to the production of vehicles and material for the war. However, the Office of Defense Transportation (ODT) allowed some buses to be built. The first reported bus, built under the ODT authorization, was this Yellow Coach Model PGA 3701 for Southwestern Greyhound Lines. The new bus had a new livery with the Greyhound dog and a bull's eye.

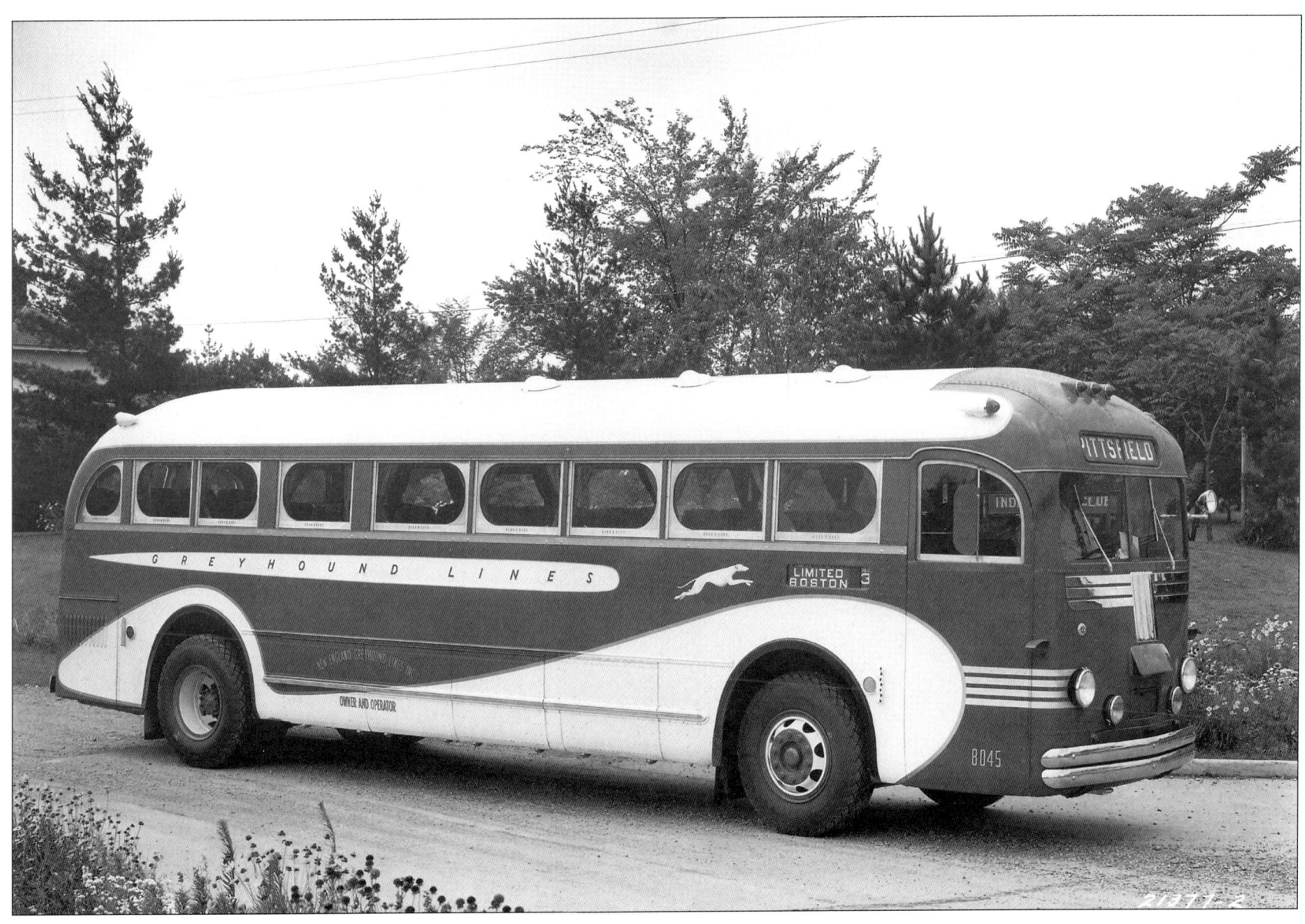

New England Greyhound Lines was one of the few bus companies owning a Yellow Coach Model 1210. New England Greyhound took delivery of this and seven other Model 1210s in June 1939. They took eight more of the same model bus in 1940, but then the model was re-designated as PG 3701. It was powered by a General Motors 707 gasoline engine and had seats for 37 passengers.

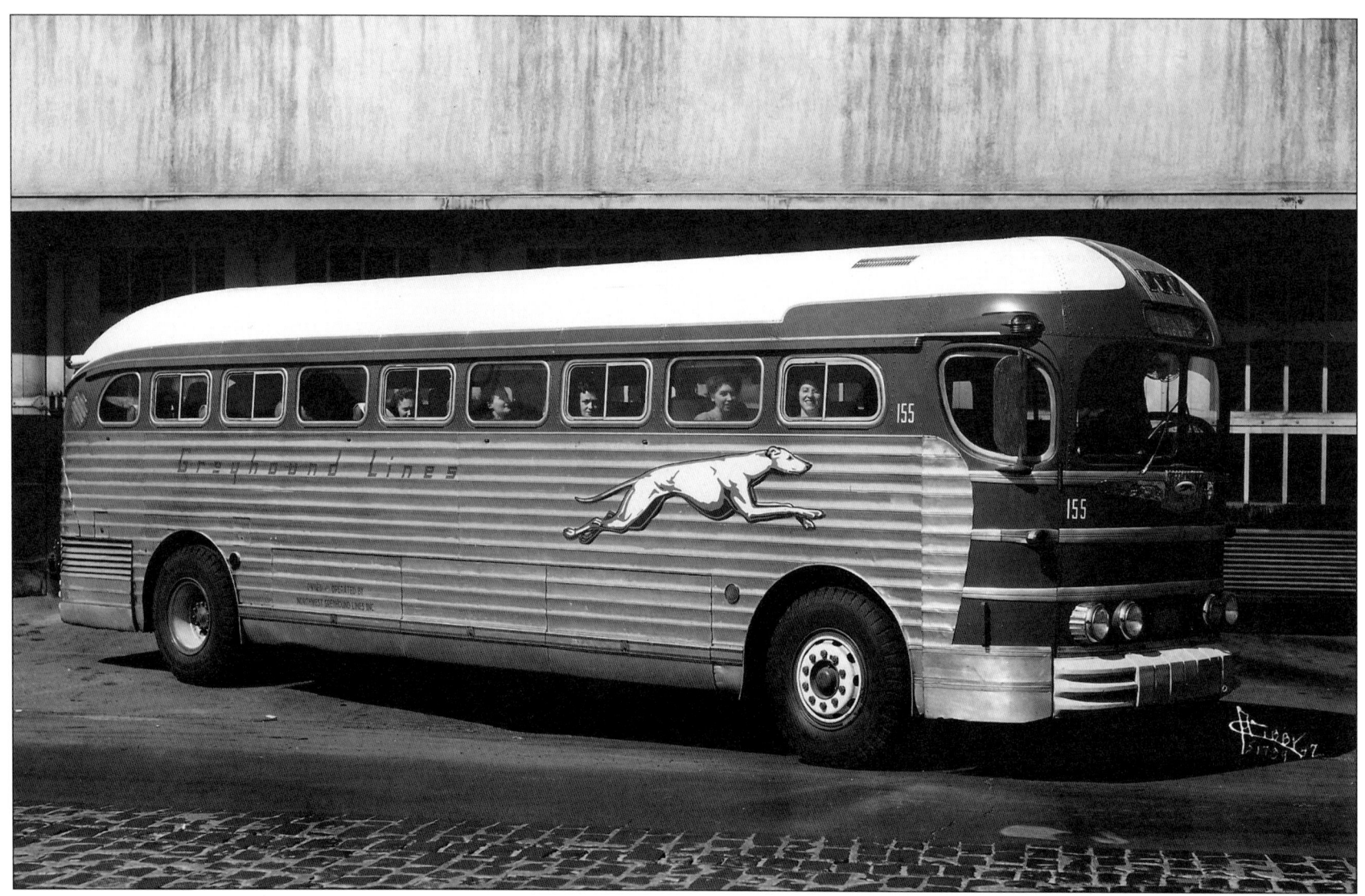

In 1940, the Silversides buses for Greyhound began service. They were built by Yellow Coach and the model was PGG or PDG 3701. The difference was that some were gasoline powered (PGG) and others were diesel-powered (PDG). About 600 of these pre-war Silversides were built. Companies that connected or had a close working arrangement with Greyhound, were allowed to purchase these buses. Washington Motor Coach Company originally acquired the bus pictured here. When Greyhound bought this company, the orange and blue Silversides in the Washington Motor Coach Company fleet were changed to the blue and white of Greyhound.

Greyhound Buses in the Movies

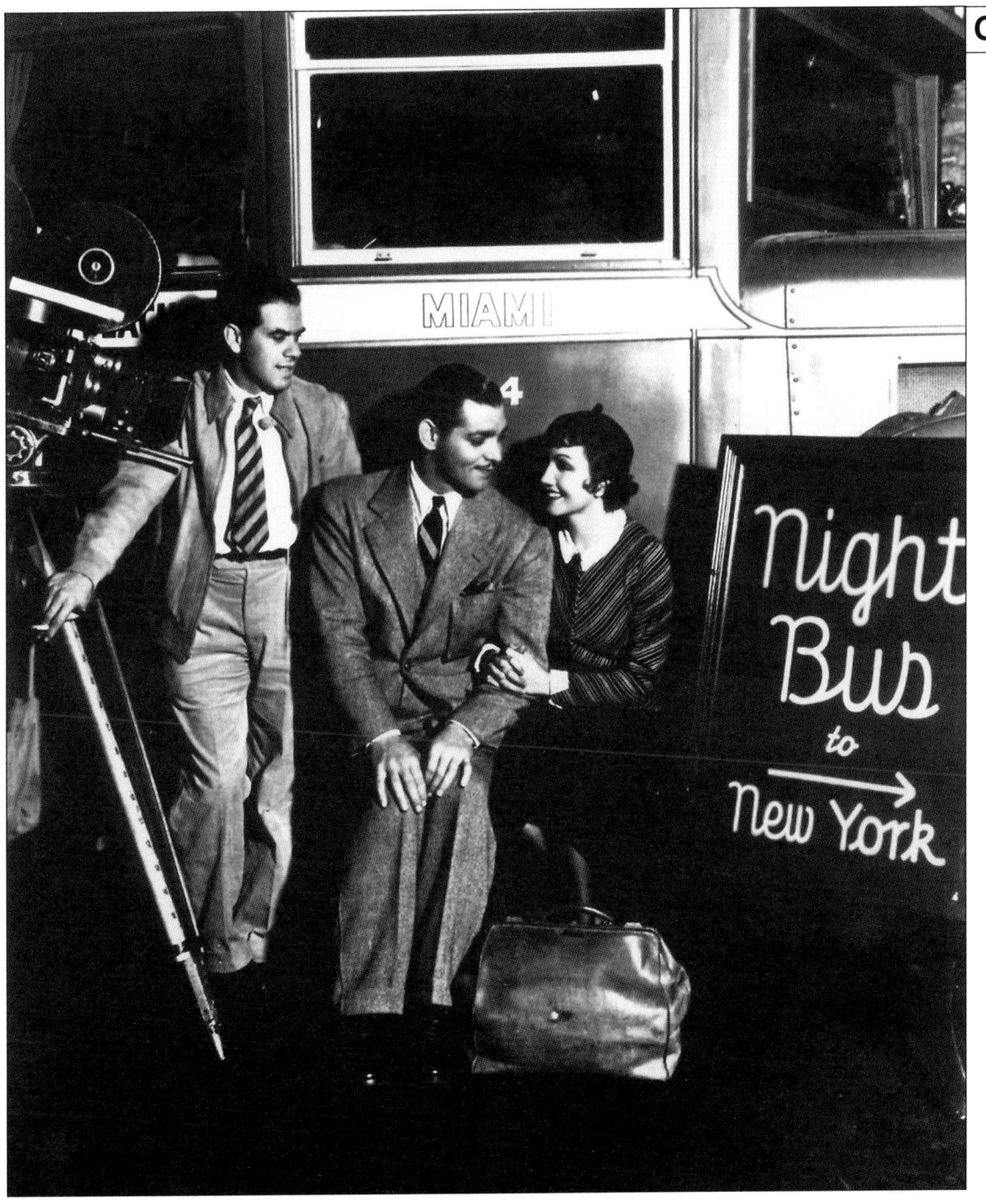

Greyhound received favorable publicity in 1934 when an Atlantic Greyhound Yellow Coach Model 670 Z-250 appeared in an award winning Hollywood film, "It Happened One Night." Clark Gable and Claudette Colbert, the stars in the film, received Academy Awards for their roles. Roscoe Karns also appeared. The Z-250 did not receive an award! The presence of the Greyhound bus in the film gave Greyhound publicity that was very important at that time.

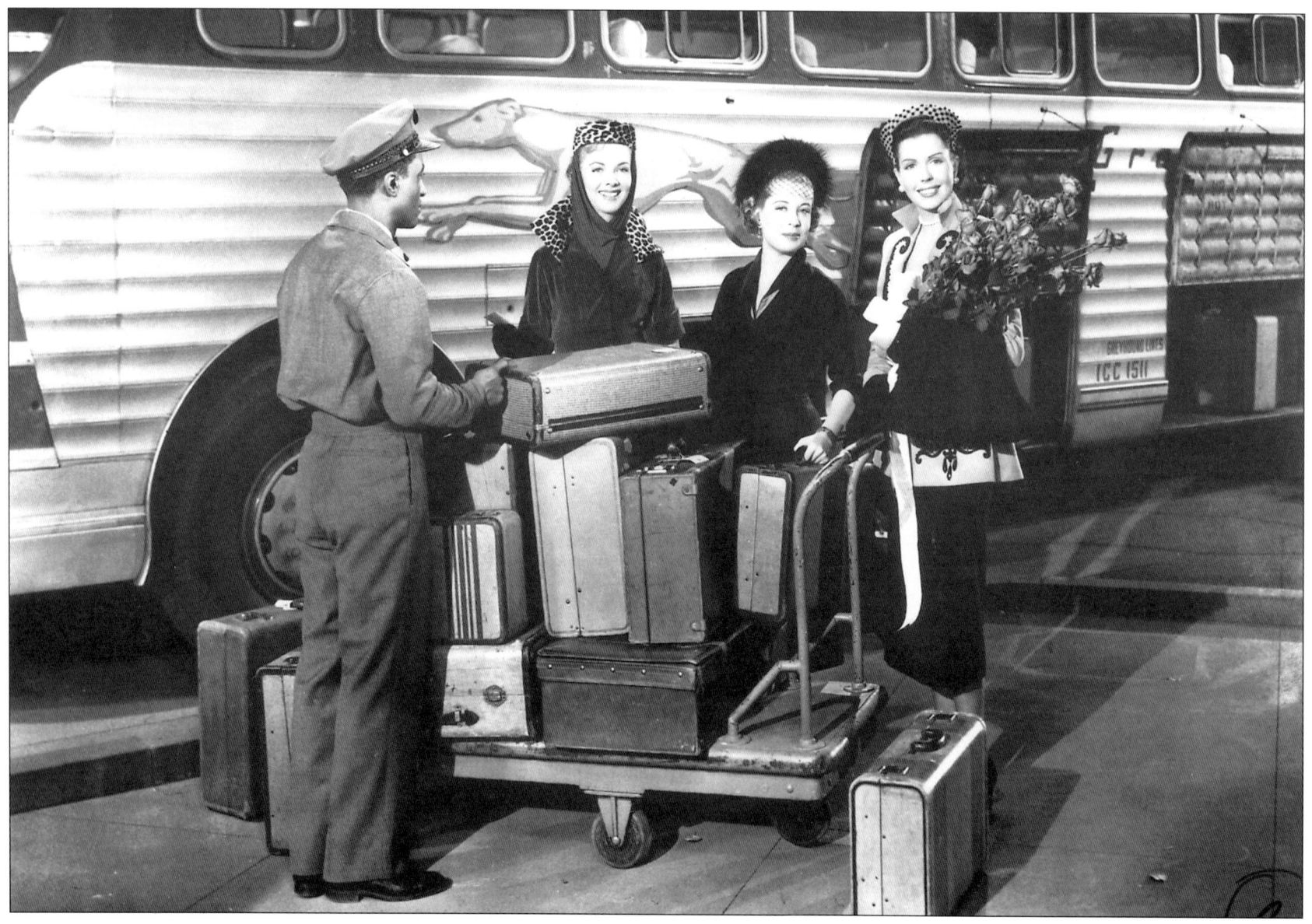

A Greyhound GM PD3751 "Silversides" bus appeared in the 1951 Hollywood film, "Two Tickets to Broadway." Starring in the film, shown standing alongside the Silverides collecting their baggage, were Gloria DeHaven, Vivian Blaine, and Ann Miller. The Silversides appeared in the film frequently. Scenes at Greyhound bus terminals were also featured in the film.

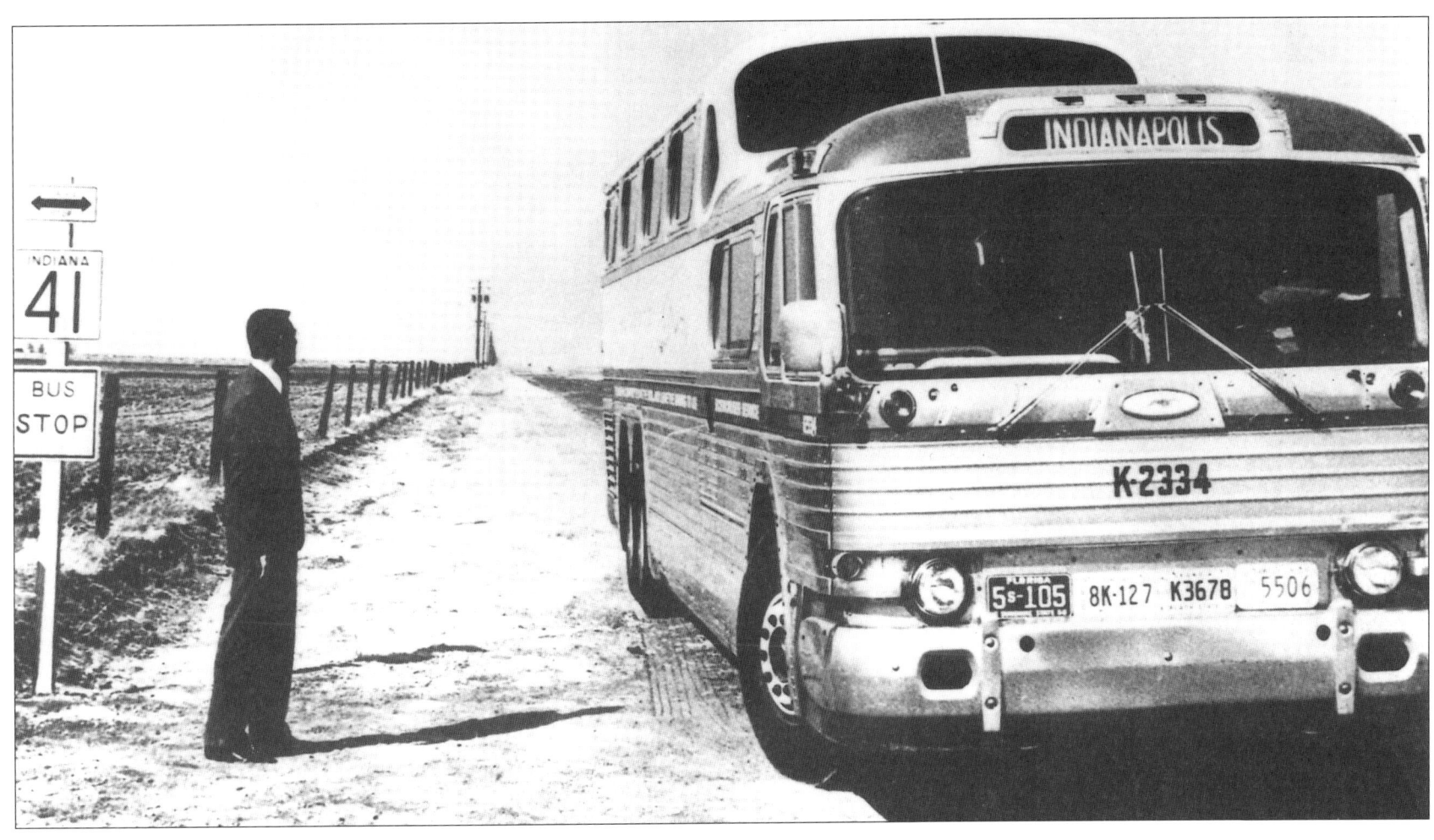
In 1956, a Greyhound Lines Scenicruiser was used in the movie, "North by Northwest." The film was an Alfred Hitchcock thriller. It starred Cary Grant, Eva Marie Saint, and John Mason.

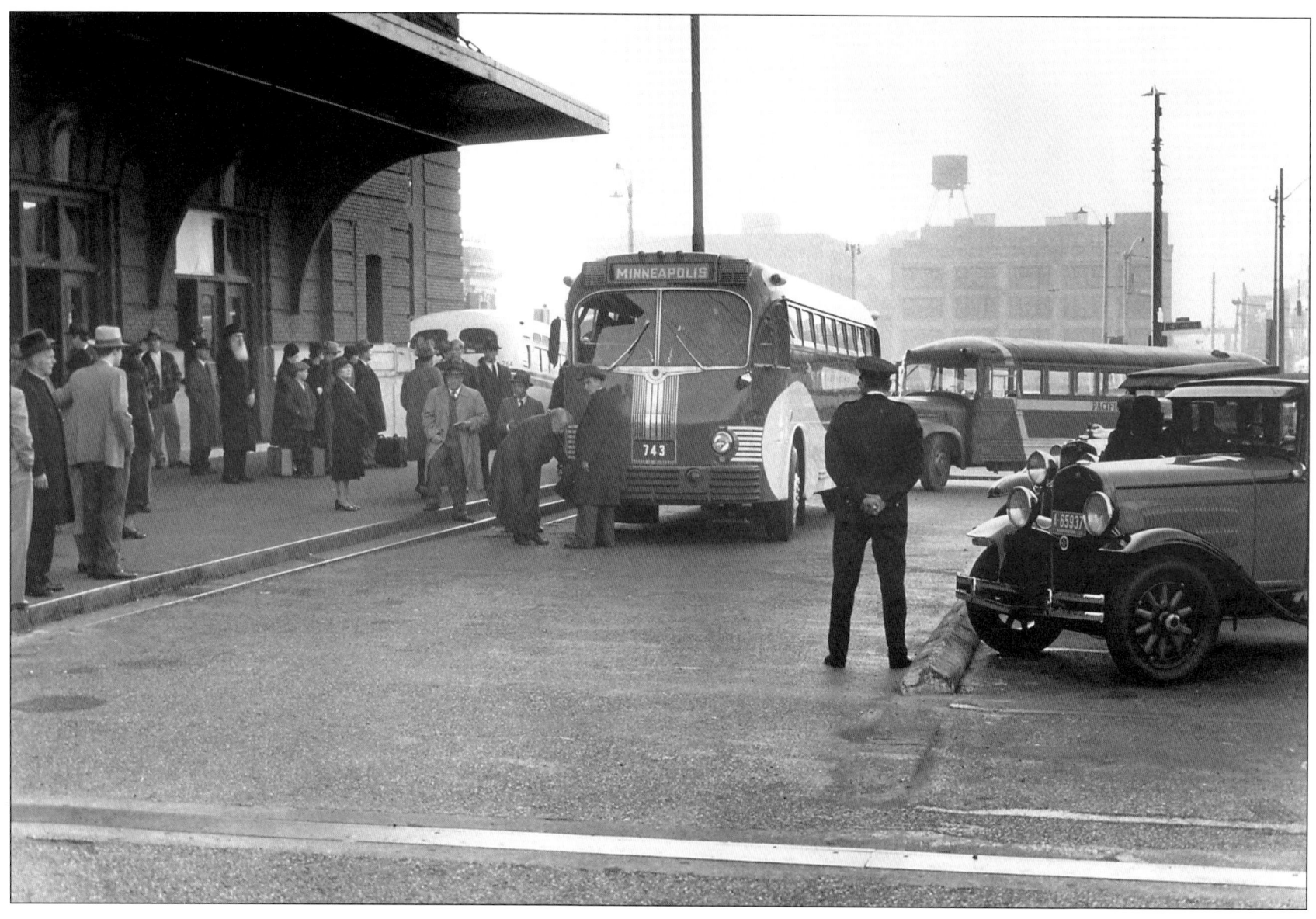

Greyhound has restored several buses, and a 1937 Yellow Coach Model 743 restored bus was used in the 1982 Hollywood film entitled "Frances." The movie deals with the life of Frances Farmer (played by Jessica Lange). The scene pictured here shows the Yellow Coach at Seattle's Union Station on a foggy day.

Small Greyhound Buses

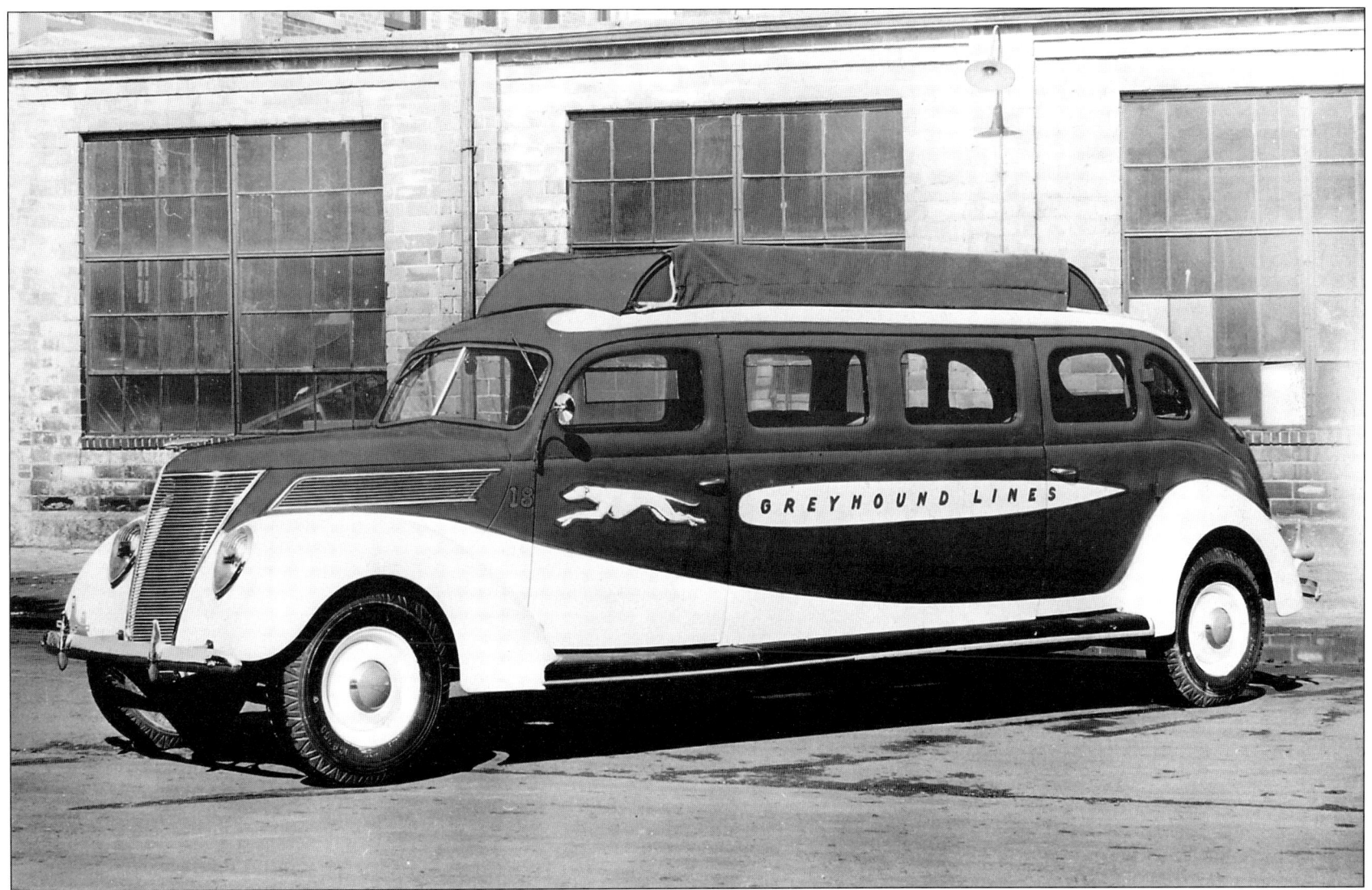

After cold Minnesota winters, the ground would thaw, causing uneven surfaces to roads for several weeks. Heavy vehicles, including buses, were not allowed on specified roads during that period. To maintain bus service, Northland Greyhound would operate a variety of lightweight buses. One of Northland Greyhound's "spring breakup buses" was this 1937 Ford V-8 stretchout, seating 10-11 passengers.

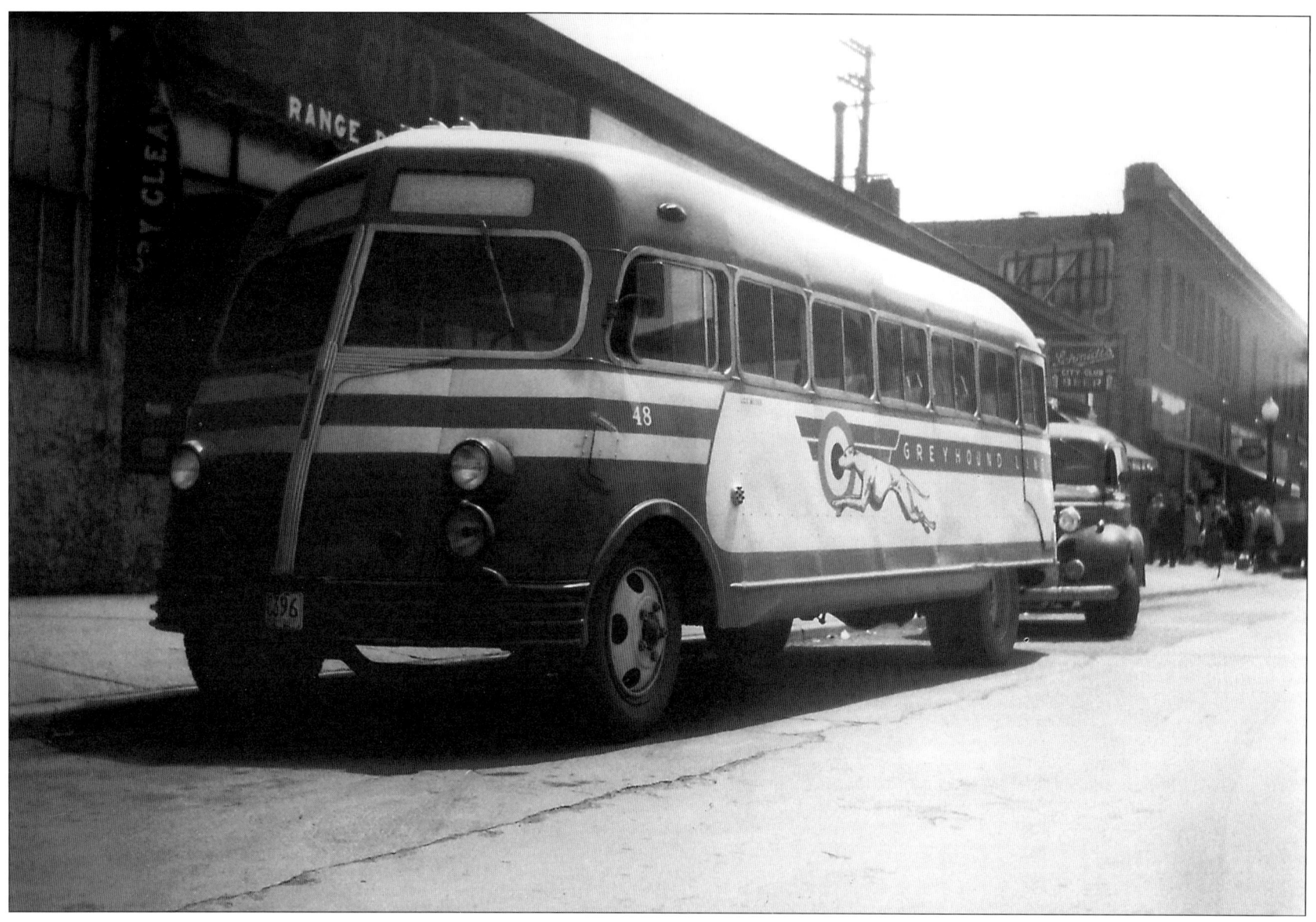

A number of small buses were in service on some routes of Northland Greyhound Lines in Minnesota each spring. This was because vehicle weight restrictions were in effect when the "spring breakup" occurred. Pictured here in Virginia, Minnesota, is an Aerocoach EFI used on the restricted Virginia-Ely route. Greyhound acquired a number of Aerocoaches of this type when several Wisconsin bus lines were acquired.

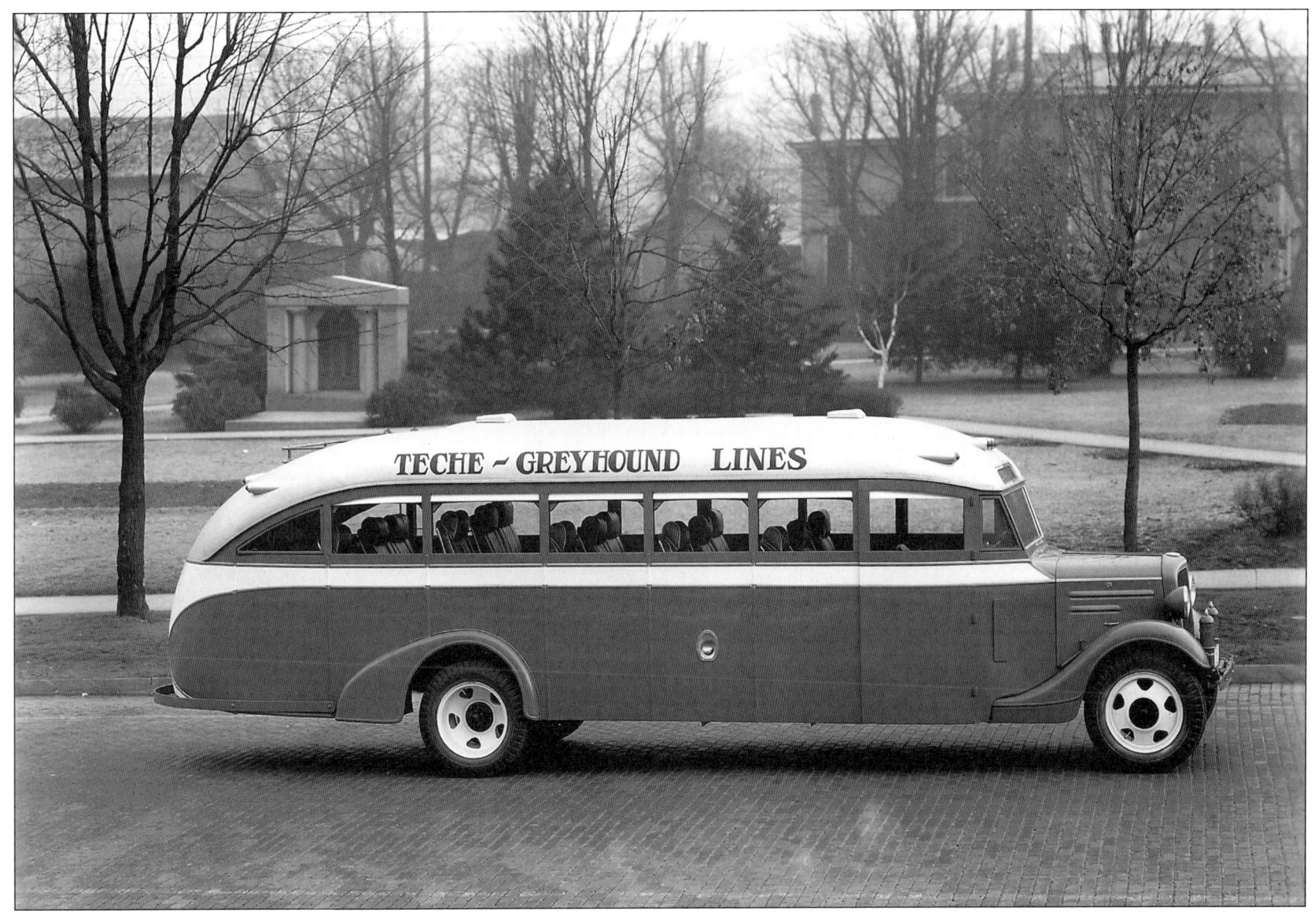

In 1936, Teche Greyhound Lines, which operated primarily in southern Louisiana, purchased four 19-passenger Flxible Airway Model 19C76 buses. These buses were used mainly on branch lines. The Teche Greyhound Flxible Airway buses were mounted on a 1936 Chevrolet truck chassis with a six-cylinder valve-in-head gasoline engine with 29.5 horsepower.

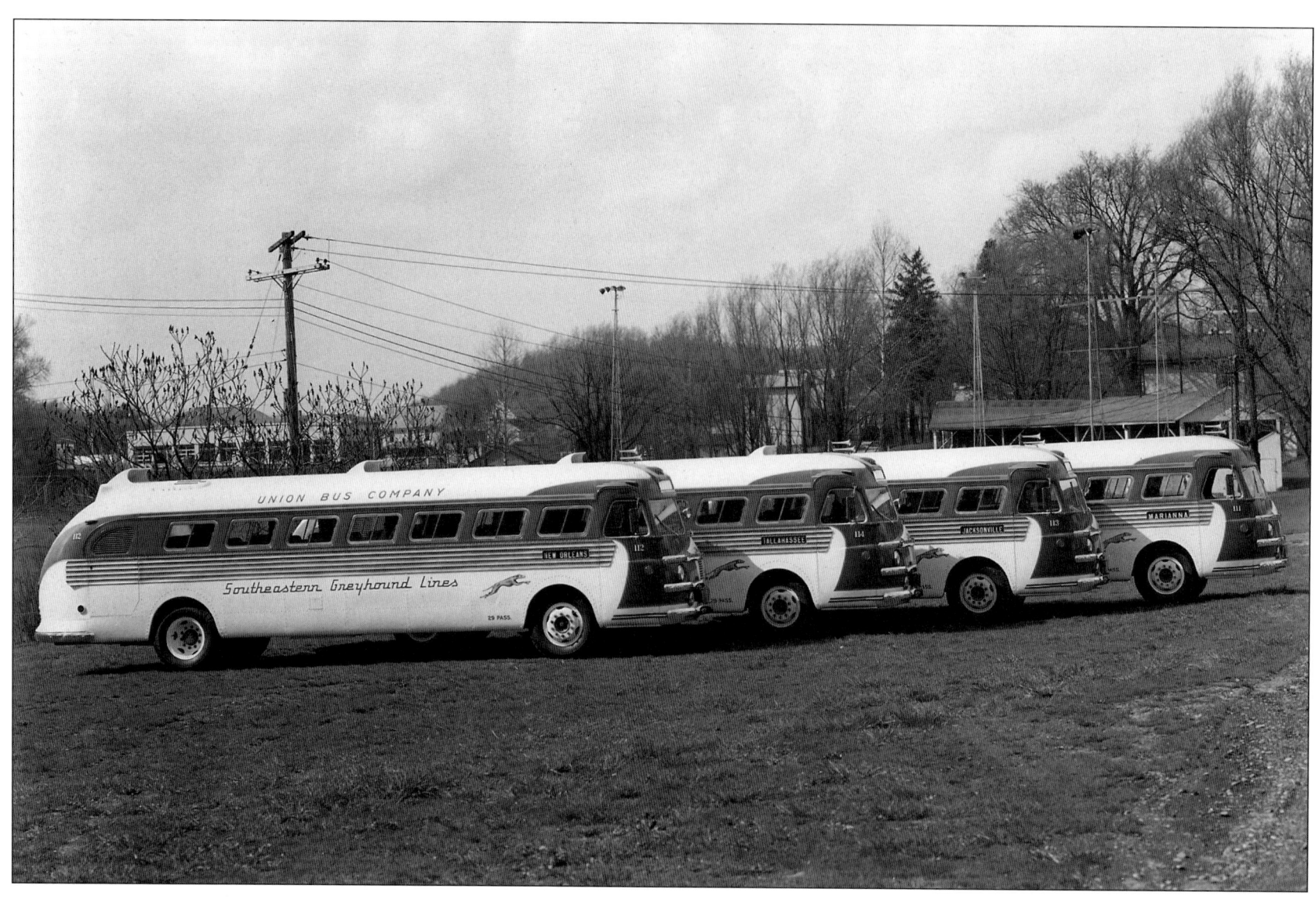

Pictured are four of six Flxible Clipper Model 29-BR-41 buses delivered to Union Bus Company of Jacksonville, Florida, in 1941. The Model 29-BR-41 Flxible Clipper had a FB Buick straight-eight bus engine mounted in the rear of the bus. Seating was for 29 passengers and there was a large luggage compartment at the rear. Union Bus Company operated routes west of Jacksonville as a part of Southeastern Greyhound Lines service. Southeastern Greyhound later acquired Union Bus Company.

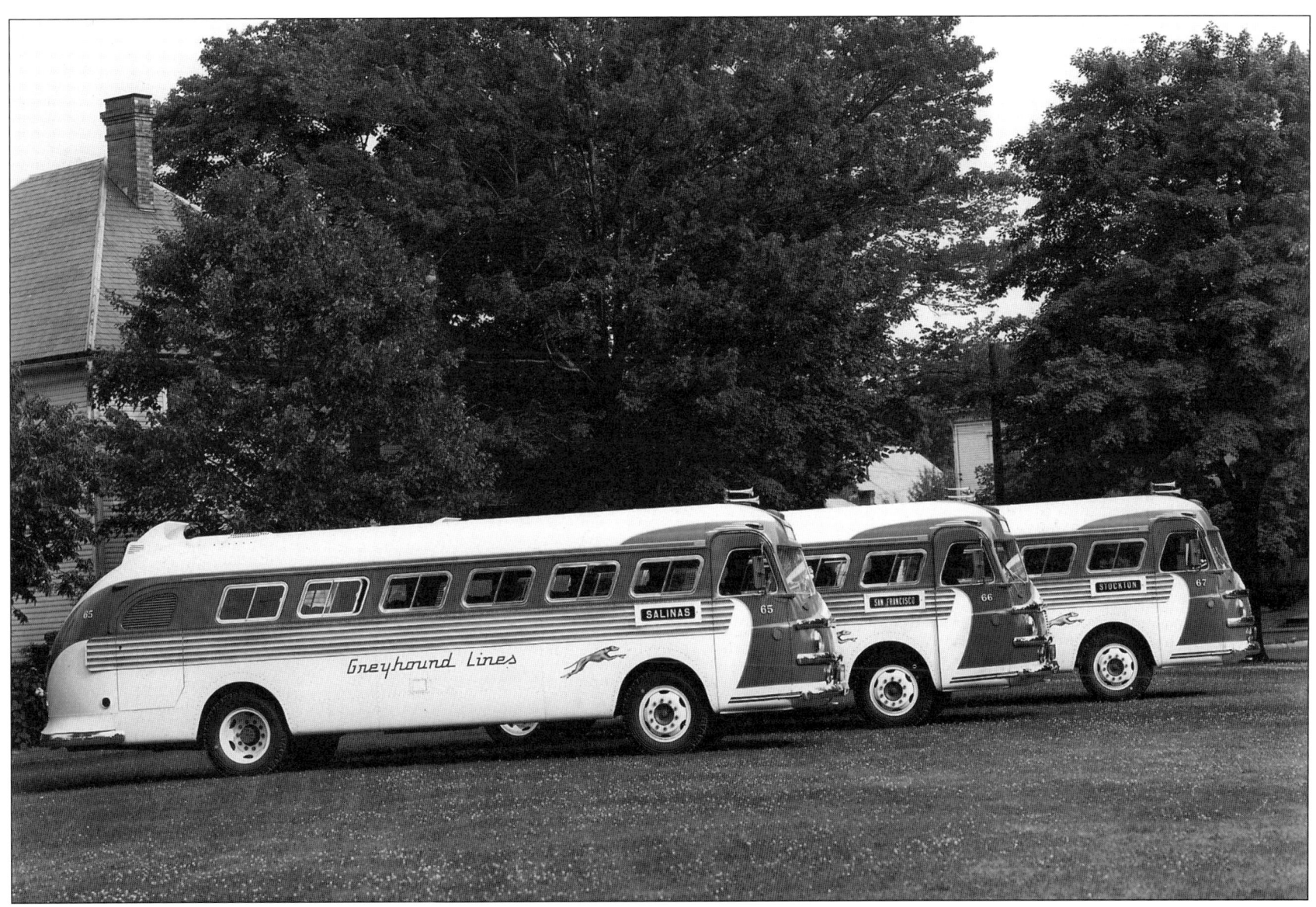

Three 25 CR-41 Flxible Clippers were delivered to Pacific Greyhound Lines in 1941. These buses were used on secondary routes of Pacific Greyhound. Chevrolet six-cylinder engines, mounted in-line at the rear, were used. Note the horns at the top of the bus. They were air horns and were typically used on most buses of that day.

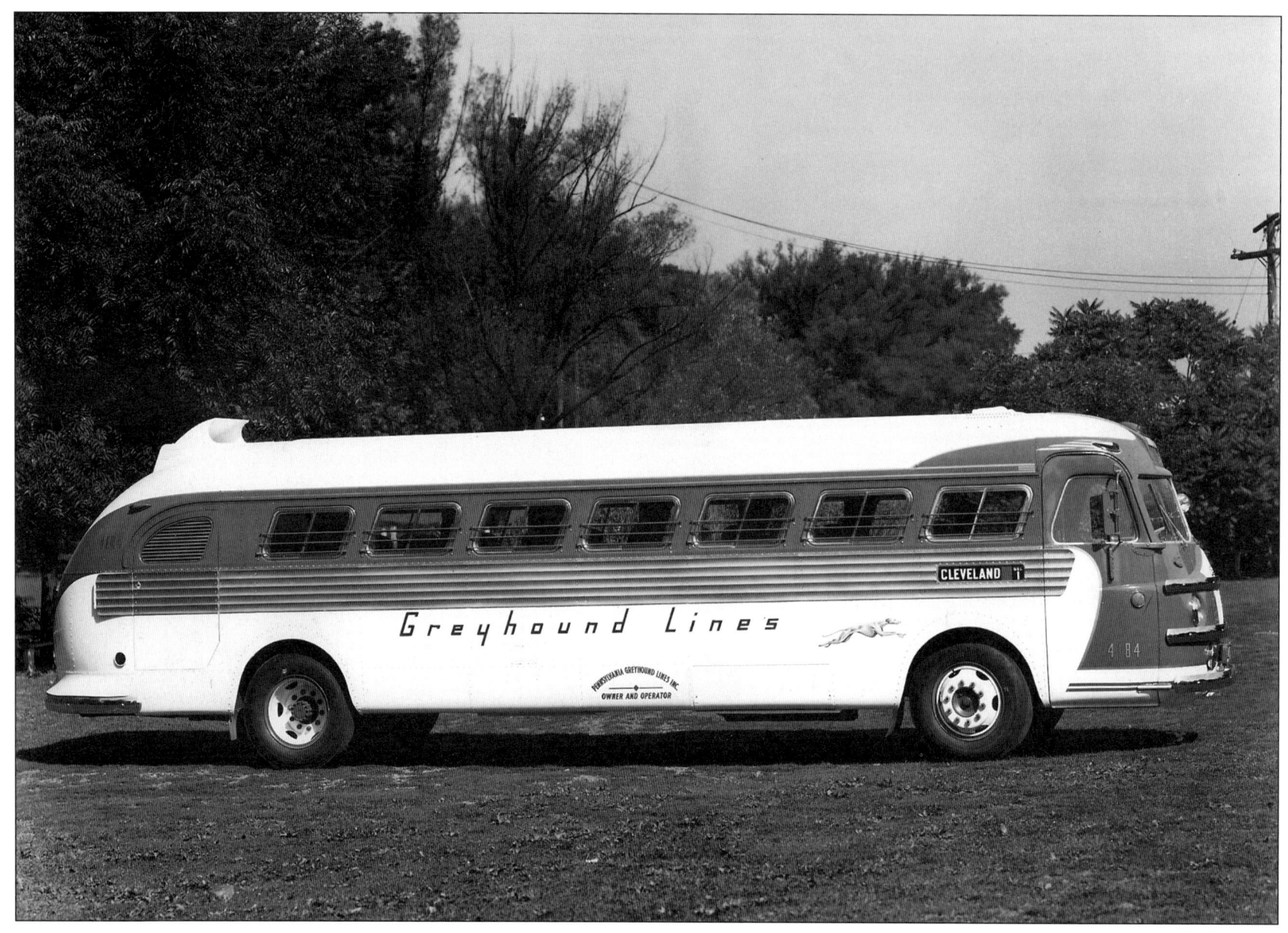

Pennsylvania Greyhound took delivery of 20 Flxible Clipper 29-BR-41 buses in 1941. The 29-passenger Flxible Clipper was a very popular bus for many bus companies in the early 1940s. The Model 29-BR-41 had a Buick straight-eight bus engine.

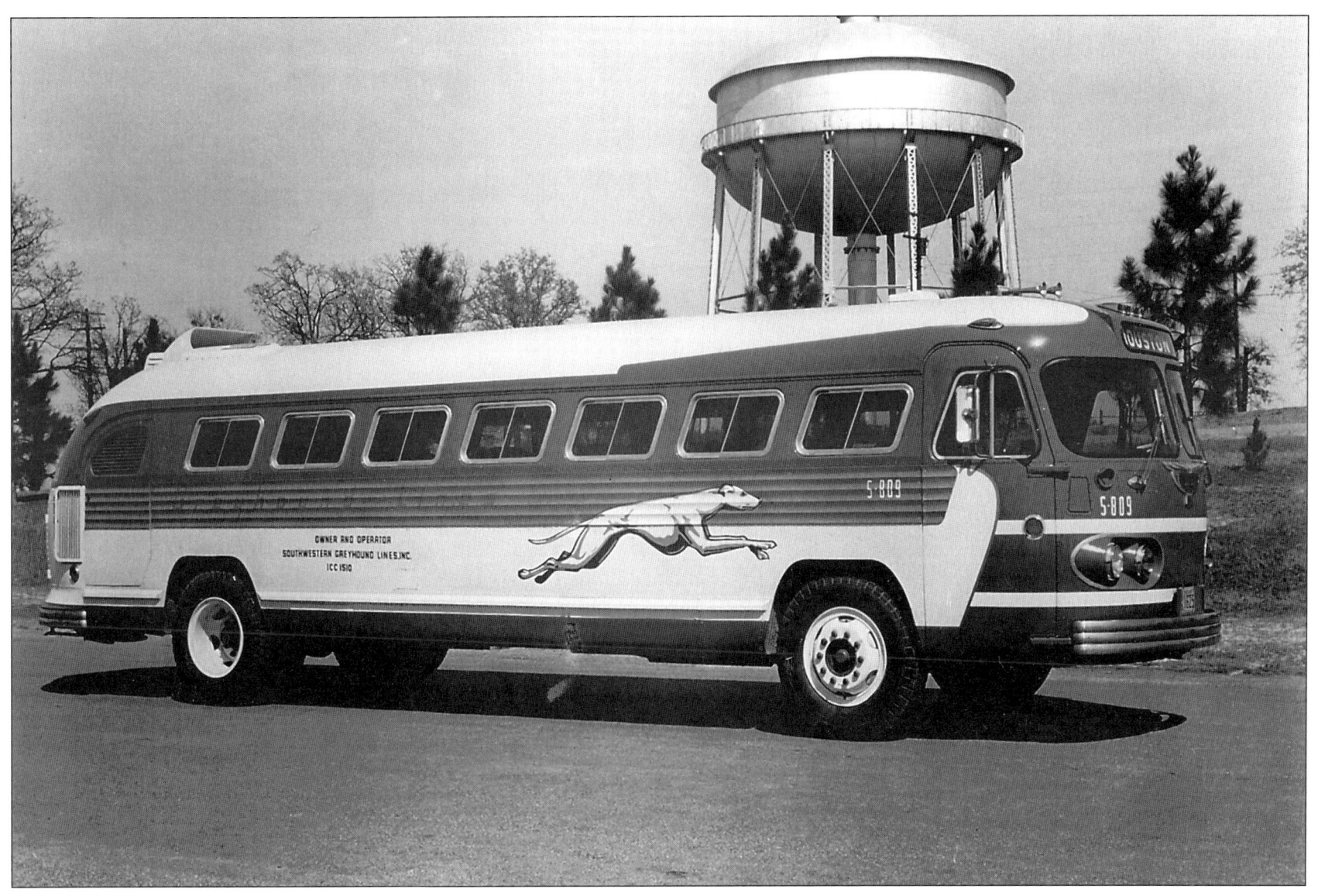

In 1949, Southwestern Greyhound bought 10 Flxible Clipper Model 19B1-49AC buses for service on light lines on its system and for overloads. The post-war Flxible Clipper had a rounded front and the three bumpers common on the front of the pre-war Clipper were not used. These buses were air-conditioned.

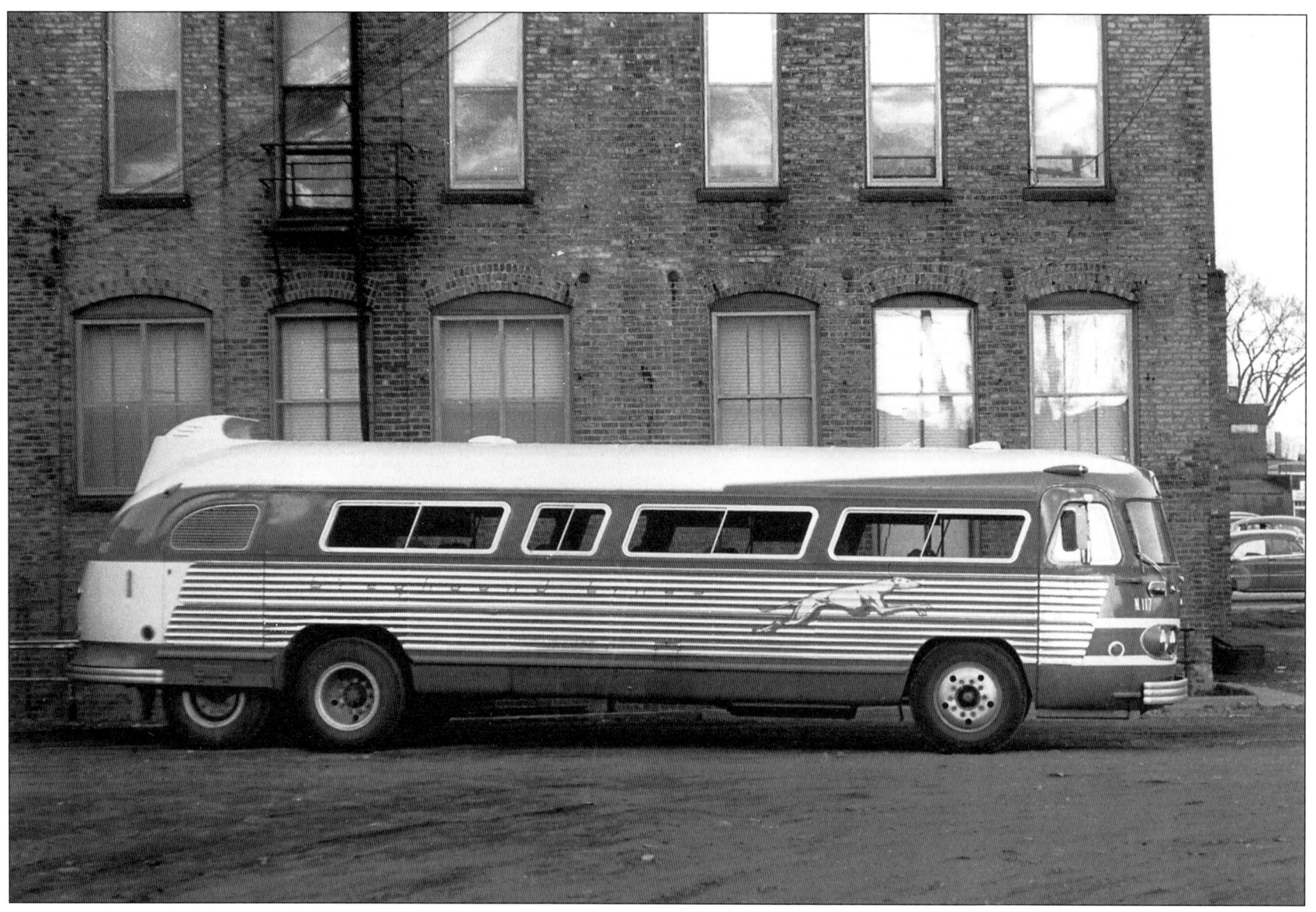

Northland Greyhound Lines purchased 16 Flxible Clipper 218B 29-passenger buses in 1953. A unique feature of these buses was that they had an extra set of wheels behind the rear driving wheels. The extra wheels were said to provide better weight distribution, allowing the bus to use weight-restricted roads during the Minnesota "spring breakup." The buses were also used at other times for second sections.

World's Fair Buses

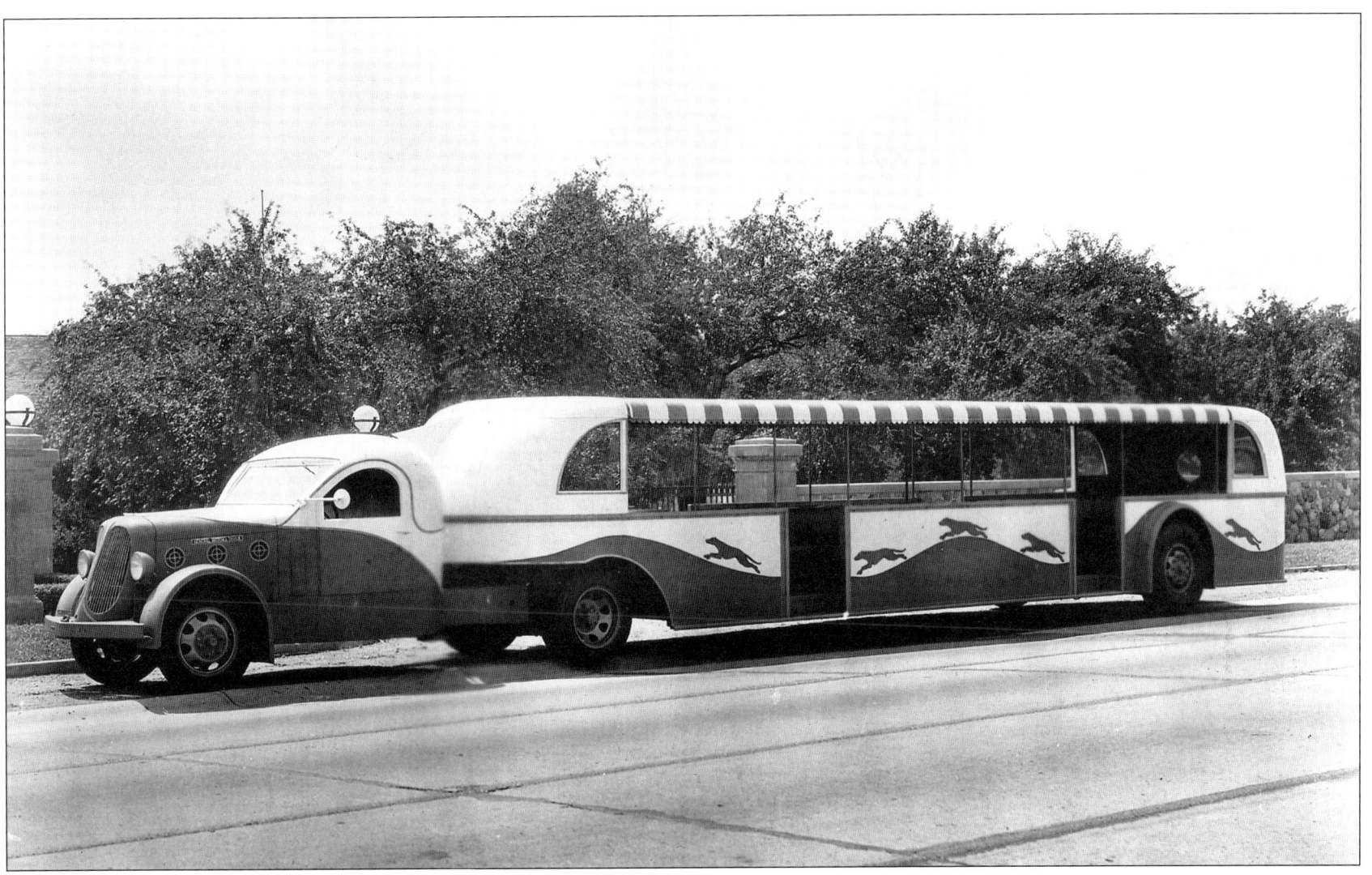

Greyhound Lines had a contract to supply buses for transportation on the site of the Chicago Century of Progress World's Fair in 1933-1934. Shown here is one of the 60 buses Greyhound had built by General Motors. The tractor was a Model T-26 GMC truck. James J. St. Croix, a well-known industrial designer, designed the vehicle.

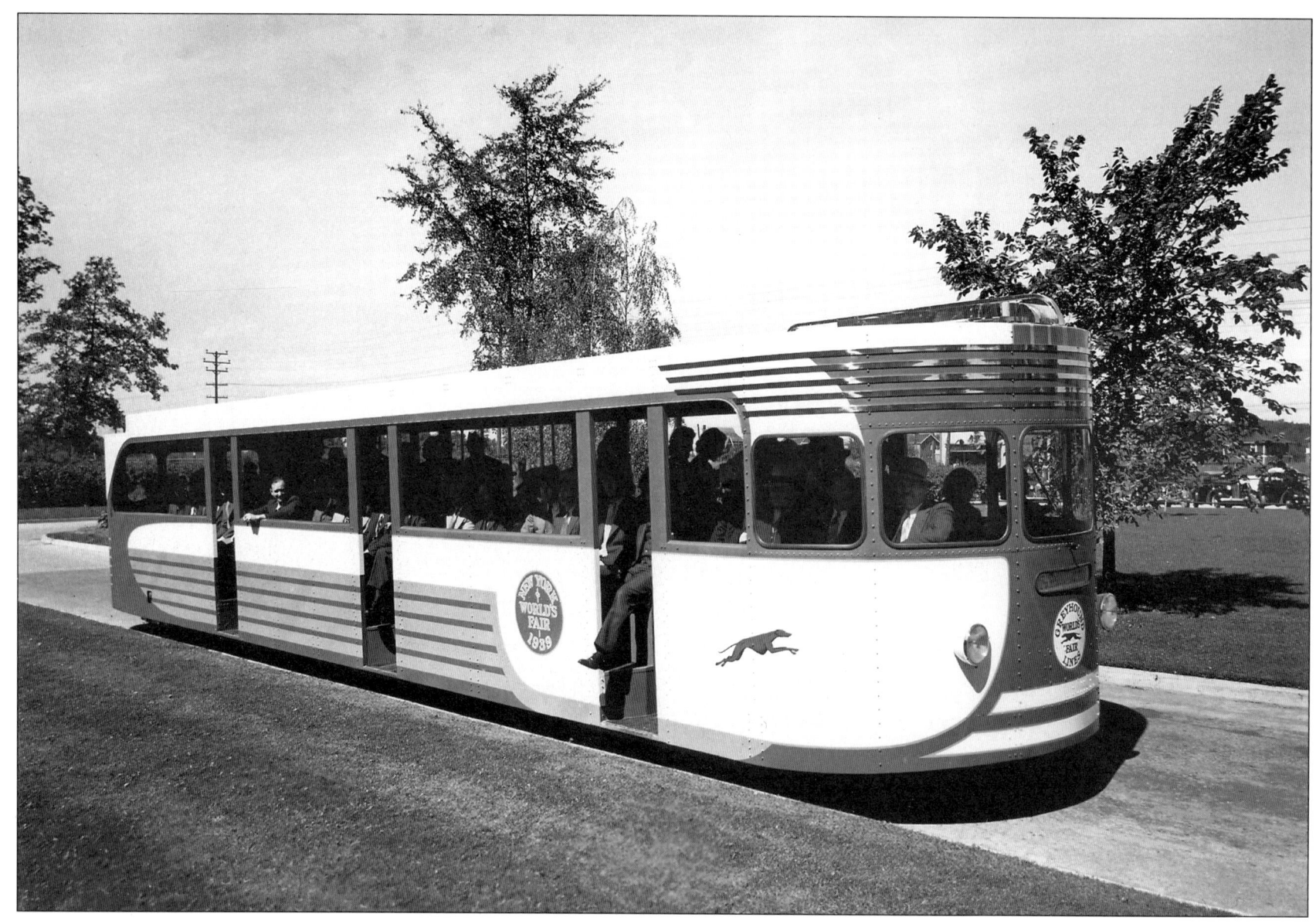

During the 1939-1940 World's Fair in New York City, Greyhound Lines was contracted to operate buses on the grounds of the fair. Greyhound had 100 of these buses built by Yellow Coach. The model number assigned was 1207. Seating was for approximately 50 passengers. Some 50 or more passengers were able to stand in the space between the seats. Greyhound also had a concession to operate restaurants at the fair.

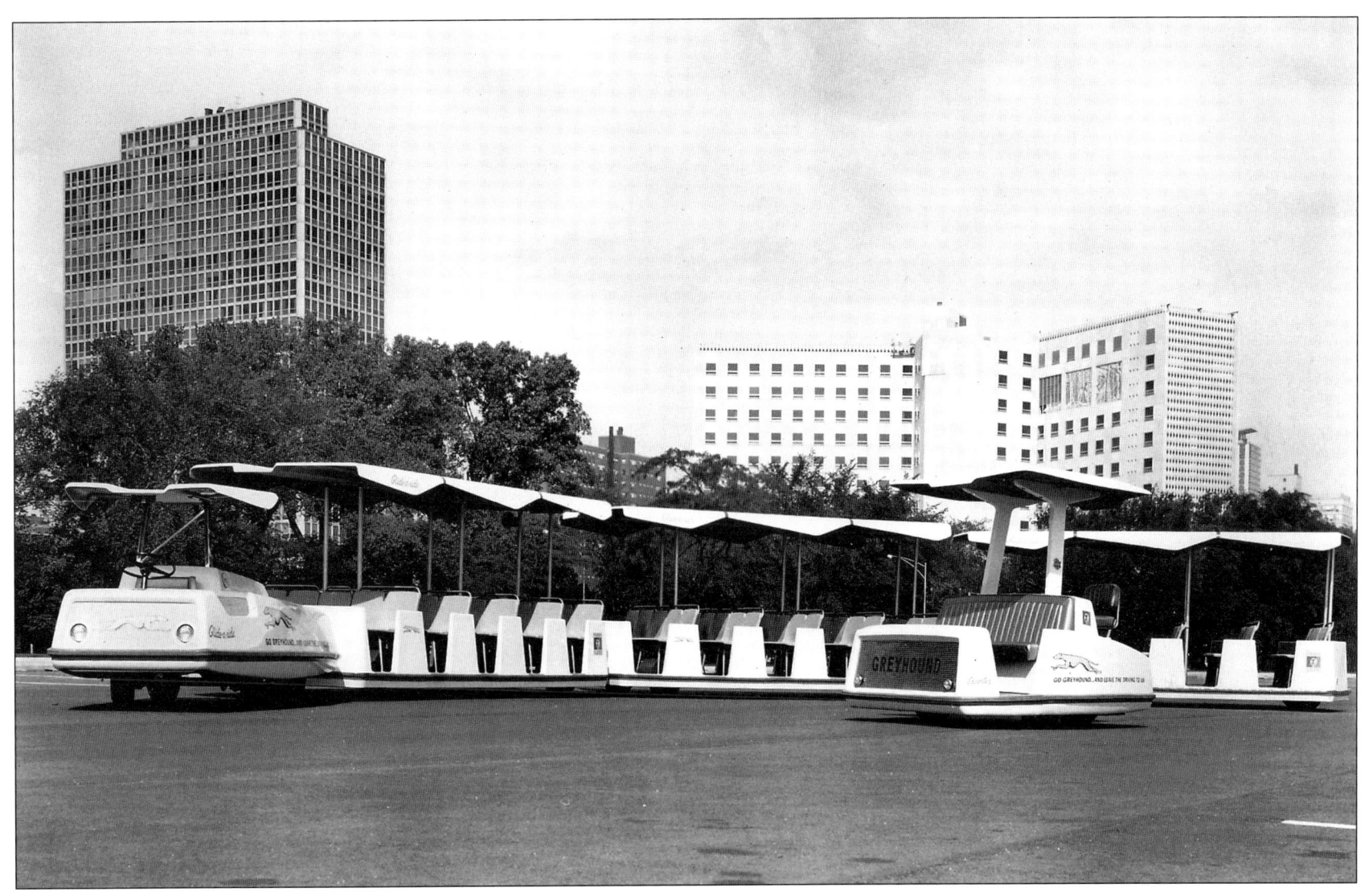

In addition to operating large General Motors TDH 5302 transit buses at the 1964-1965 New York World's Fair, two other types of vehicles were under contract by Greyhound. In the foreground is one of the four-seater "Escorters." The Escorter provided personalized sightseeing service at the fair and was designed and manufactured by Kalamazoo Manufacturing Co. In the background is the "Glide-a-Ride," 60-passenger trailer vehicles designed and manufactured by Clark Equipment Co., in Battle Creek, Michigan.

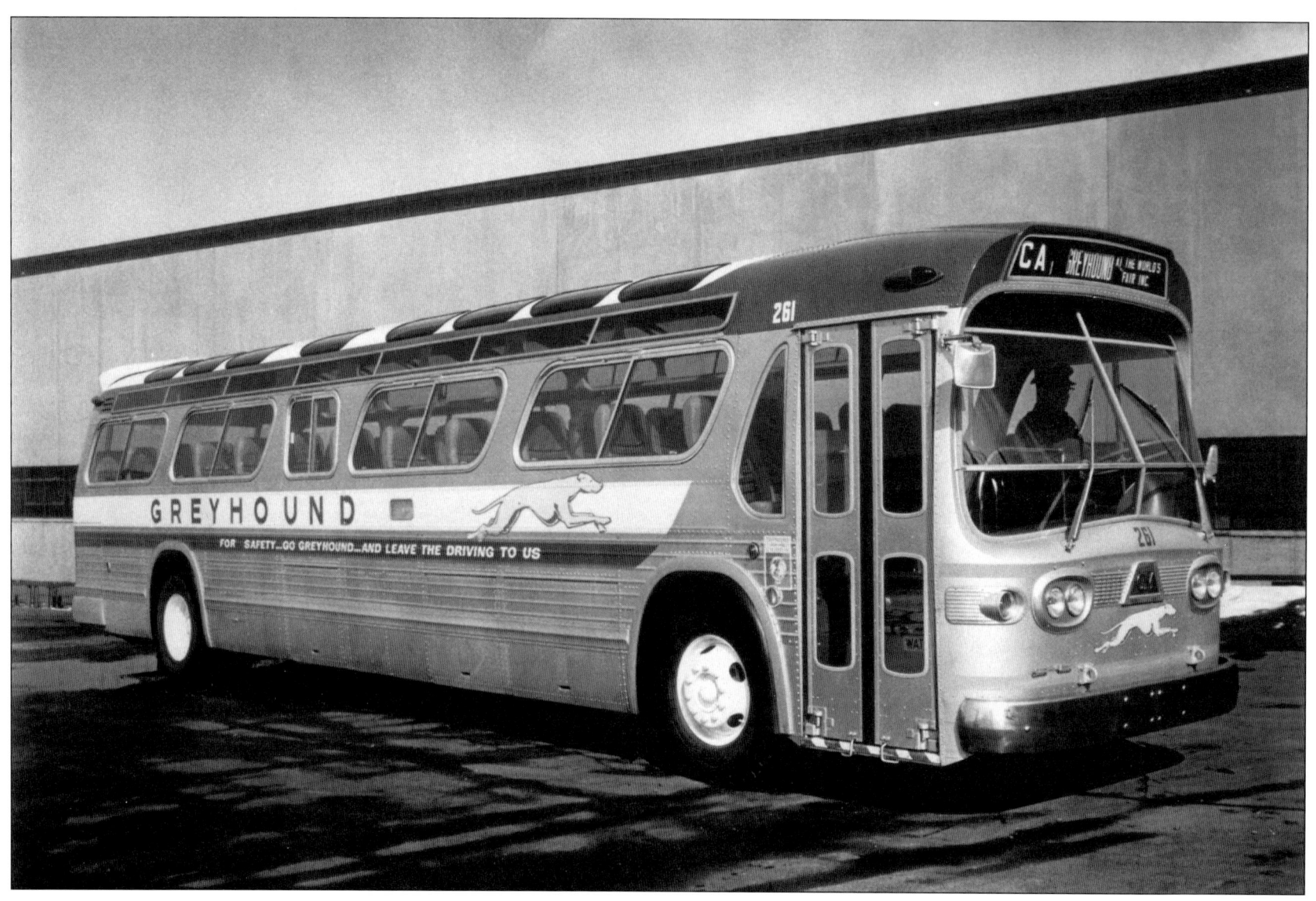

For the 1964 New York World's Fair, 40 General Motors SDM 5302 buses were in service. The windows at the top of the bus gave the passengers added viewing. These buses were sold to bus companies in the New York area after the fair closed. *Don Coffin Collection*

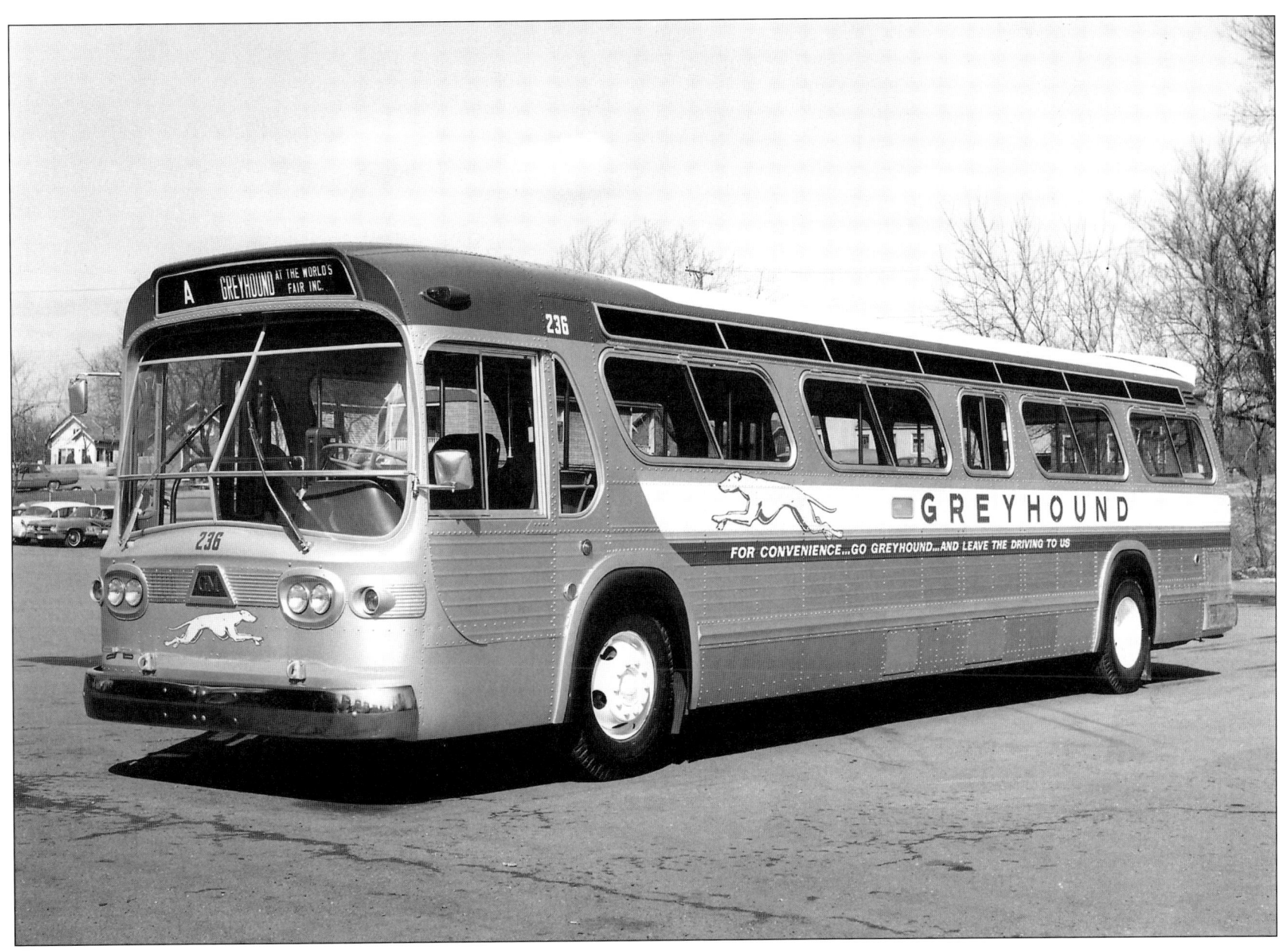

General Motors TDH 5303 transit buses were built for Greyhound Lines in 1964. They were used in New York World's Fair service at first, but were sold after the fair was over.

Greyhound Bus Stations

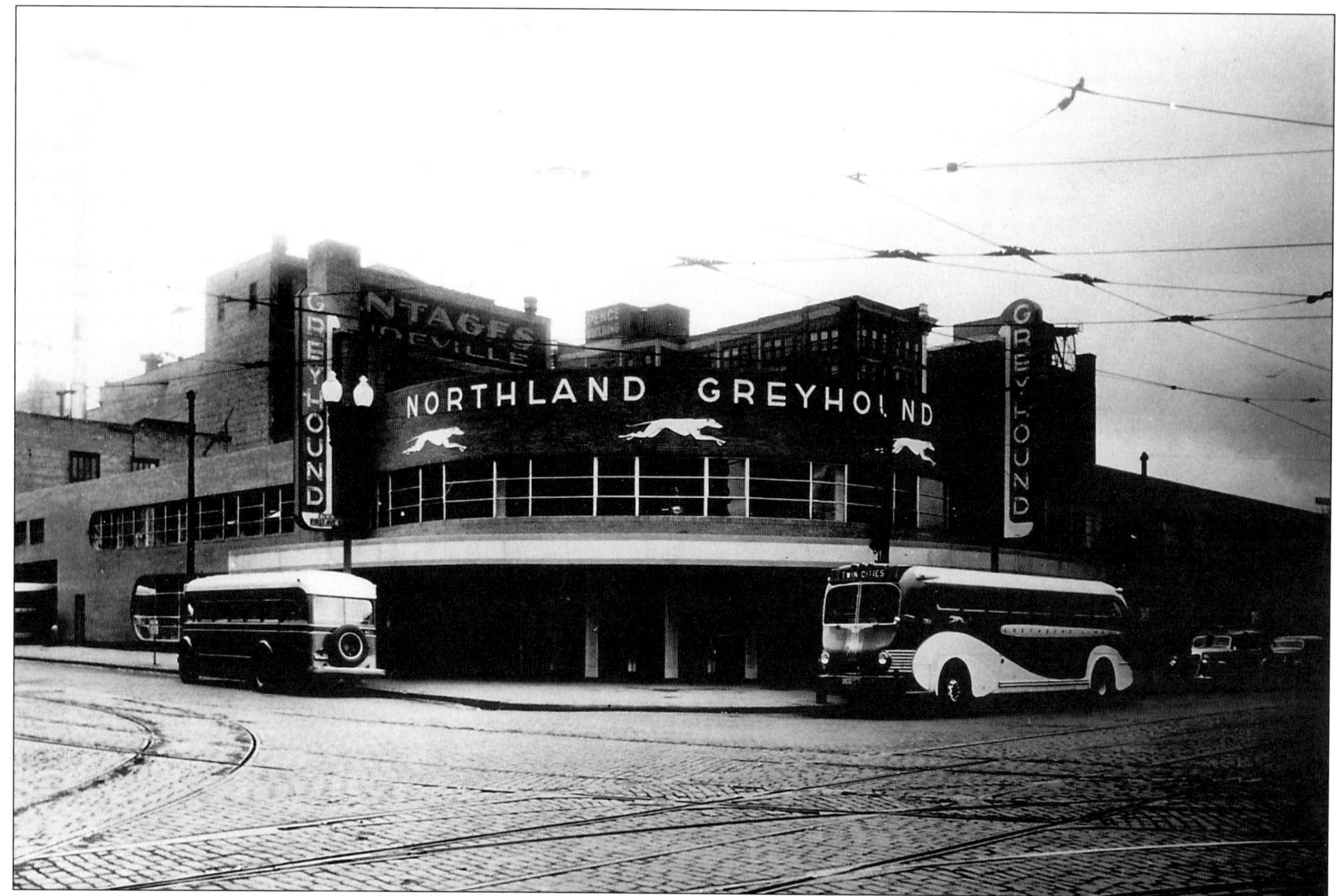

In 1937, Northland Greyhound Lines opened a new bus terminal in Minneapolis, Minnesota. The cost of the building, which featured blue glazed brick on the front, was $500,000. Inside loading for the buses was featured. There was a sizable waiting room, restaurant, ticket office, express room, travel bureau, and lavatories.

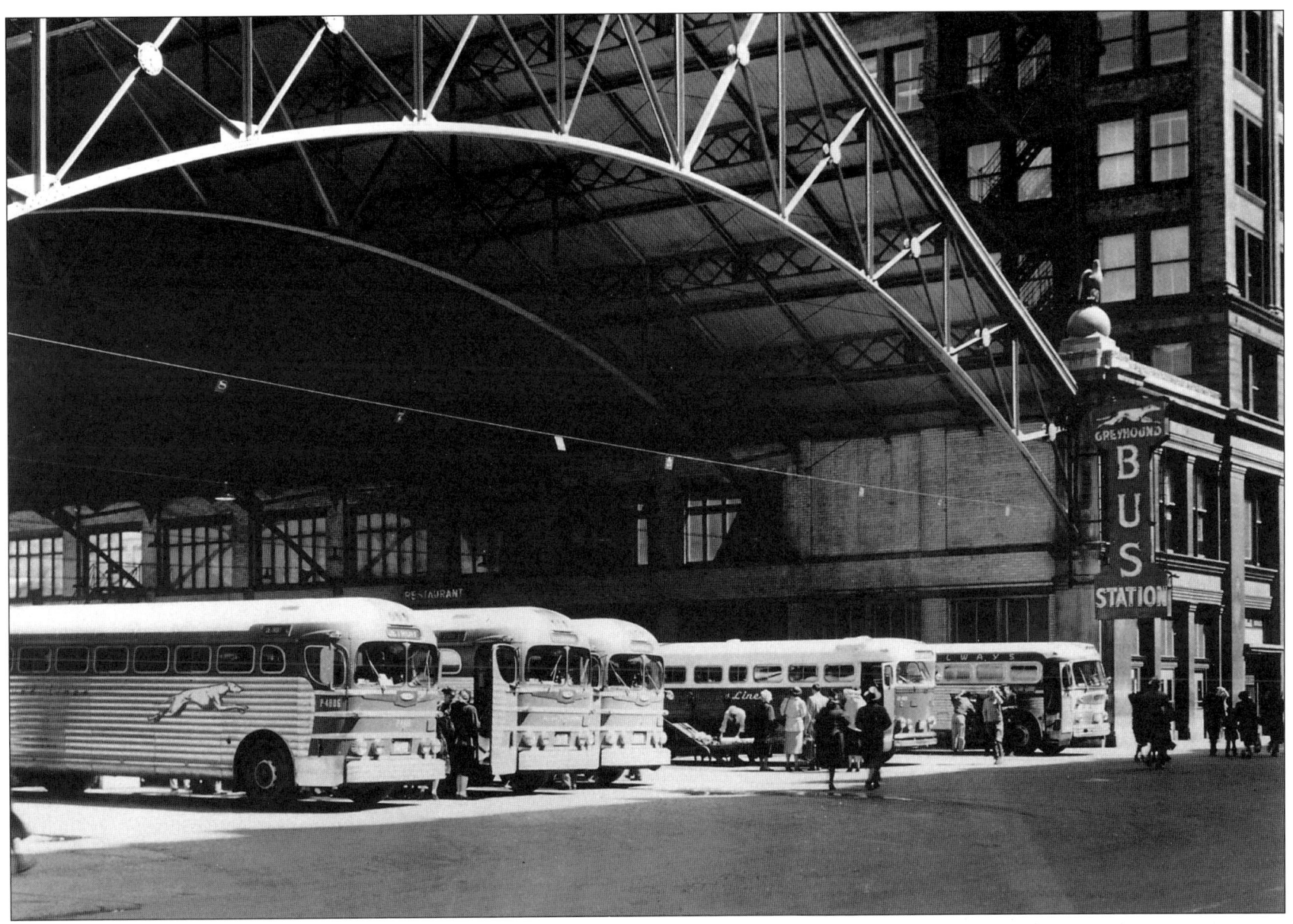

The Indianapolis, Indiana, Traction Terminal Bus Station served Pennsylvania Greyhound Lines and 12 other bus companies from the early 1930s. It was originally a busy terminal for the electric interurban railways that served Indiana. For a number of years, both interurban railways and bus lines shared the terminal. *Tom Jones Collection*

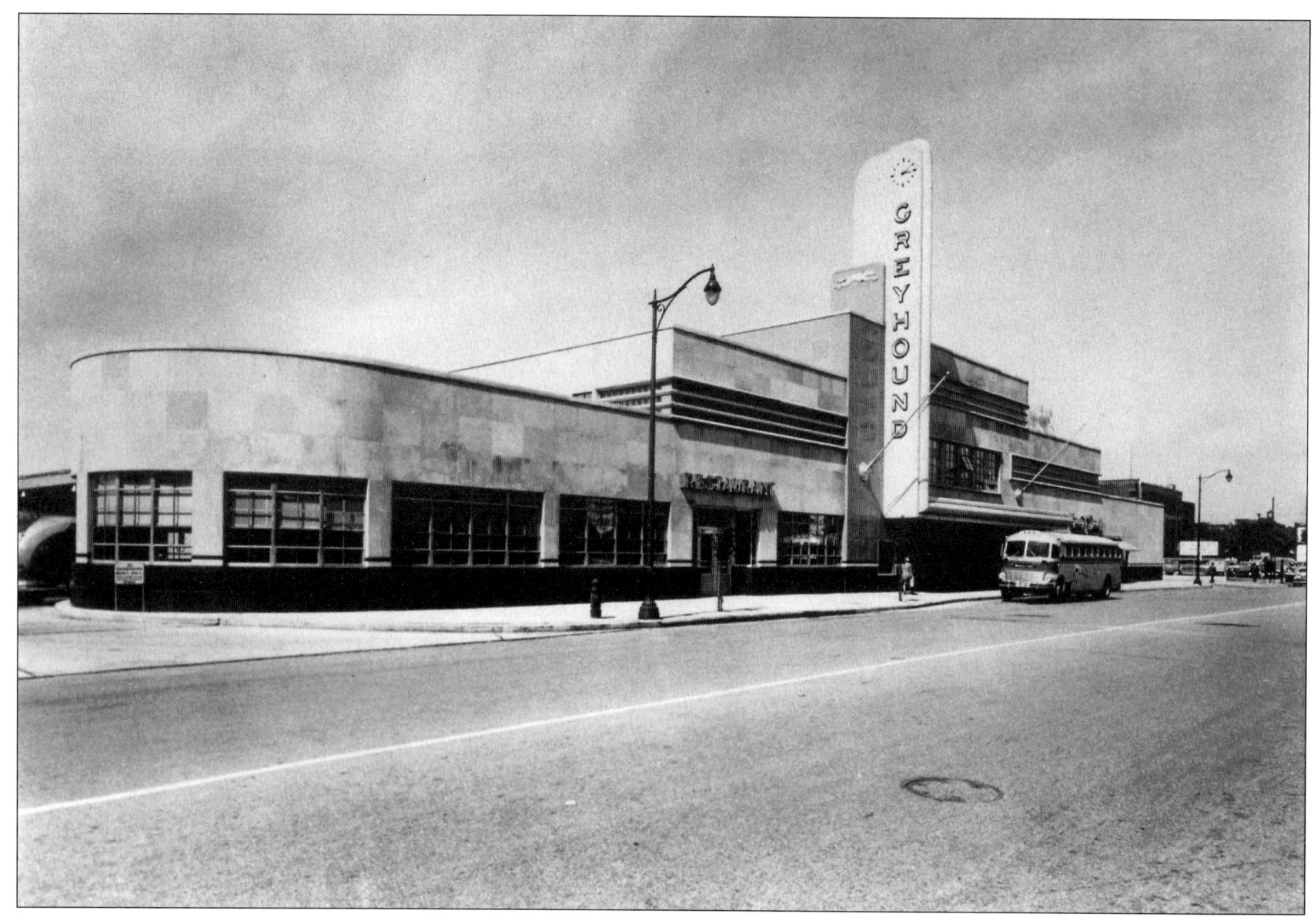

The Greyhound Bus Terminal in Cleveland, Ohio, was built in 1948 and continues to serve Greyhound schedules. The terminal has recently been renovated. It has an Art Deco style – popular from 1935 to 1950 – and is now on the National Register of Historic Places. The Cleveland Terminal architect, William Sudwick Arrasmith, was involved in the design and construction of approximately 60 other Greyhound terminals. *Don Coffin Collection*

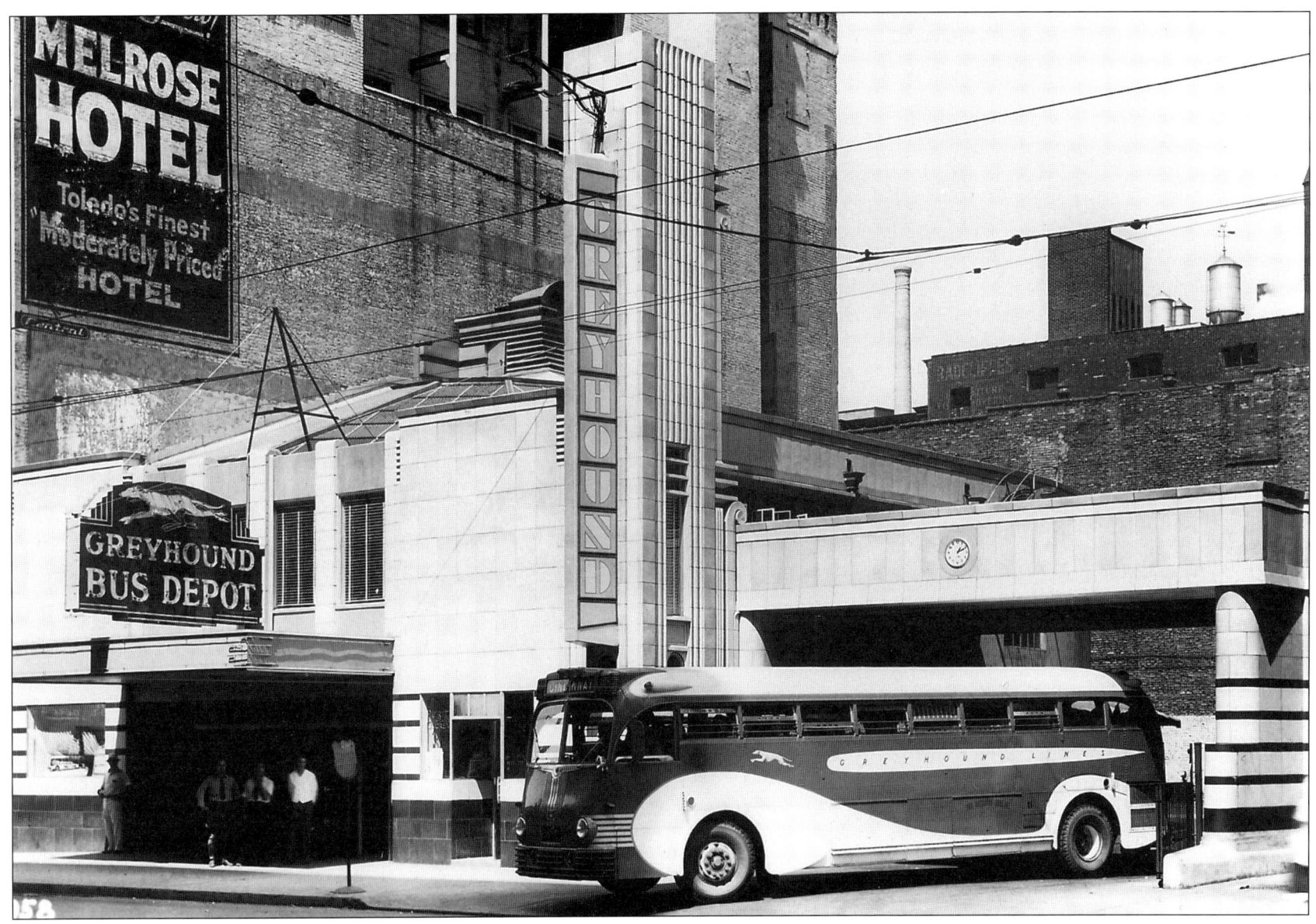

Many medium-sized cities had convenient bus terminals in the downtown areas in the 1930s and 1940s. This is a view of the Greyhound bus terminal in Toledo, Ohio. A Yellow Coach Model 743 is pictured just leaving the loading area in the back of the terminal. Note the impressive Greyhound signs. The running dog on the sign had neon lighting that made it appear that the dog was running when illuminated at night.

Buses of Companies Acquired by Greyhound and Affiliated Companies

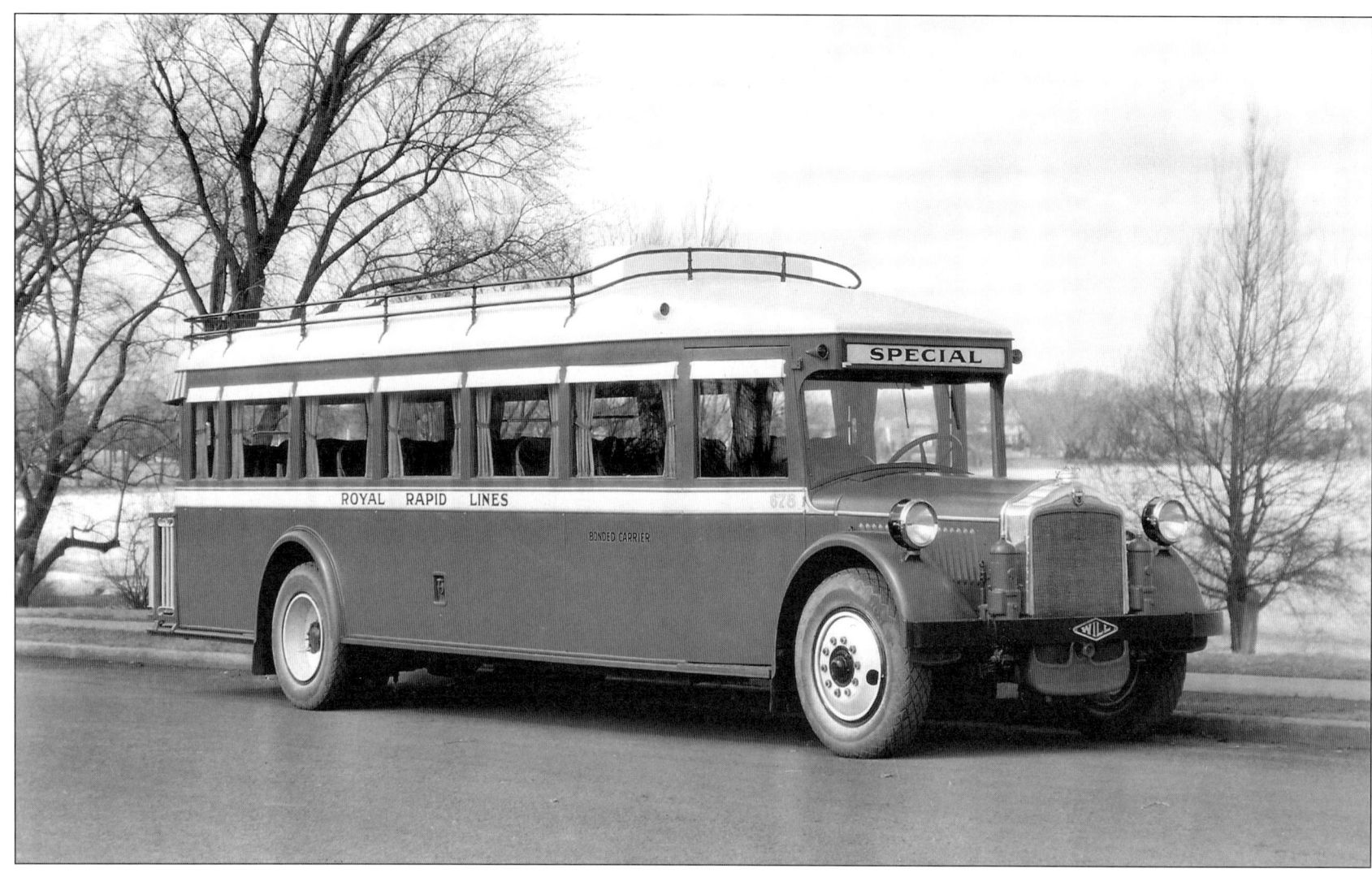

Royal Rapid Lines was a bus company, which had its roots on Minnesota's Iron Range. E. Roy Fitzgerald and his brothers operated Range Rapid Transit in Eveleth, Minnesota. They sold to Northland Transportation Company and went to Madison, Wisconsin, forming Royal Rapid Lines with routes between Chicago and Minneapolis. The Fitzgeralds then sold Royal Rapid Lines to Greyhound and later established the National City Lines. This Will/Eckland bus was one operated by Royal Rapid Lines in 1929.

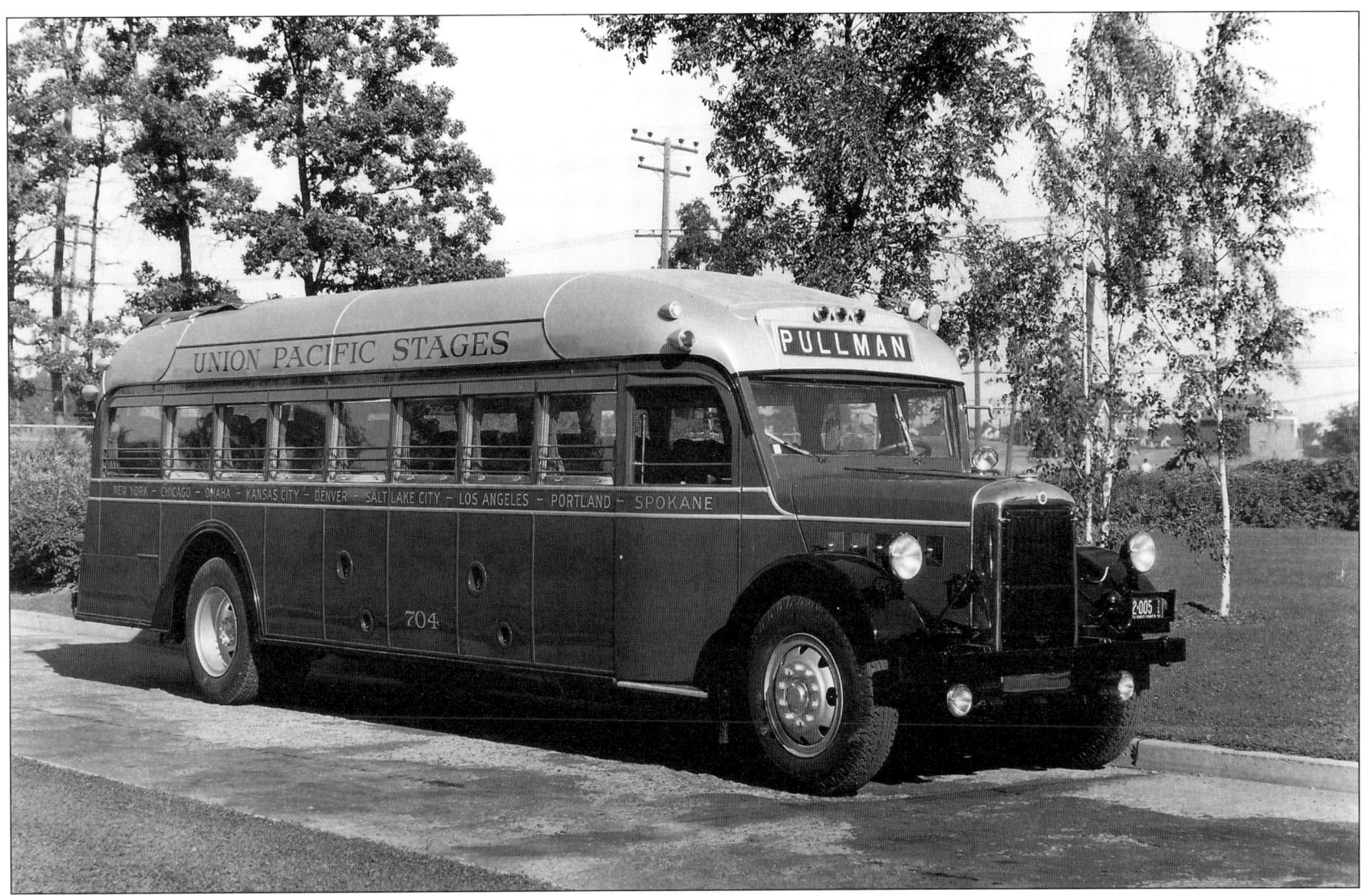

Union Pacific Stages, along with Interstate Transit Lines and Chicago and Northwestern Stages, worked together for many years to provide thru service between Chicago-Salt Lake City-Los Angeles and Salt Lake City-Portland. They were also affiliated with the Union Pacific Railroad and the Chicago North Western Railway. The system did not become fully owned by Greyhound until 1952. Greyhound had an interest from 1943 and the name Overland Greyhound Lines was used beginning then. Pictured here in 1935 is a Yellow Coach Z-250 Model 843 Streamliner in Union Pacific livery.

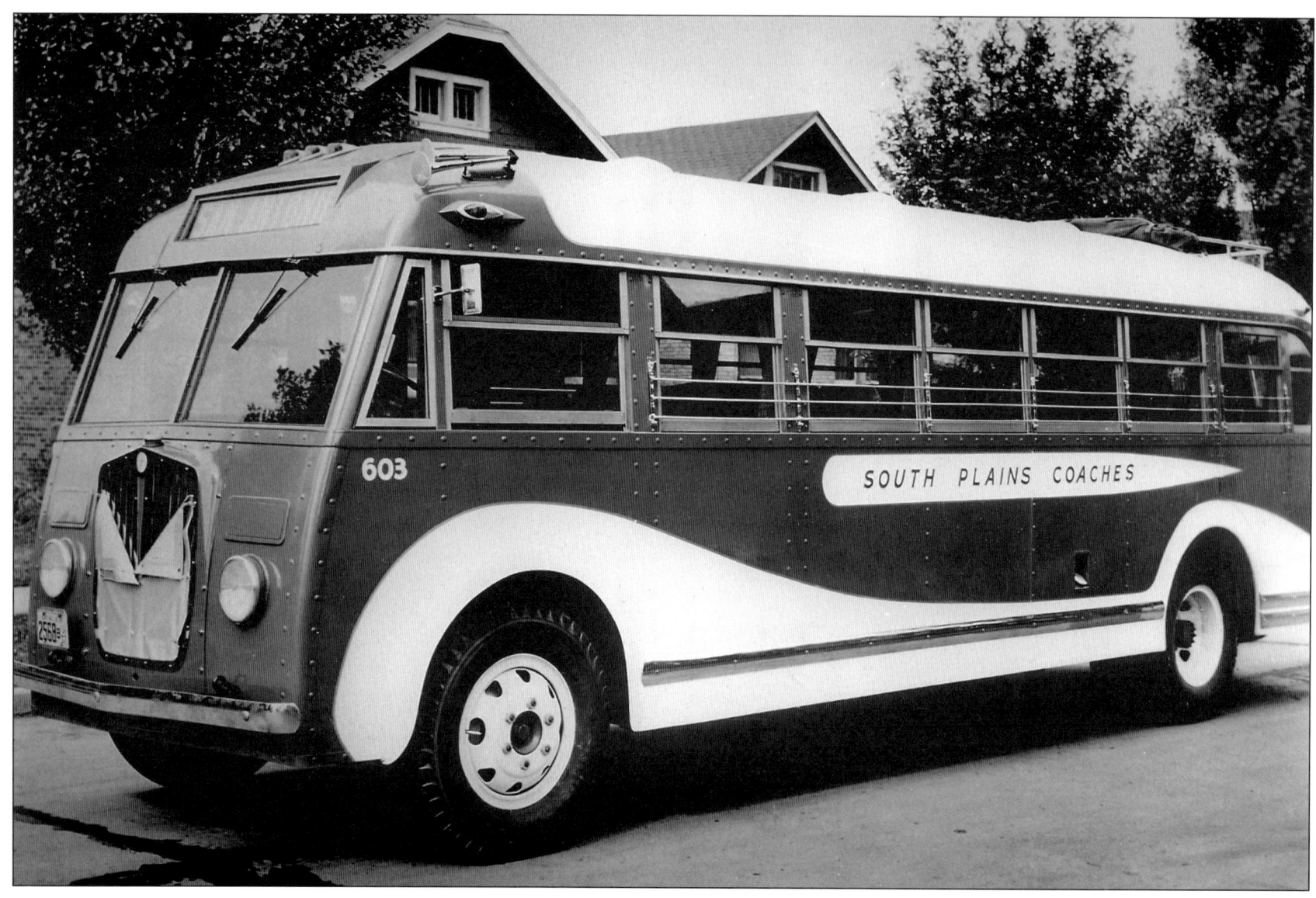

South Plains Coaches was a company operating in the Texas panhandle. In 1939, it merged with two other Texas bus companies, and the new company became known as Texas, New Mexico & Oklahoma Coaches (TNM&O). Greyhound became a majority owner of TNM&O in 1967 and in 1988 Greyhound became the full owner. TNM&O Coaches continues to operate as a separate company. Pictured here is a DMX manufactured by the Dittmar Manufacturing Company in Chicago, which was operated by South Plains Coaches in 1937.

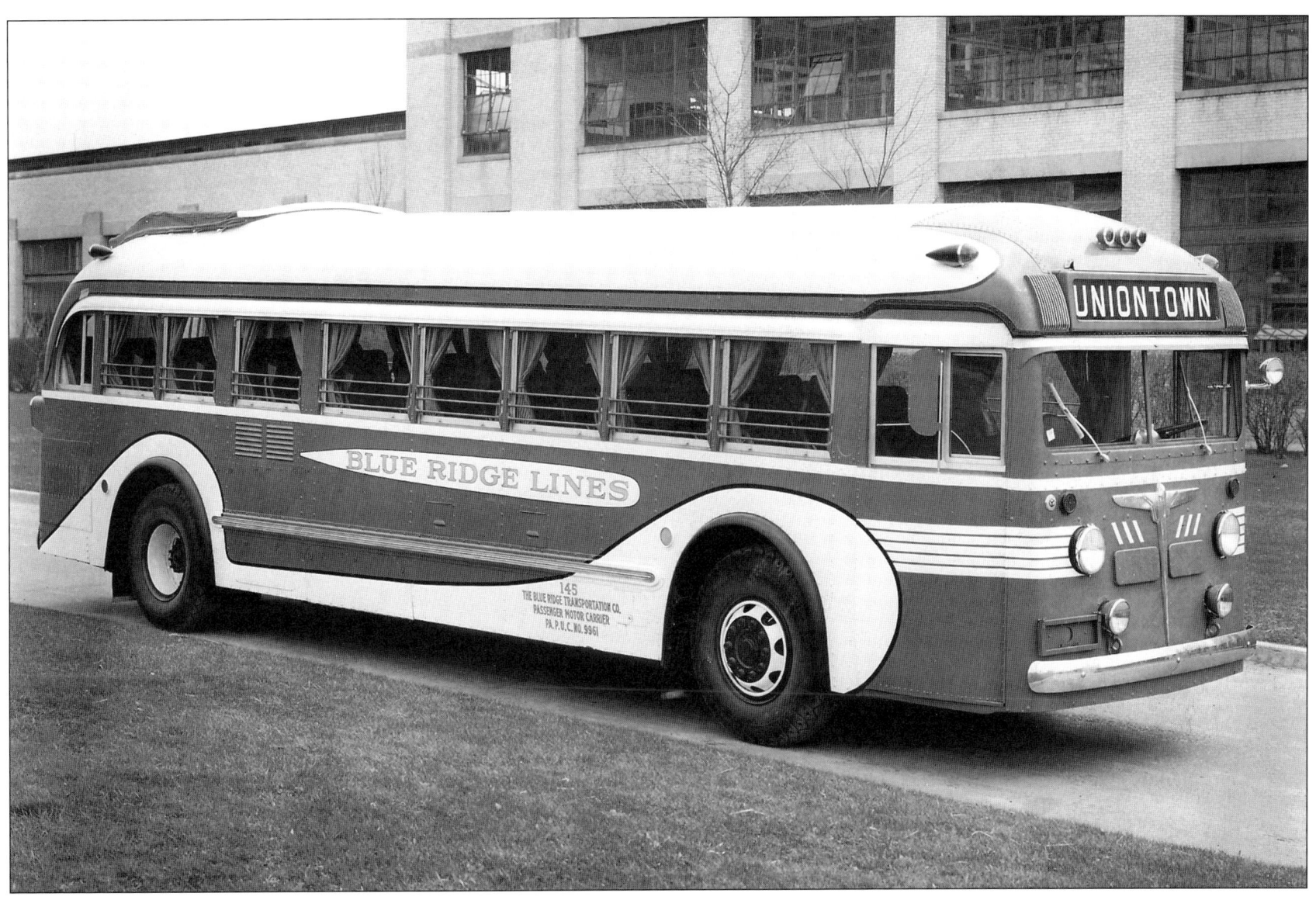

Blue Ridge Transportation Company of Hagerstown, Maryland, operated an important bus system in the east. The main routes were between Washington/Baltimore and Pittsburgh. Another route went to Cleveland, and there was considerable suburban service in the Pittsburgh area. Blue Ridge cooperated closely with Greyhound Lines for many years, and Greyhound purchased the company in 1956. At the time Blue Ridge had some 175 buses. In 1938, Blue Ridge operated these Model 742 Yellow Coaches.

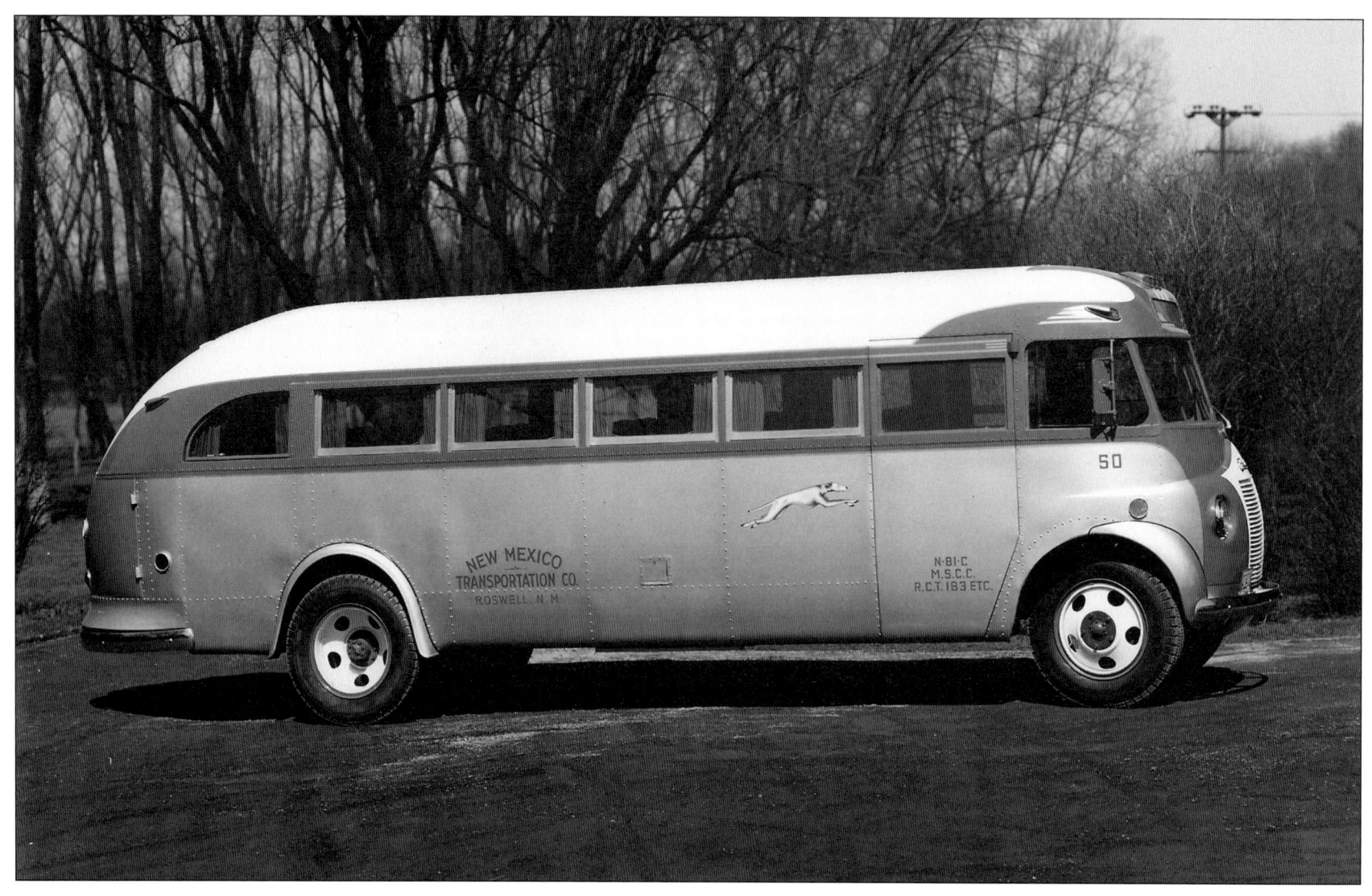

New Mexico Transportation Company operated considerable service throughout New Mexico, and Greyhound had a major interest in the company. Eventually, it was merged into the Texas, New Mexico & Oklahoma Coaches system, which became a fully owned Greyhound company in 1988. Pictured here in 1941 is a Flxible Model 18 CF 41, 18-passenger bus. It had a Chevrolet engine mounted at the front.

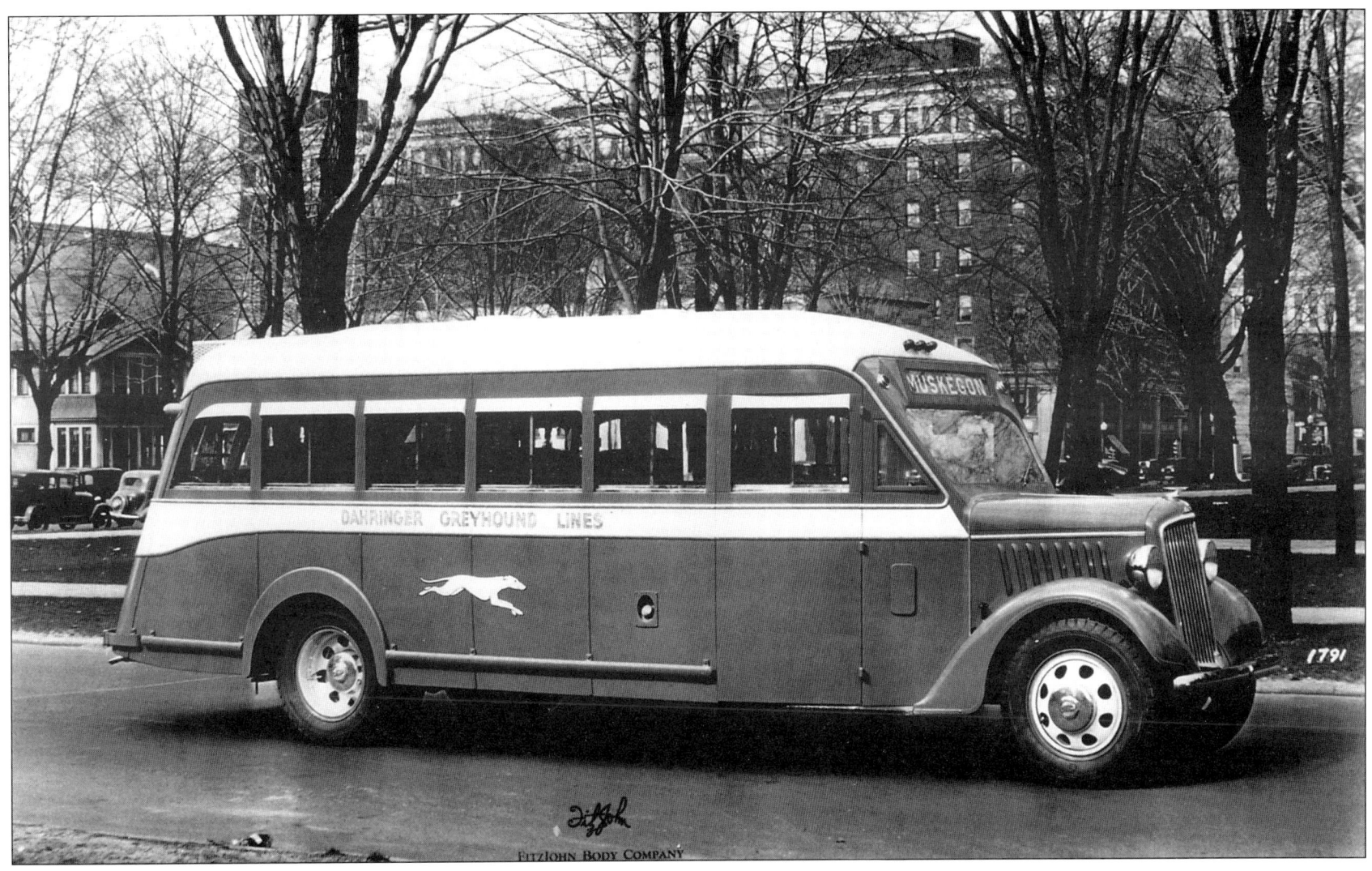

Dahringer Greyhound Lines was not a well-known bus line but carried the Greyhound name and the running dog emblem. Dahringer's main route was between Ludington, Michigan, where the company headquartered, and Traverse City, Michigan. It was thought that the use of the Greyhound name and emblem was the result of an early-day agreement. Pictured here is a 1935 Reo bus with a Fitzjohn Model 130 body. The Fitzjohn company was located in Muskegon, Michigan. Enders Greyhound, also a Michigan company, had a similar Greyhound name agreement. Northeast Missouri Greyhound Lines, another small line with the Greyhound name, was an actual division of Greyhound Lines.

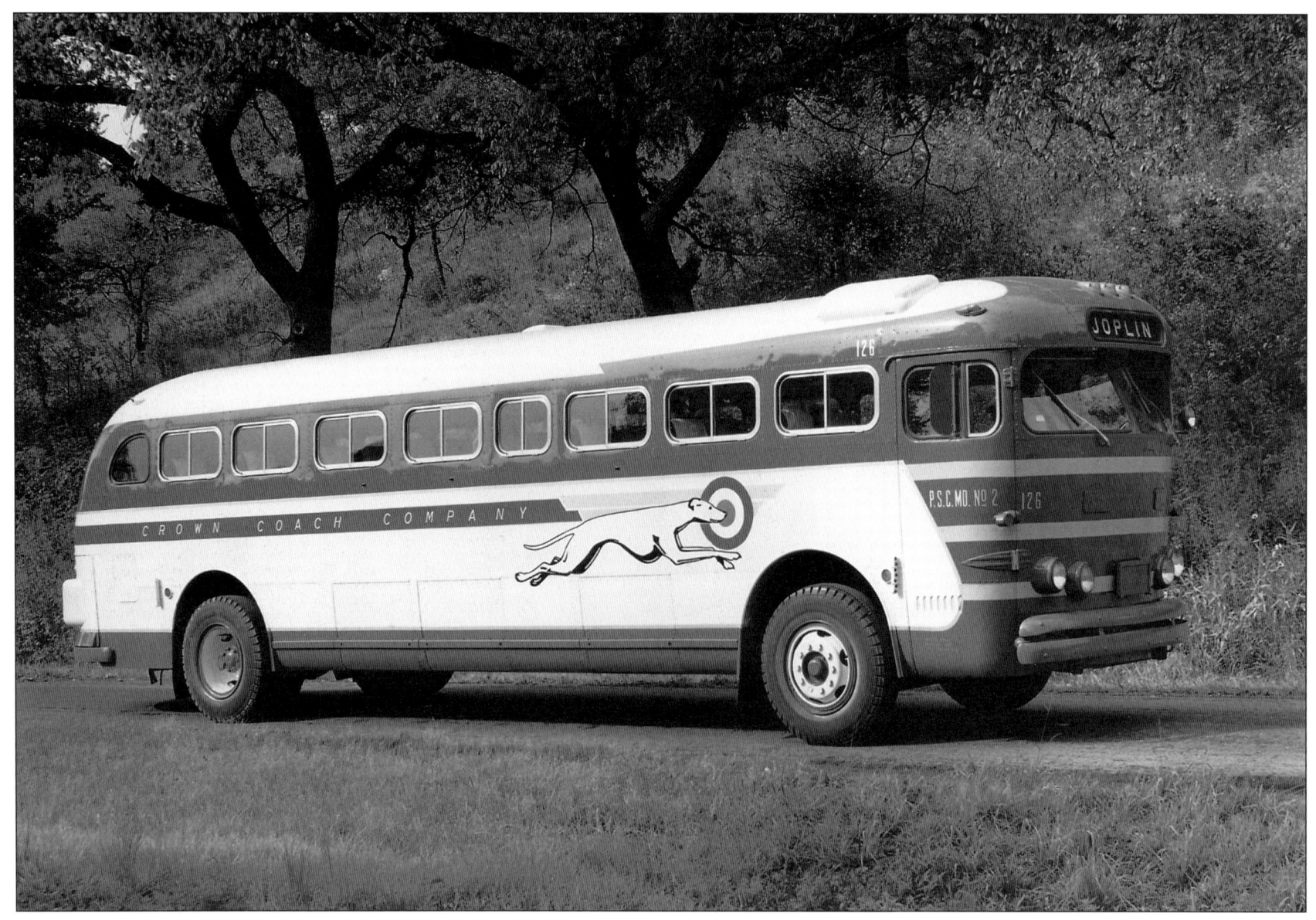

Crown Coach Company of Joplin, Missouri, was 40 percent owned by Greyhound Lines for several decades. Crown Coach was allowed to use the Greyhound colors and the Greyhound dog logo. Crown Coach was established in 1923, and was sold to Jefferson Lines in 1966. The main route of Crown Coach was between Kansas City and Texarkana, Arkansas/Texas. Pictured here is a Crown Coach Model PGA 3702 in 1943.

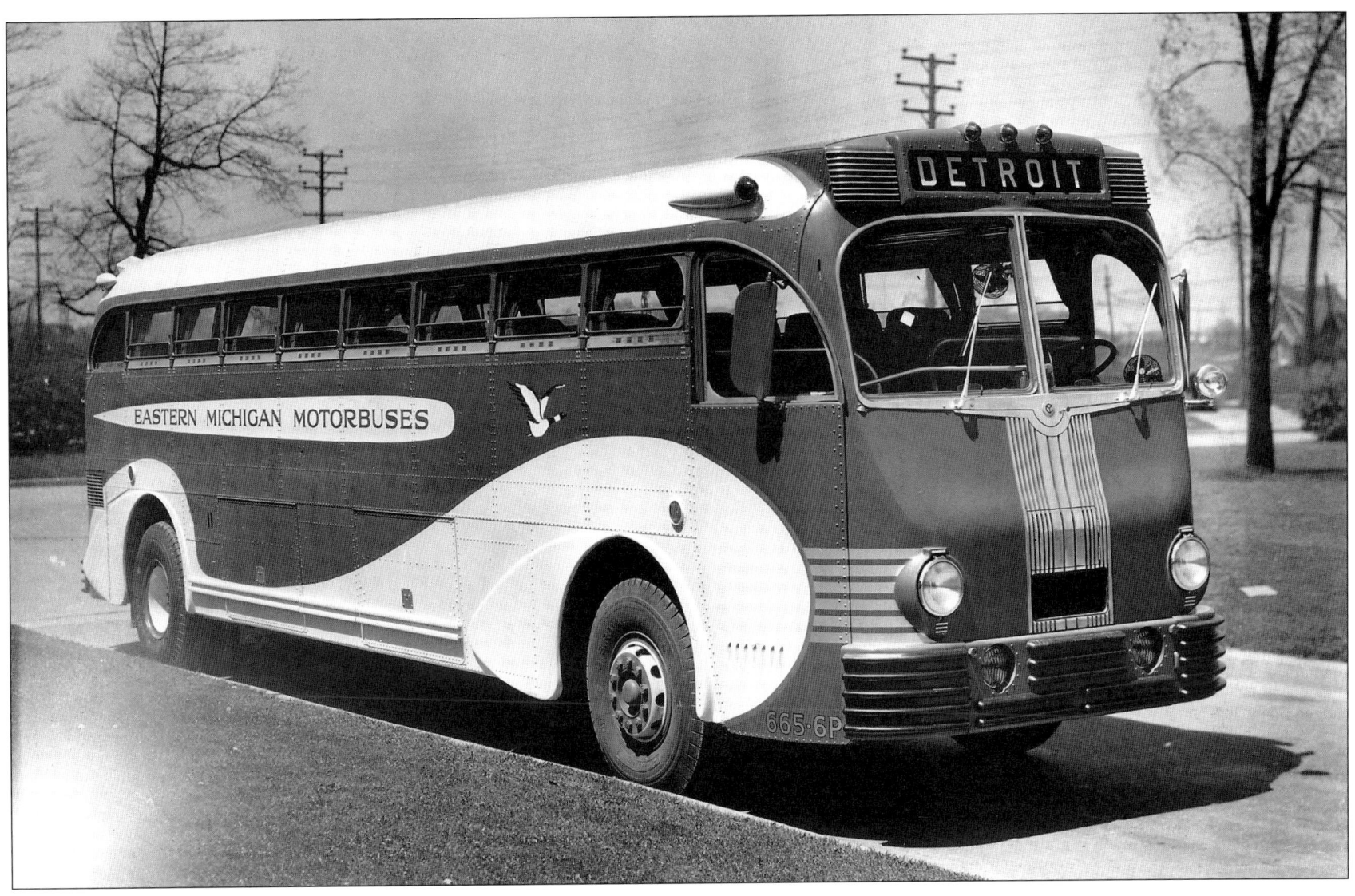

Eastern Michigan Motorbuses, also known as Blue Goose Lines, had a sizable bus operation throughout Michigan. In 1939, the Greyhound Corporation acquired an interest in Eastern Michigan Motorbuses. In 1941, Greyhound acquired a majority control of the Michigan company and it became Great Lakes Greyhound Lines. Pictured here is a Yellow Coach Model 743 of Eastern Michigan Motorbuses, which was added to the fleet in 1939. The Model 743 was a Greyhound-designed bus, as Greyhound-friendly companies were given the opportunity to add this bus to their fleets.

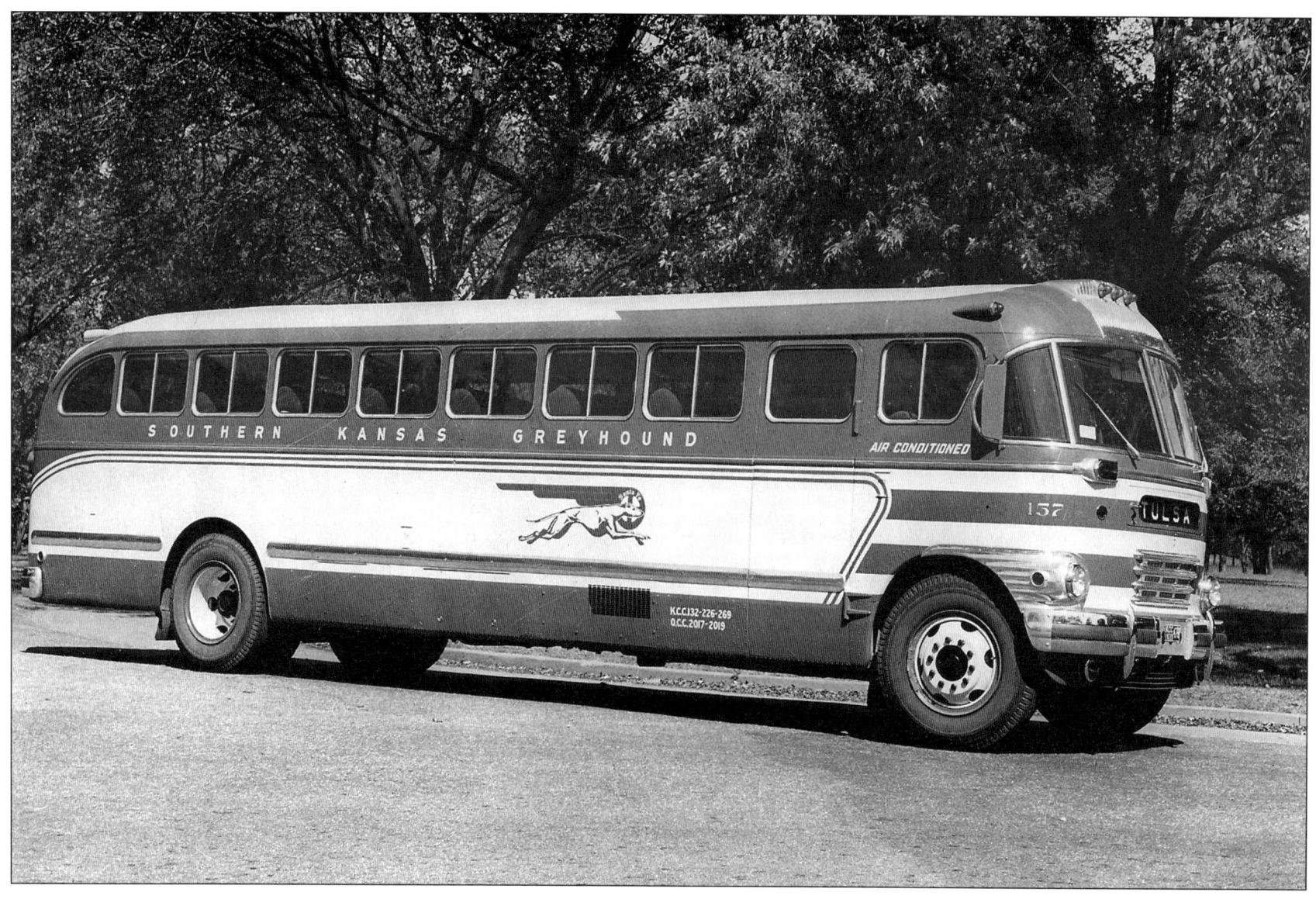

Southern Kansas Greyhound Lines, which operated this ACF-Brill IC41 in the late 1940s and 1950s, was an interesting company. It was owned jointly by Greyhound and Santa Fe Trailways. Note the emblem has both the Greyhound and Santa Fe symbols. Each company took turns maintaining and operating Southern Kansas Greyhound Lines on a year-to-year basis. Santa Fe Trailways had a link between Kansas City and the Southwest, but Greyhound did not, and Southern Kansas Greyhound provided that link.

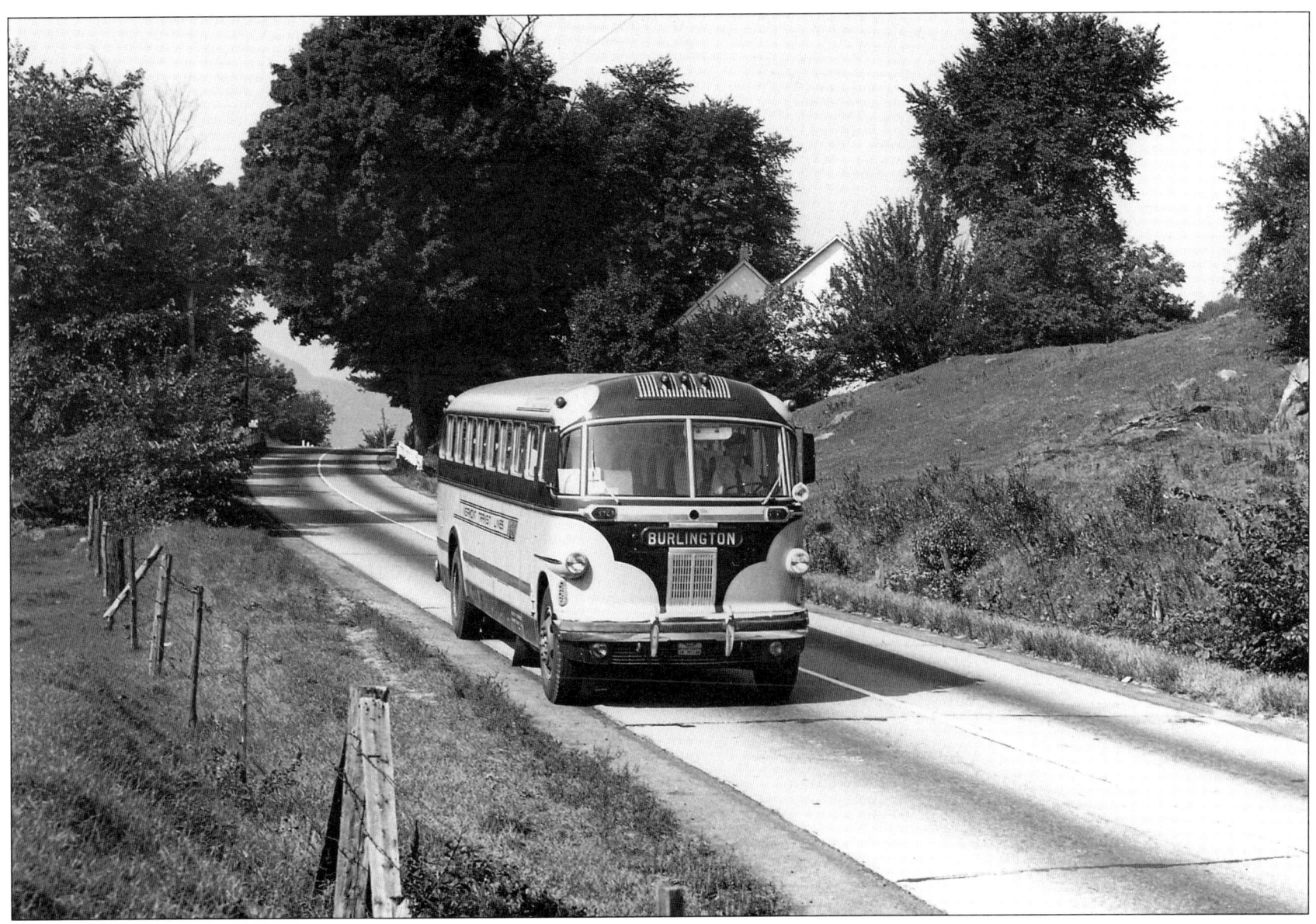

Greyhound Lines purchased Vermont Transit Lines in 1976, and Vermont Transit has continued to operate as a separate company. Connections are made with Greyhound Lines at a number of locations. In December 1945, Vermont Transit bought two ACF/Brill IC 41 buses soon after this model bus was introduced. One of the buses is pictured here on a rural Vermont highway. The buses carried the name Green Mountaineer.

Transit-Type Greyhound Buses

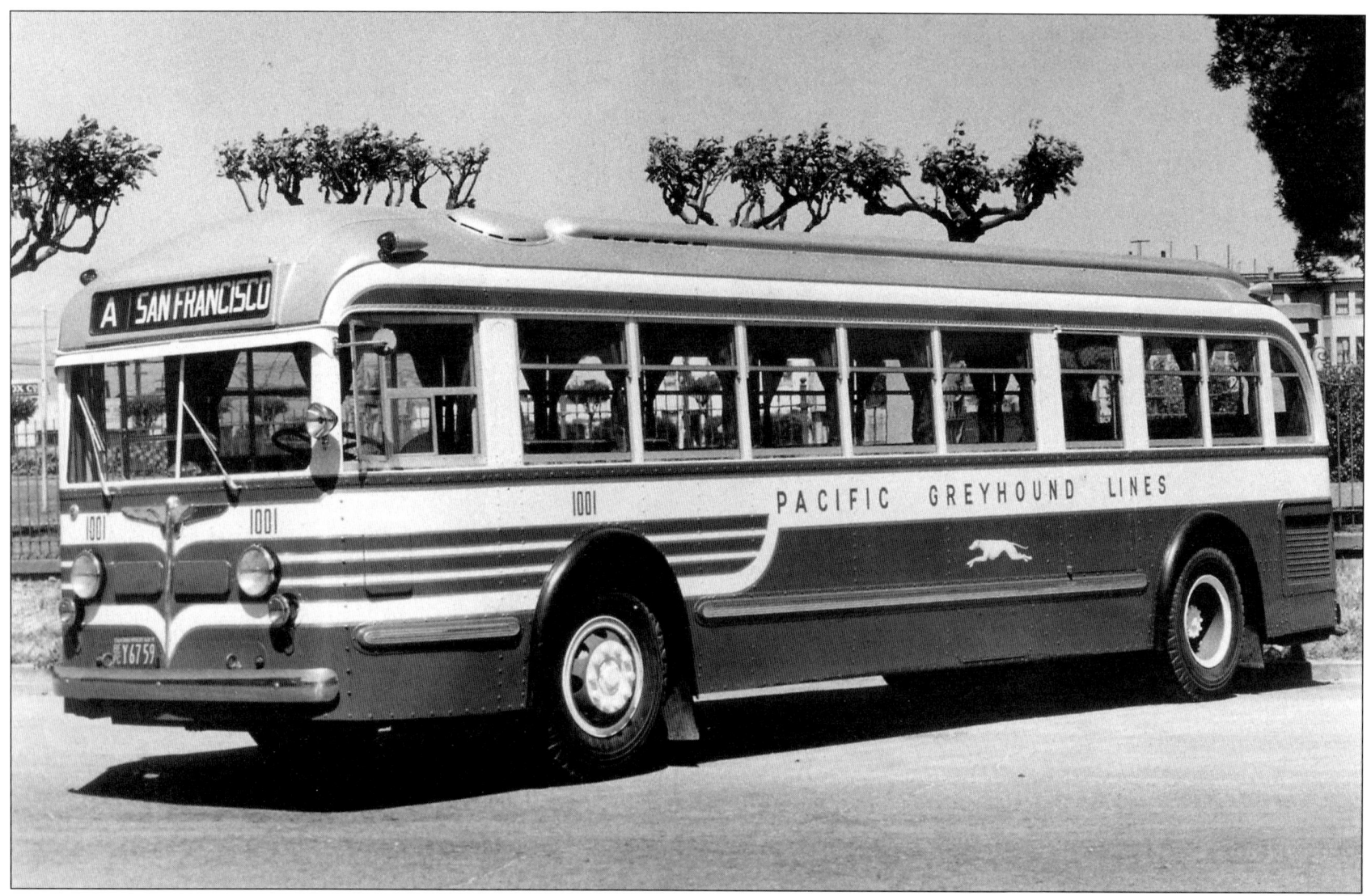

Greyhound operated extensive suburban service in the San Francisco Bay area. Some lines crossed the Golden Gate Bridge to Marin County. Other routes were operated across the San Francisco Oakland Bay Bridge to communities in Contra Costa County on the east side of the Bay. In 1939, Yellow Coach Model 740 suburban buses operated on all of the routes. *Don Coffin Collection*

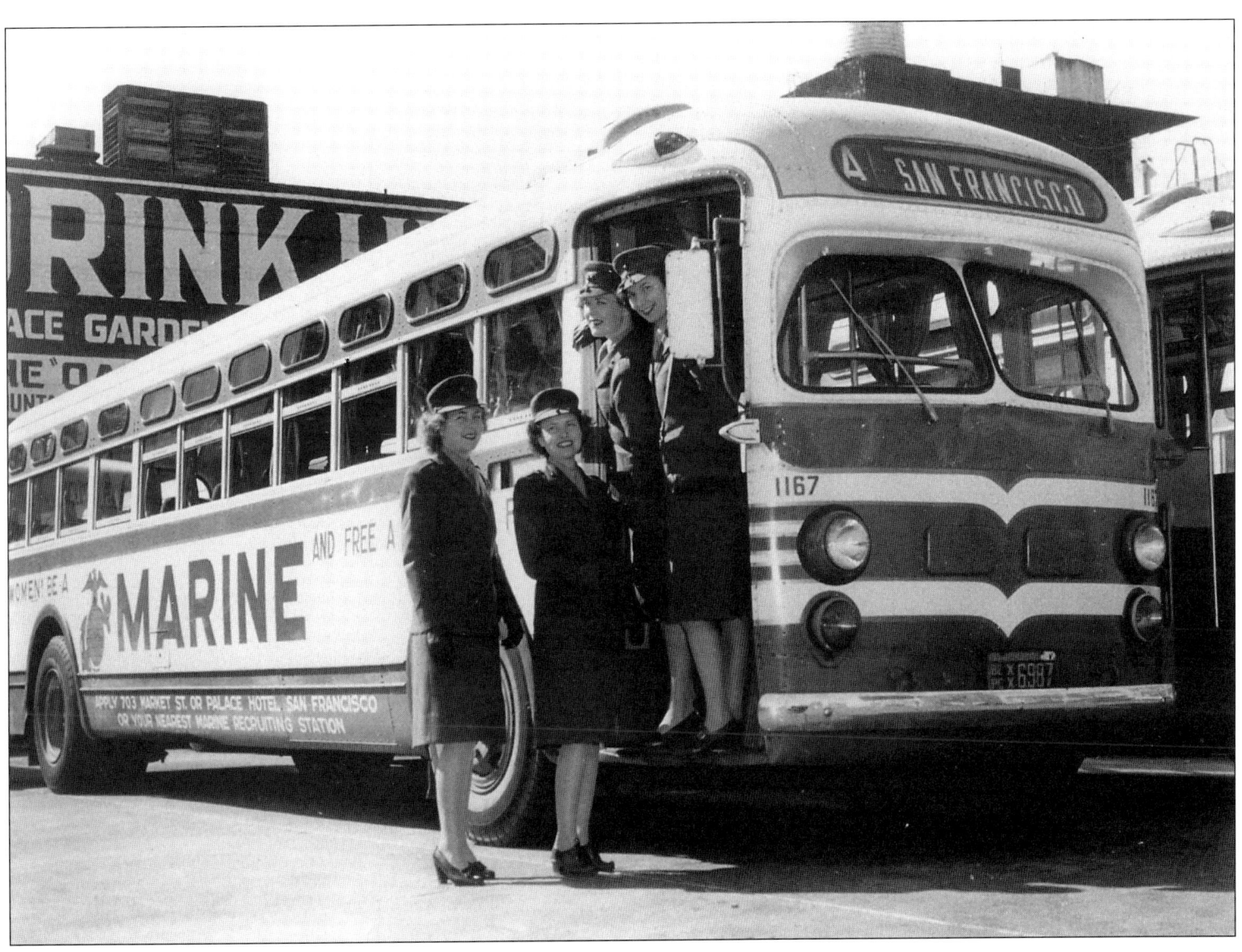

During World War II, Greyhound buses throughout the country were busy transporting enlistees, defense workers and essential workers. Buses were also frequently used for troop movements. In addition, Greyhound buses often had advertisements to recruit service personnel, like this 1941 Yellow Coach TDM 4505 in San Francisco encouraging the recruitment of marines. War Bond promotions were also presented on Greyhound buses. *Don Coffin Collection*

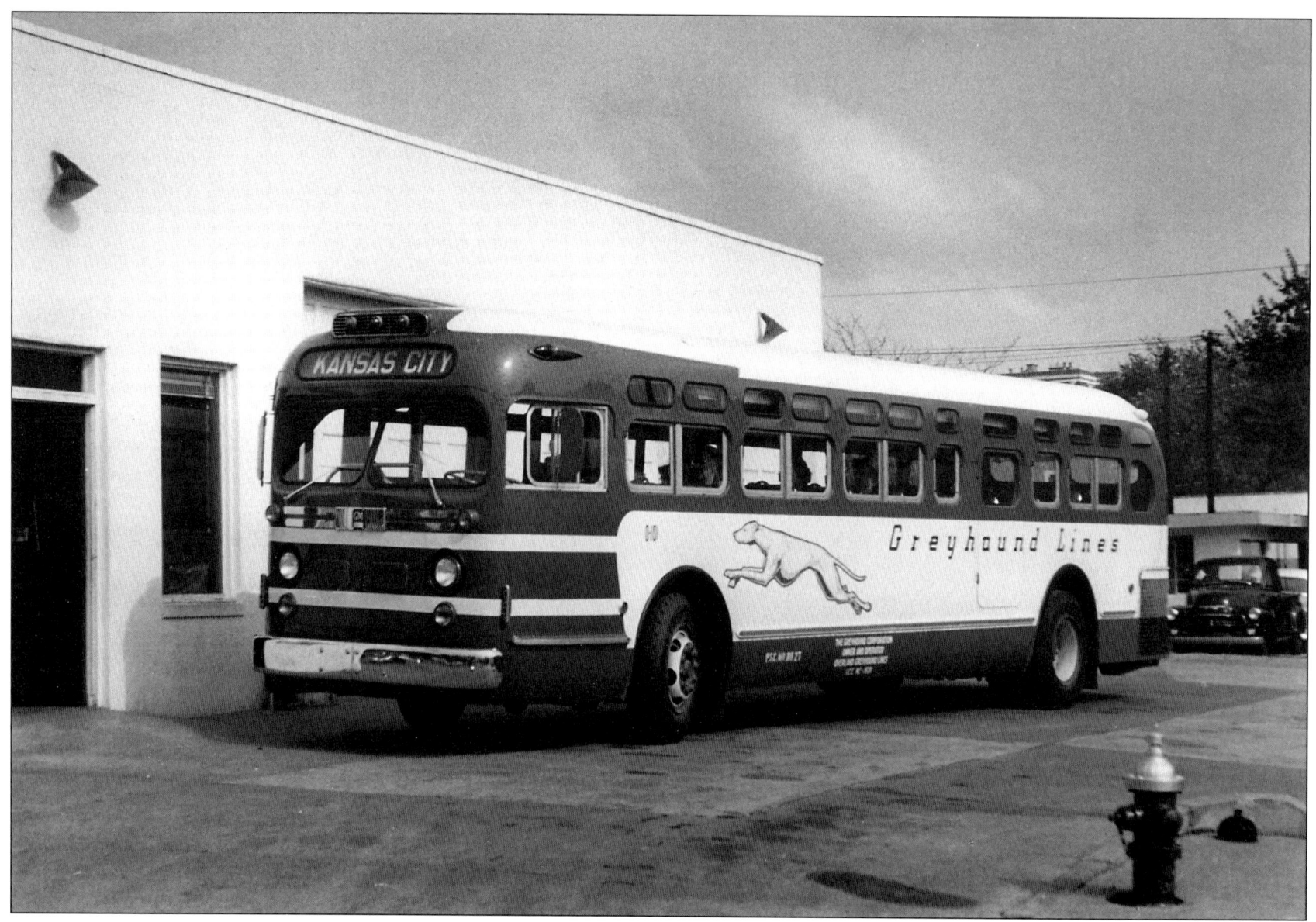

Overland Greyhound Lines operated this General Motors TDM 4512 transit bus on a route between Kansas City and the nearby Missouri communities of Liberty and Excelsior Springs. The route was acquired in 1934, along with other Kansas City suburban routes. Jefferson Lines became the operator of the service in 1964, and later it was taken over by the Kansas City Transit Authority.

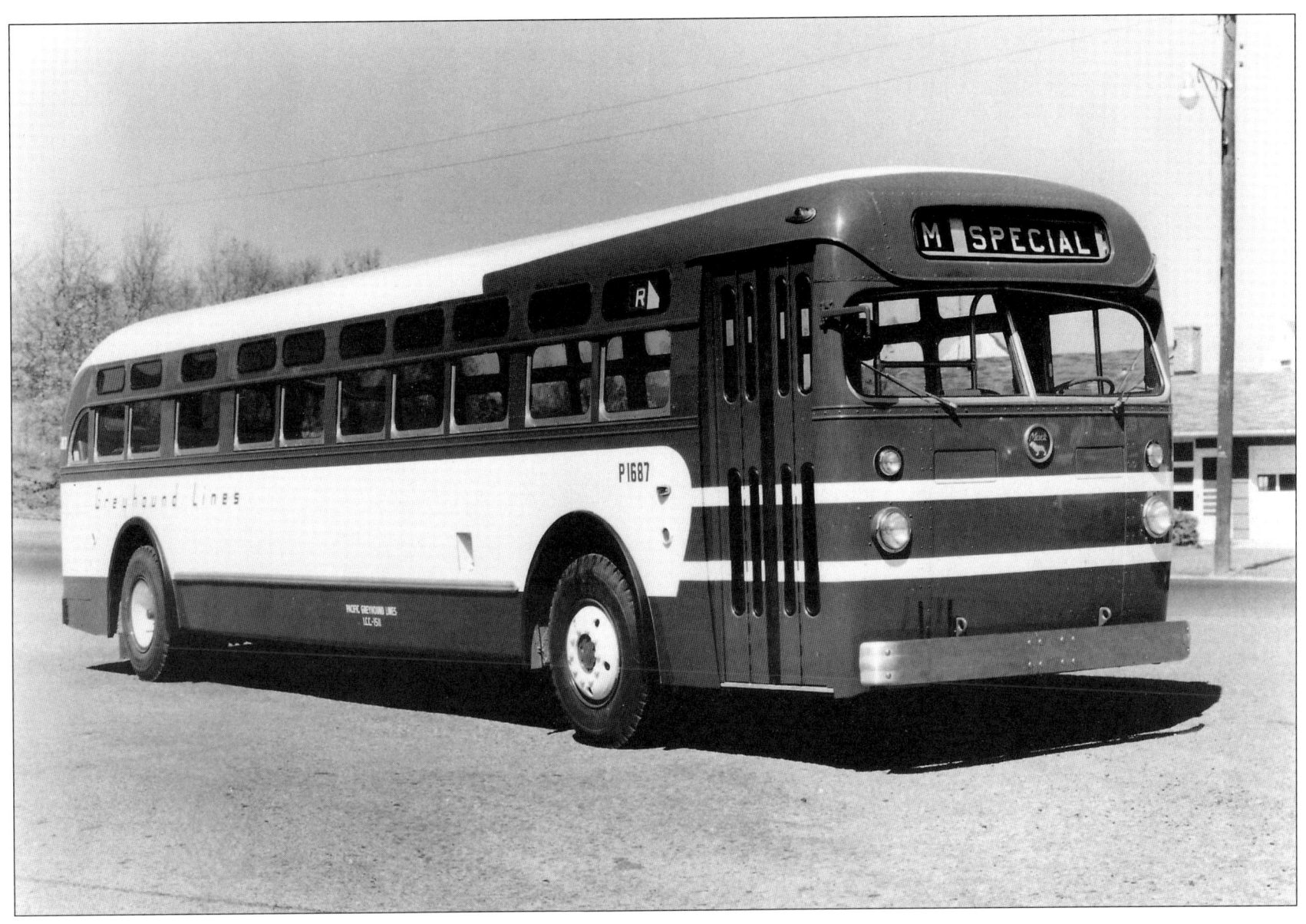

Pacific Greyhound Lines received 30 C-49 Mack transit buses in 1957 for its suburban service in the San Francisco Bay area. For less than a year, four C-49 Mack buses were in service by Richmond Greyhound Lines. The C-49s had six-cylinder Mack Thermodyne diesel engines. These 30 C-49 Macks were the only post-war Macks owned by Greyhound companies.

Mid-20th Century Greyhound Buses

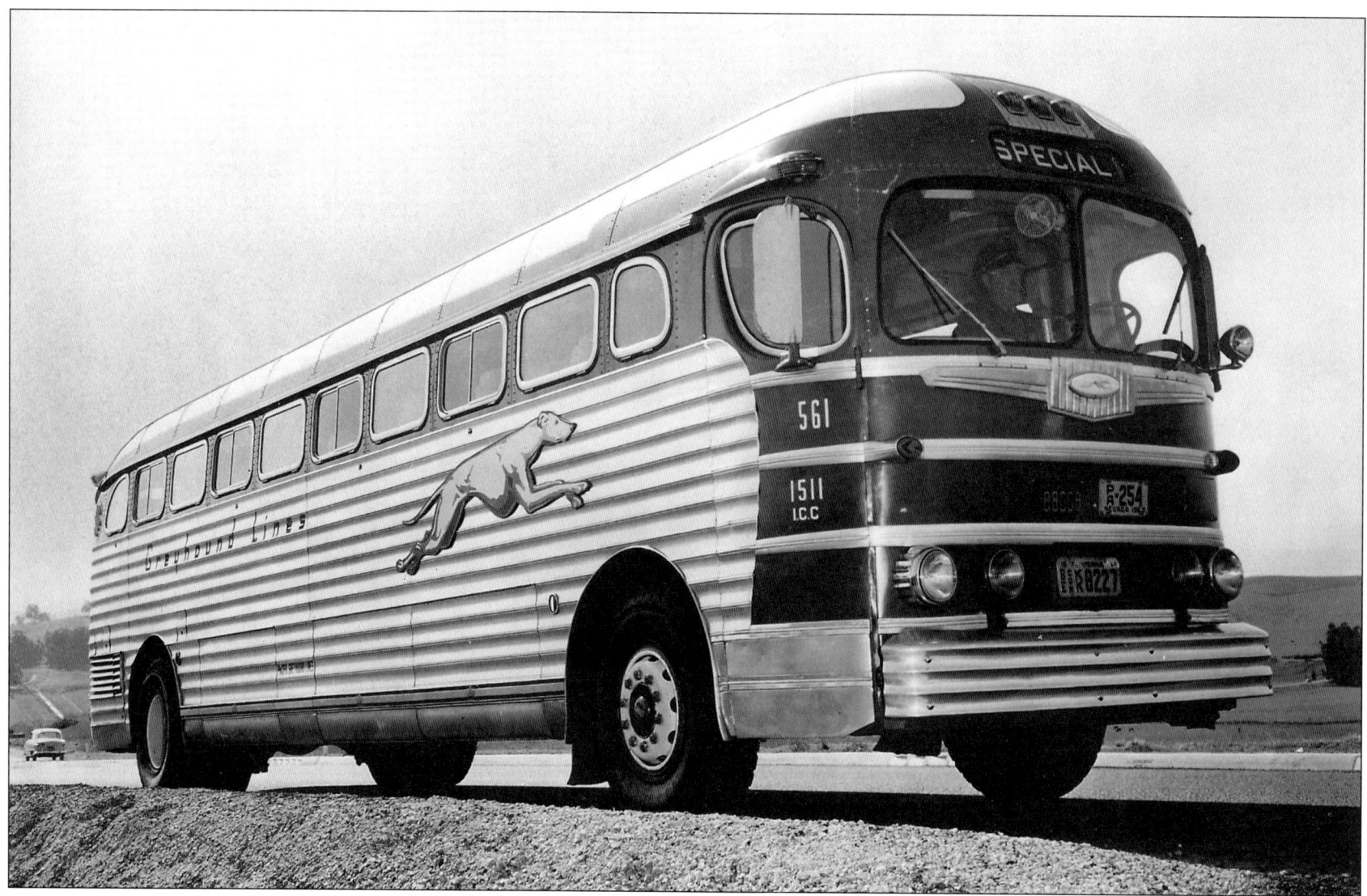

Greyhound needed new buses following World War II. In June 1947, Greyhound placed a $37 million order with General Motor Truck and Coach Division for 1,500 GM PD 3751 and PD 4151 Silversides buses. These buses were longer than most of the pre-war Silversides model and had seats for 37 passengers. The engine was a General Motors two-cycle diesel engine mounted longitudinally across the rear with the angle drive.

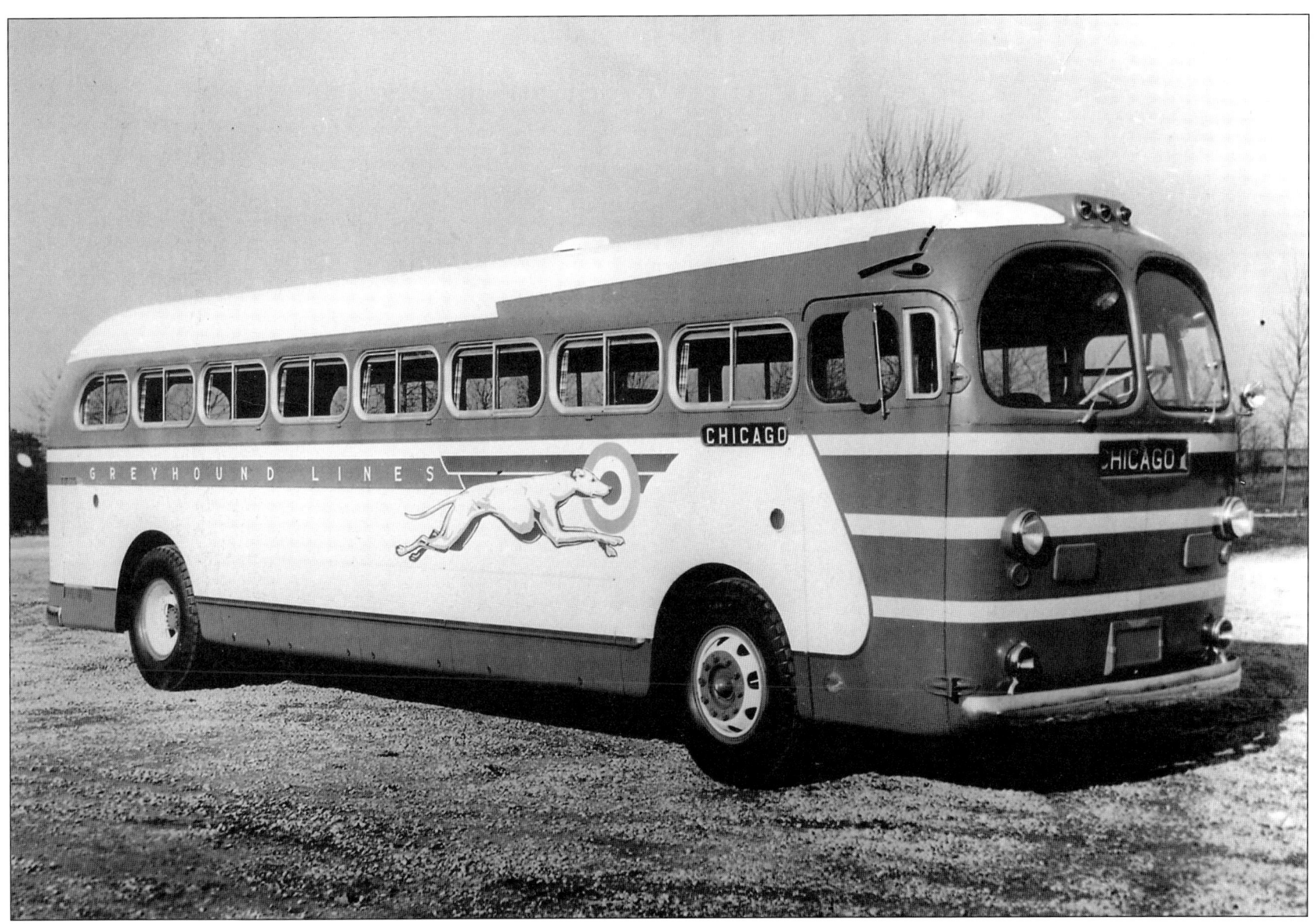

A number of Greyhound divisions operated Aerocoach buses like the one pictured here. The General American Aerocoach Company in Chicago built the Aerocoach buses. This model was the P 46-37 bus. An important feature was the all-welded tubular steel frame with aluminum paneling. An International Red diamond 450 gasoline engine and a Clark Equipment Company five-speed transmission were used.

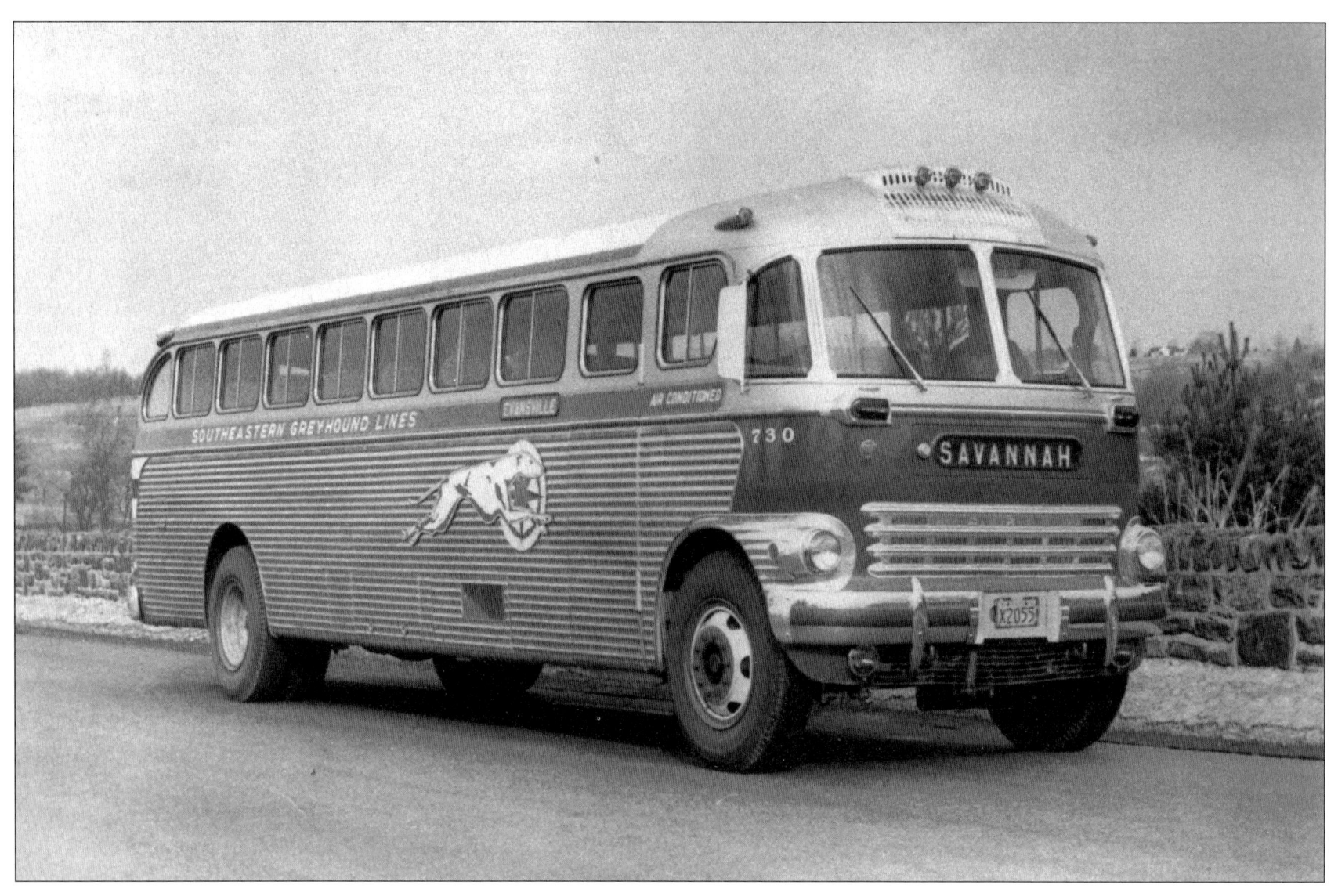

Deluxe ACF-Brill IC-41 buses were purchased by Southeastern Greyhound Lines in 1948. These luxury buses had many passenger amenities such as a water cooler, buffet counter, and coffee urn. The buses were used on Southeastern's Florida service. On this service, uniformed stewardesses were aboard to attend to passengers' requirements. These 14 ACF-Brill buses were the last ACF buses acquired by Southeastern Greyhound Lines. *Don Coffin Collection*

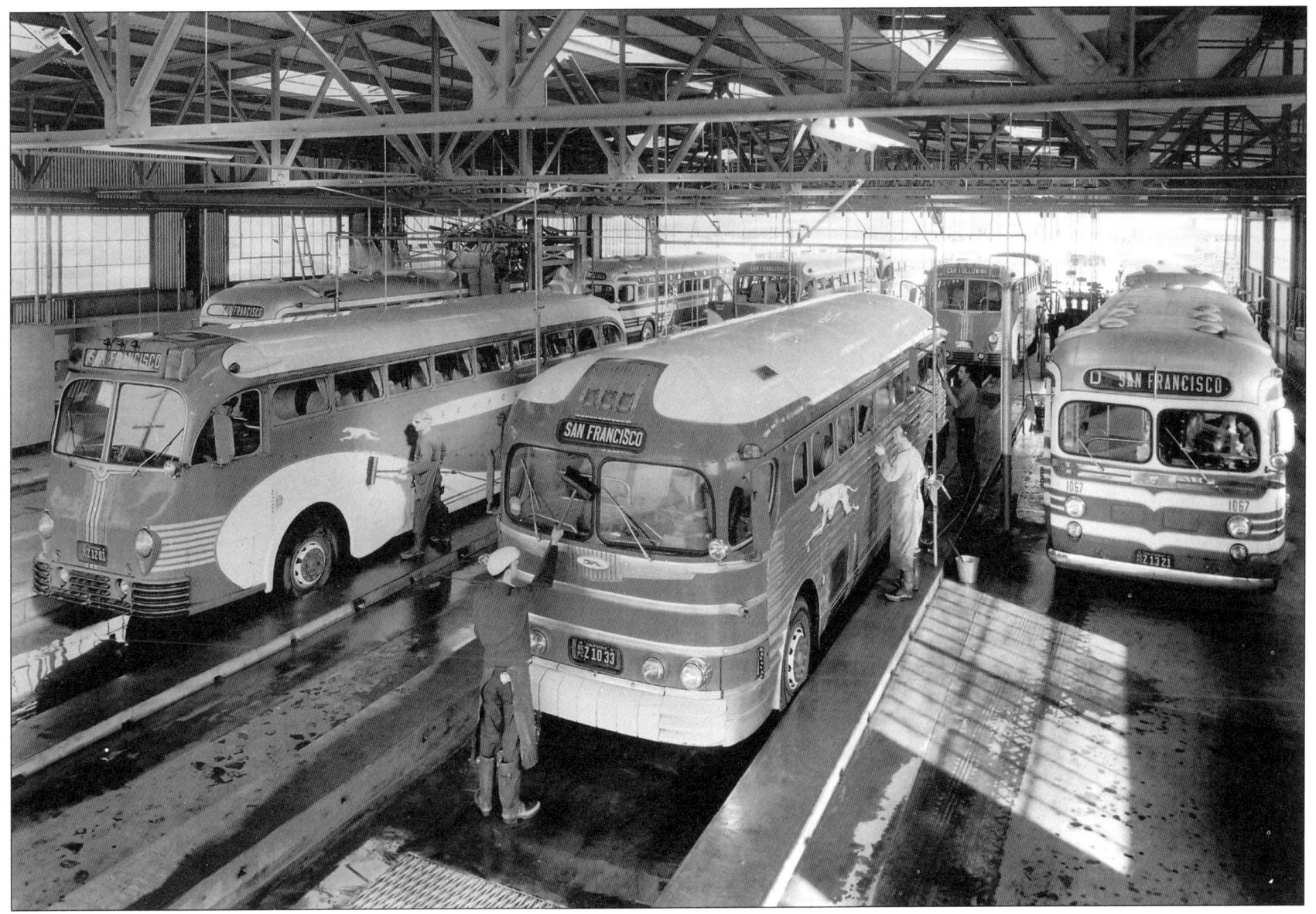

This picture shows the interior of the Pacific Greyhound Lines garage in San Francisco, California. It has been a major Greyhound maintenance facility for many years. At the right foreground is a Yellow Coach Model 719 Super Coach. In the middle is a Yellow Coach PD 4101 Silversides, and to the right is a Yellow Coach TD 4502 used in suburban service.

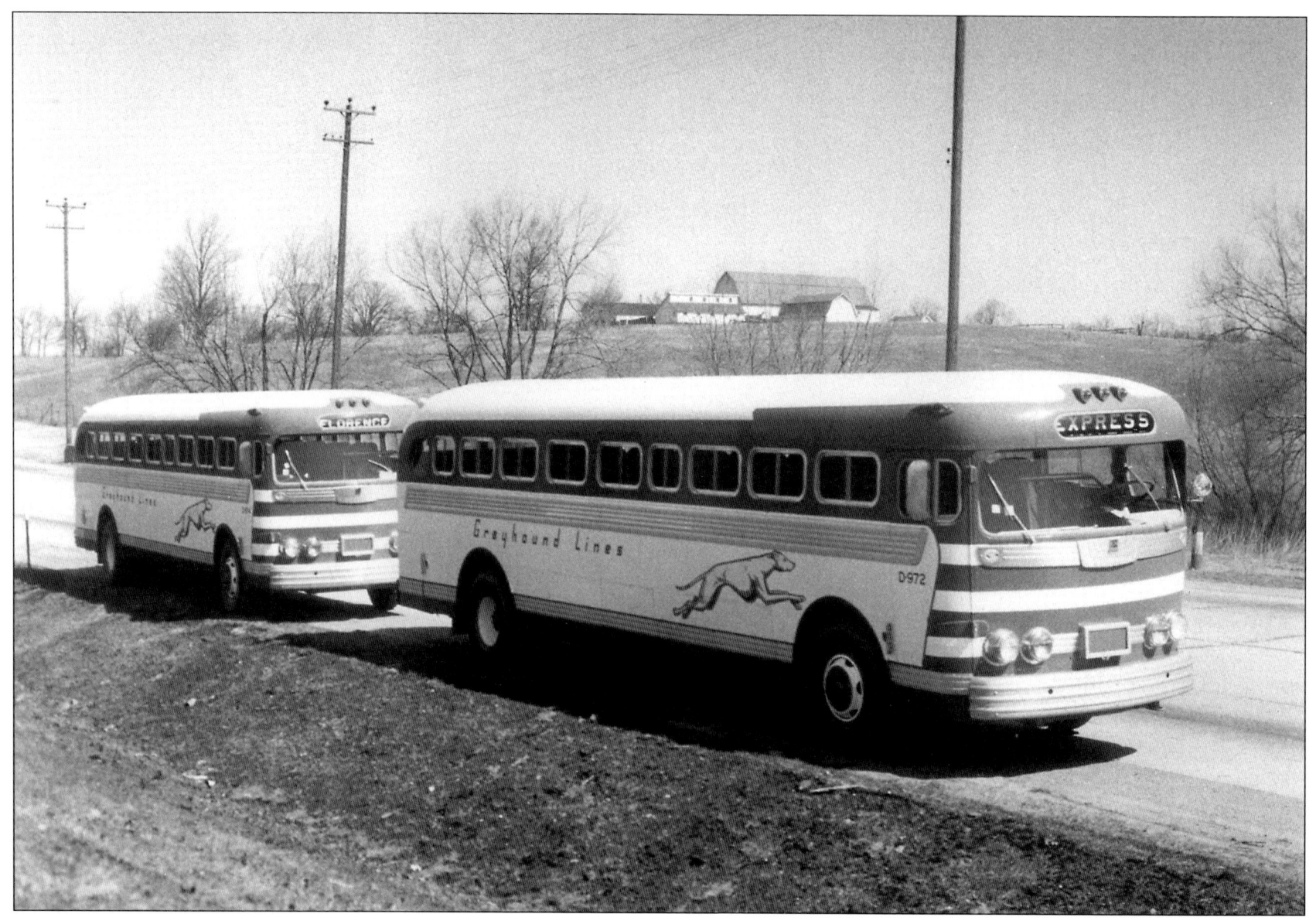

In 1949, General Motors began building the 41-passenger Model PDA 4101 buses. Pictured here are two of the ten that were purchased by the Memphis-based Dixie Greyhound Lines. Southwestern Greyhound received 25 of the Model PDA 4101 bus. These were the only two Greyhound divisions, which operated the General Motors PDA 4101 bus. *Don Coffin Collection*

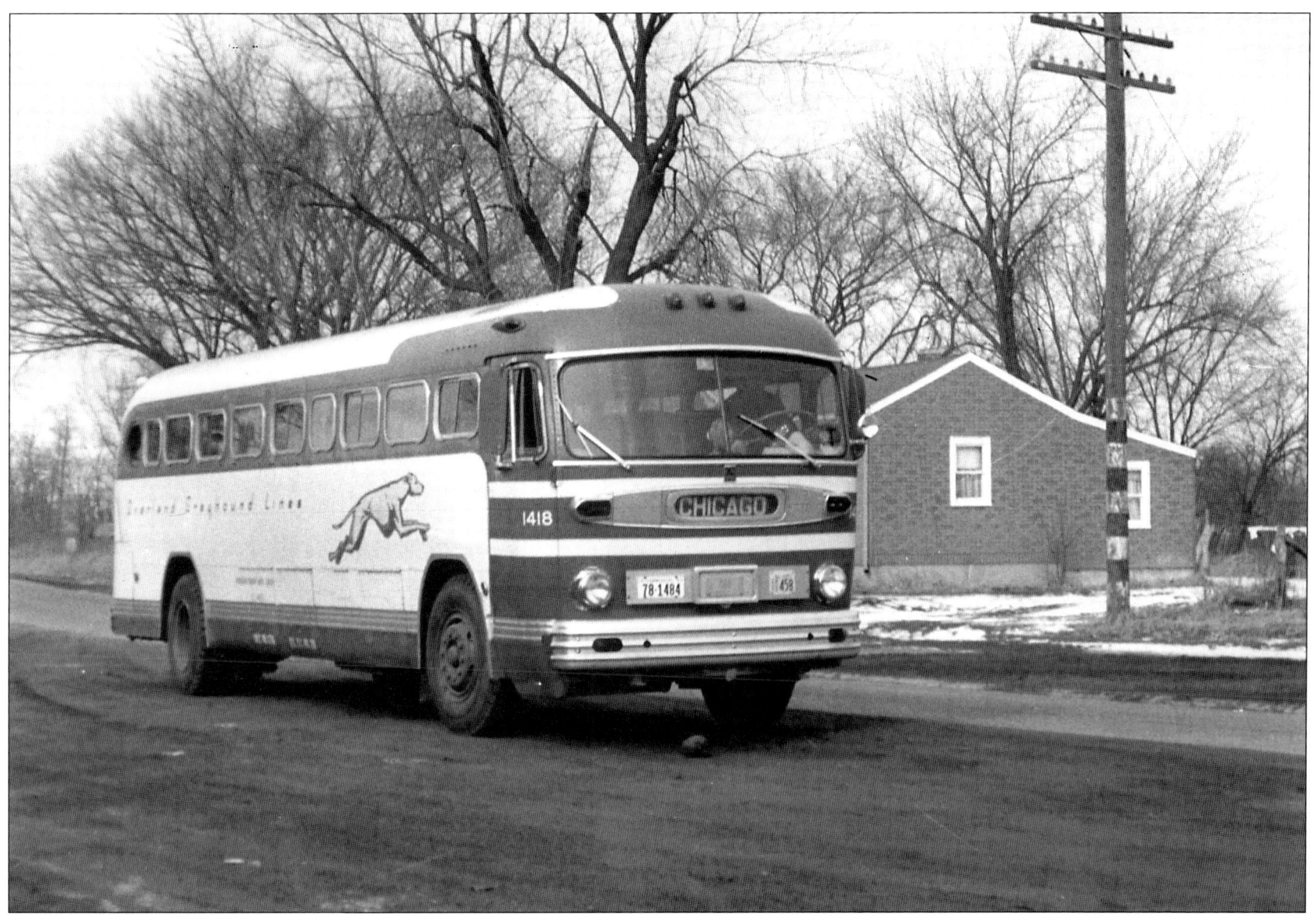

When this General Motors Model PD 4103 bus was delivered in 1951, it and 24 others were operating under the name Interstate Transit Lines. In 1952, Interstate Transit Lines became fully owned by Greyhound, although it was known as Overland Greyhound Line for several years. This Overland bus was pictured near Homestead, Iowa, on U.S. Highway 6. A number of other Greyhound divisions operated General Motors PD 4103 buses.

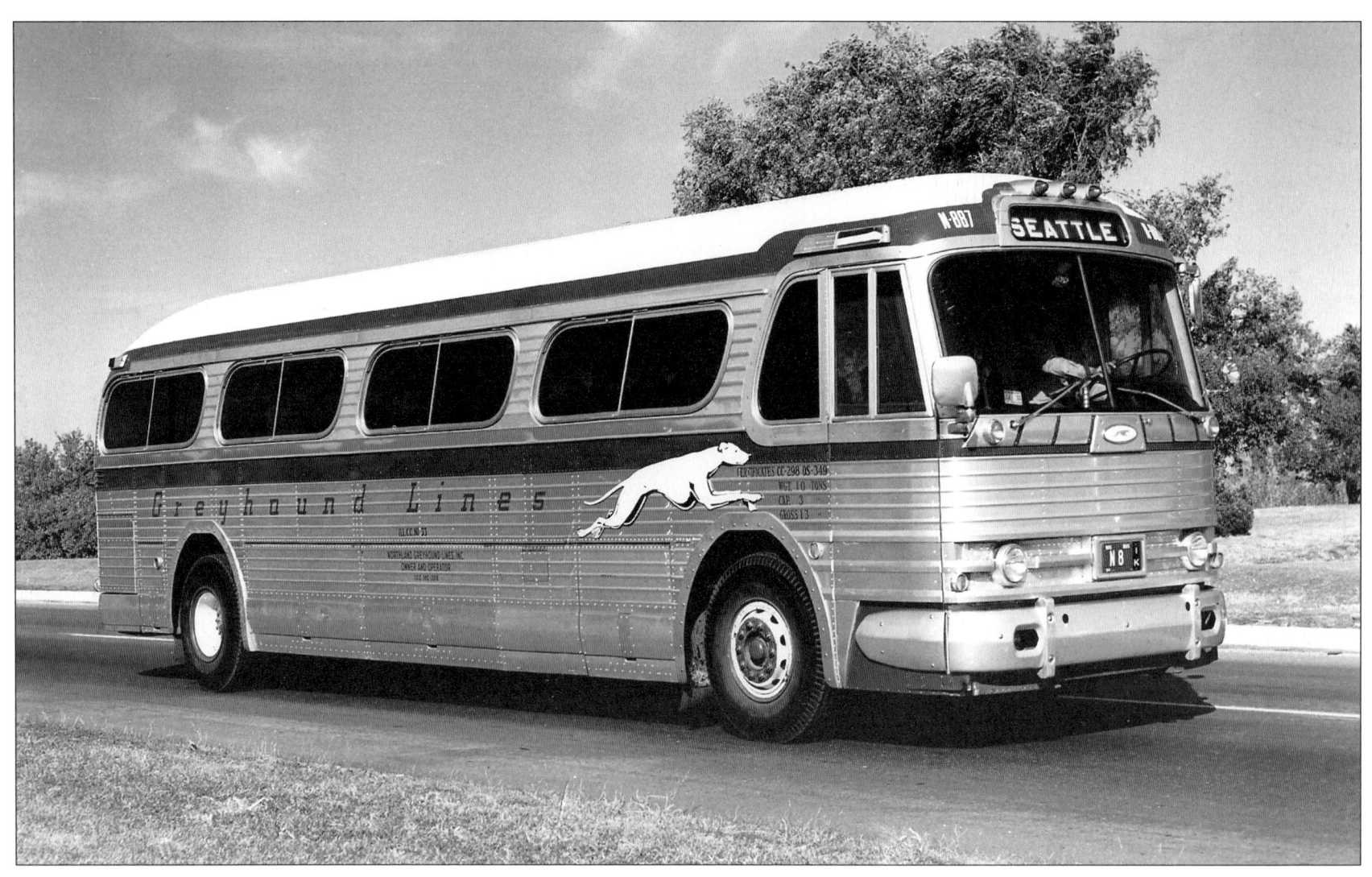

In 1952, General Motors Truck and Coach Division introduced a newly designed intercity bus, known as the Model PD 4104. One of the important new features was air suspension, which gave a more comfortable ride for the passengers than the metal leaf springs used on previous buses. All Greyhound divisions had fleets of the new bus, which Greyhound named the Highway Traveler. The PD 4104 pictured here was in the Northland Greyhound Lines fleet.

Experimental Greyhound Buses

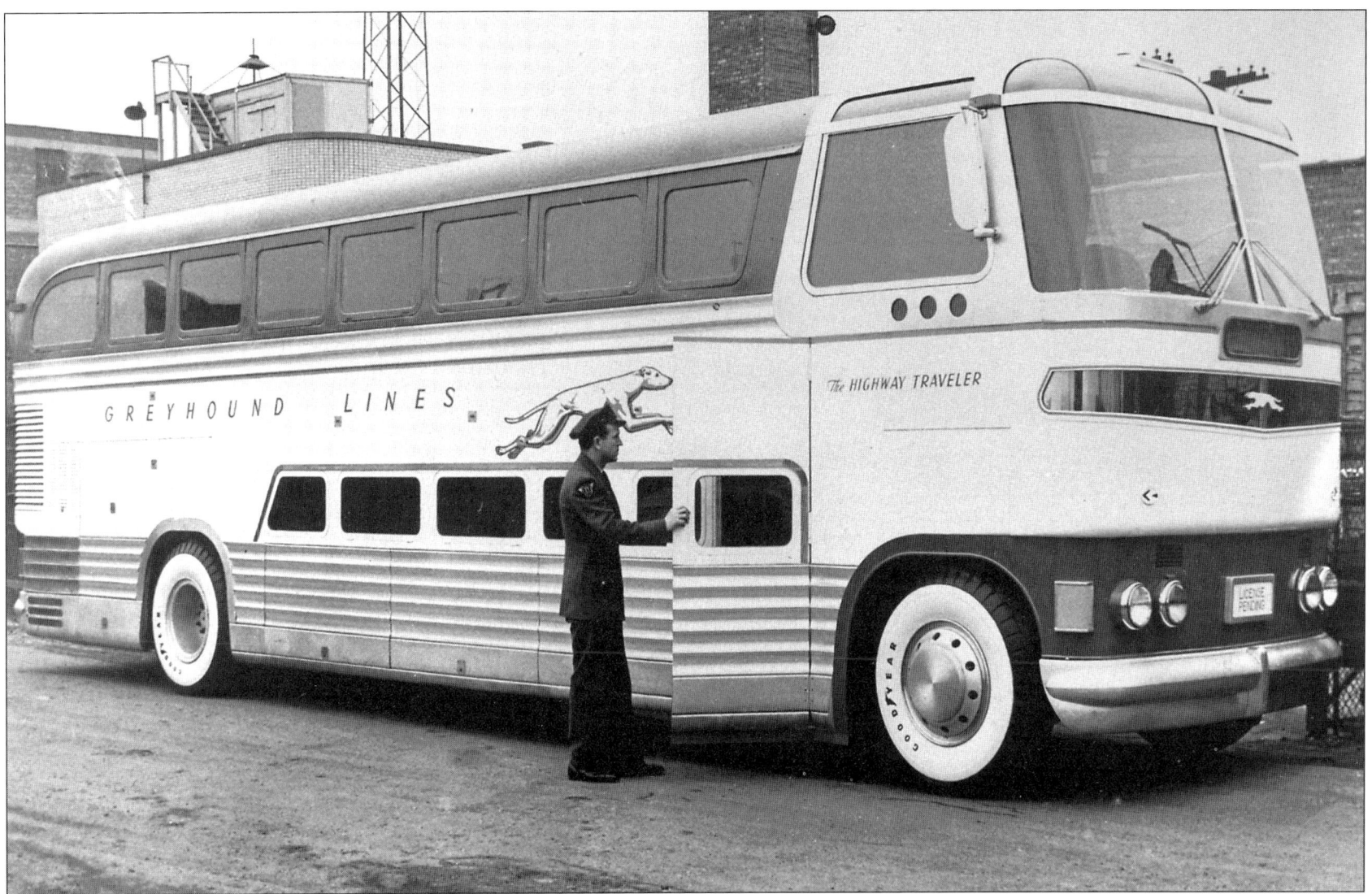

The GX-1 was a Greyhound Lines experimental bus envisioned in 1945 and completed for testing in 1947. It had three levels: 13 passengers in a lower level, 31 passengers on the upper deck, and six in a section behind the driver. Two air-cooled engines were mounted in the rear. The bus never went into production and GX-1 was only briefly in service.

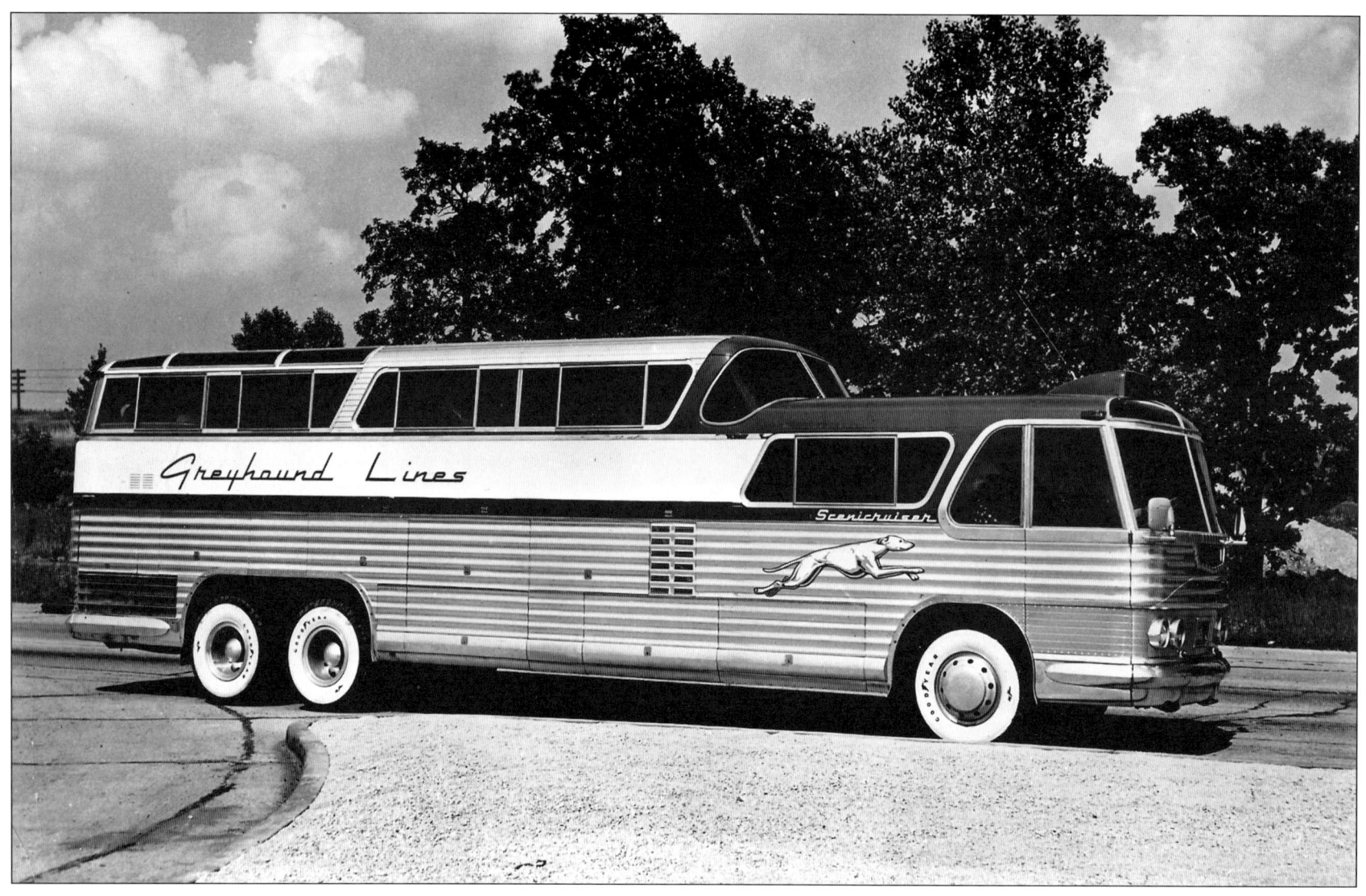

The GX-2, a Greyhound experimental bus, was completed in 1949. It was a cooperative project between Greyhound and General Motors. Its deck-and-a-half design led to the production of the PD 4501 Scenicruiser. The GX-2 was 40 feet long, accommodated 43 passengers, had a lavatory, and large underfloor space for luggage. The power plant was a GM 6-71 diesel engine. The GX-2 toured in many areas for promotion and evaluation for the new type of bus that Greyhound would be operating during the 1950s. The GX-2 only operated in regular service for Greyhound for a time.

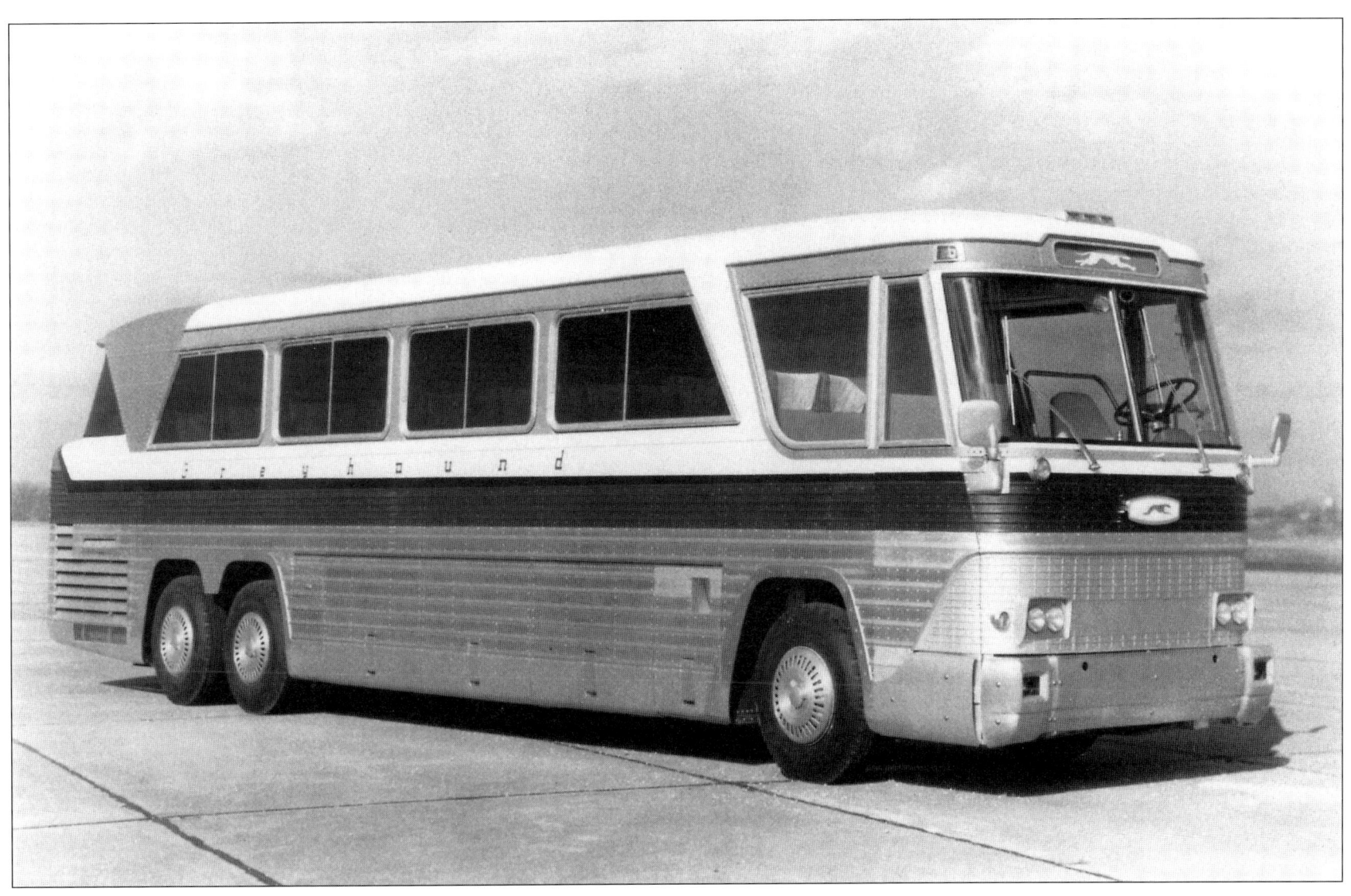

Mack Trucks, Inc. built this Model MV 620-D bus for testing by Greyhound Lines in 1957. The MV 620-D made many trips between Chicago and San Francisco and logged 260,000 miles through 1960. However, Greyhound did not accept this particular bus, and no more were built. This bus originally had a Mack six-cylinder ENDLT 674 diesel engine. *Charles Wotring Collection*

Scenicruisers

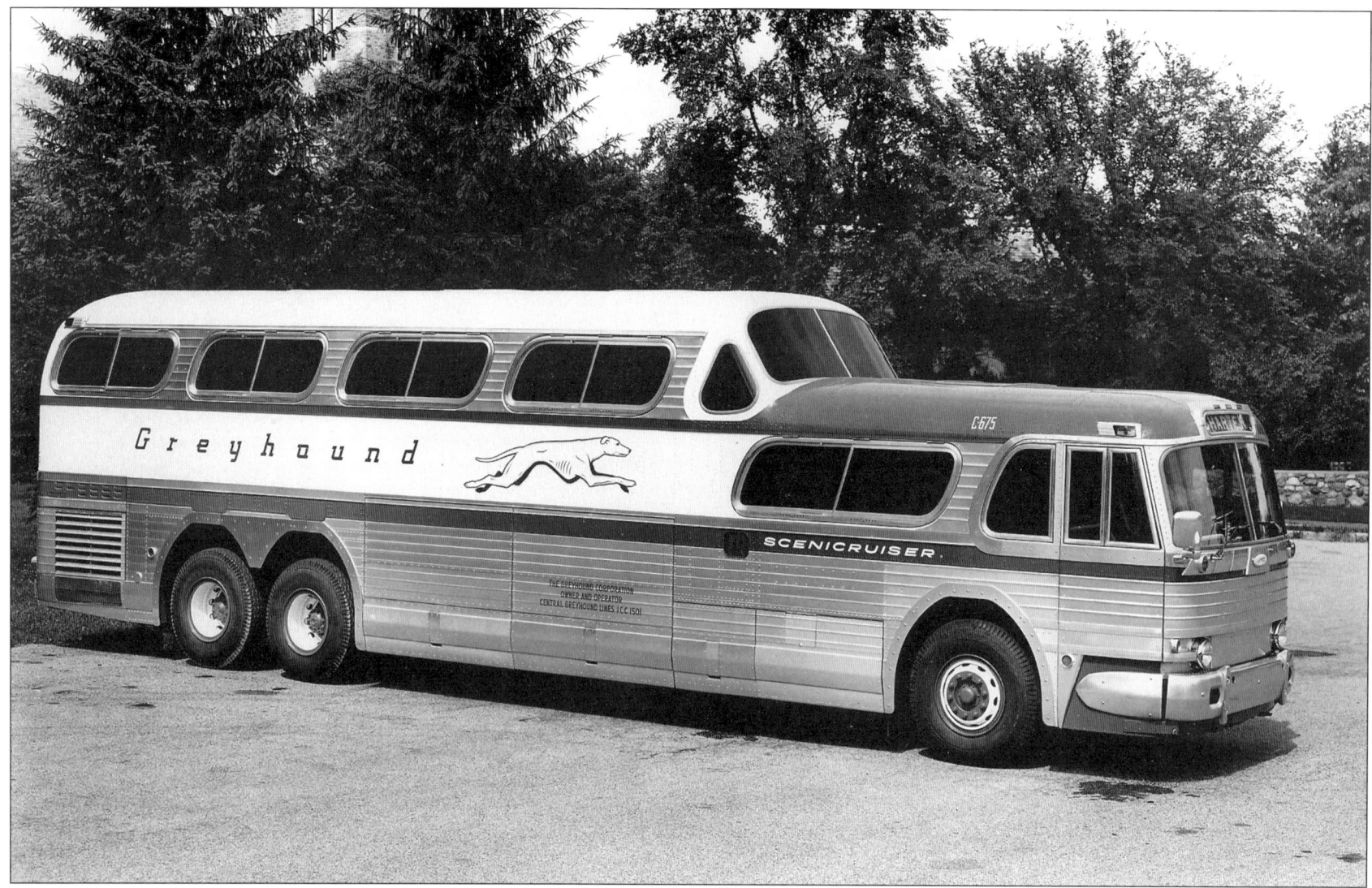

The Greyhound Scenicruiser of 1954 was the production model of the experimental GX-2 bus of 1949. It was built by General Motors. The model was designated as the PD 4501. The deck-and-a-half design attracted passengers and was reported to be Greyhound's most famous bus. There were 1,001 of the Scenicruisers built exclusively for Greyhound.

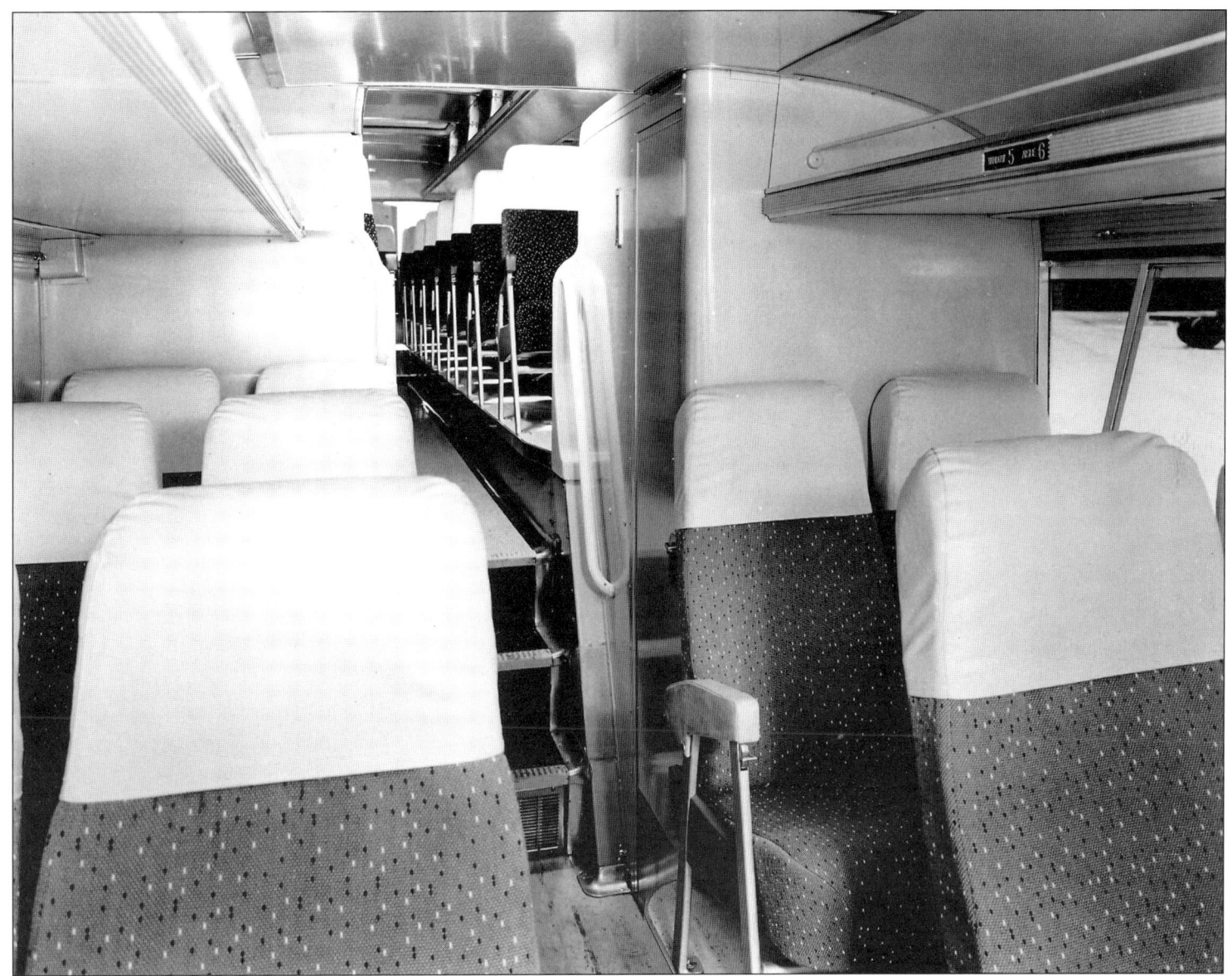

This is the interior view of the famous Greyhound Scenicruiser. It had seating for 10 passengers on the lower level behind the driver. A restroom is shown located at the left below the stairway to the upper deck, which had seats for 33 passengers. There were parcel racks above the seats. Under the upper deck were very large luggage compartments.

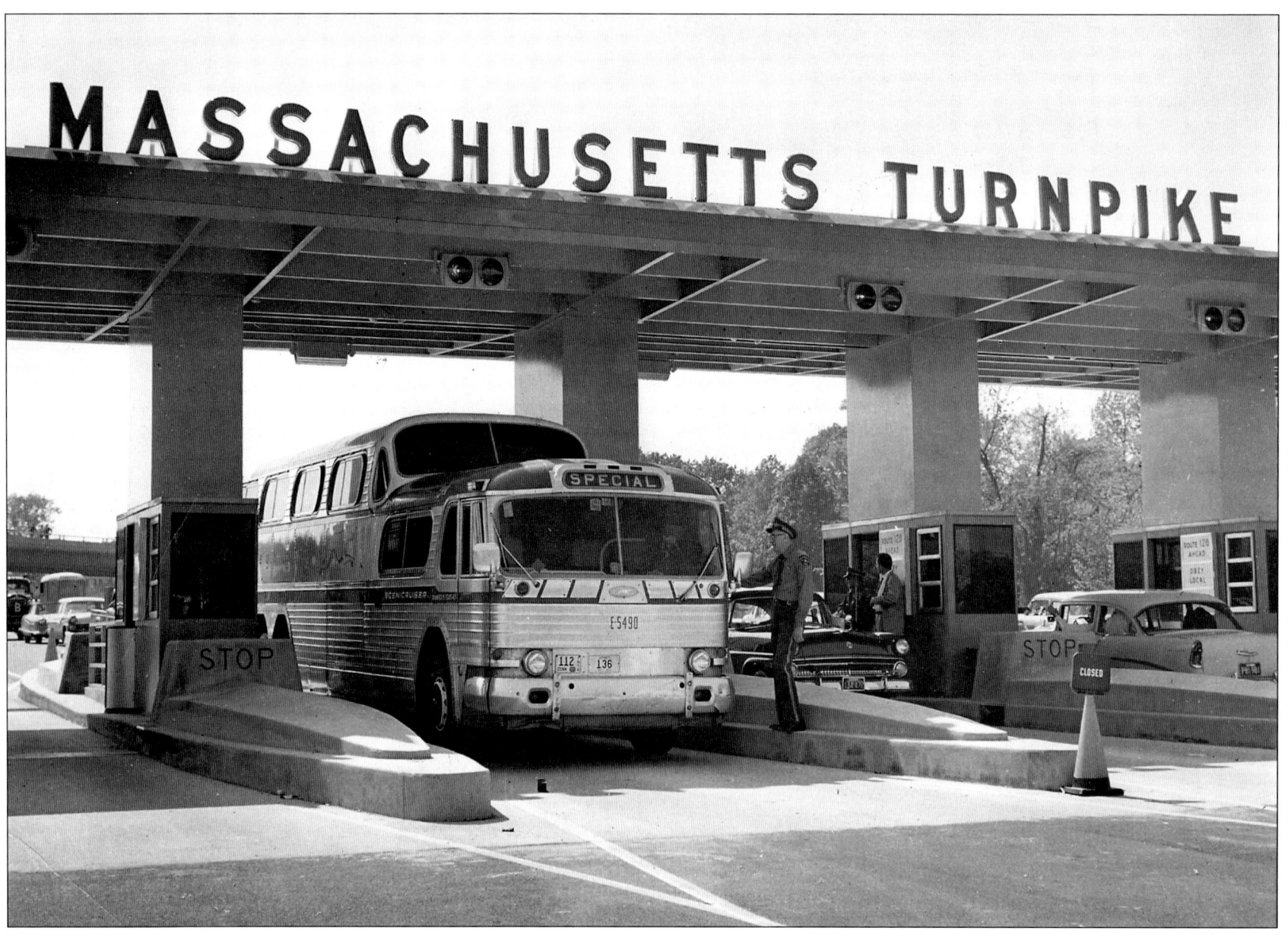

Toll roads like the Massachusetts Turnpike gave Greyhound the opportunity to operate express non-stop service between many metropolitan centers. The new turnpikes, interstate freeways, and the popular Scenicruiser bus contributed to good growth for Greyhound Lines in the 1950s.

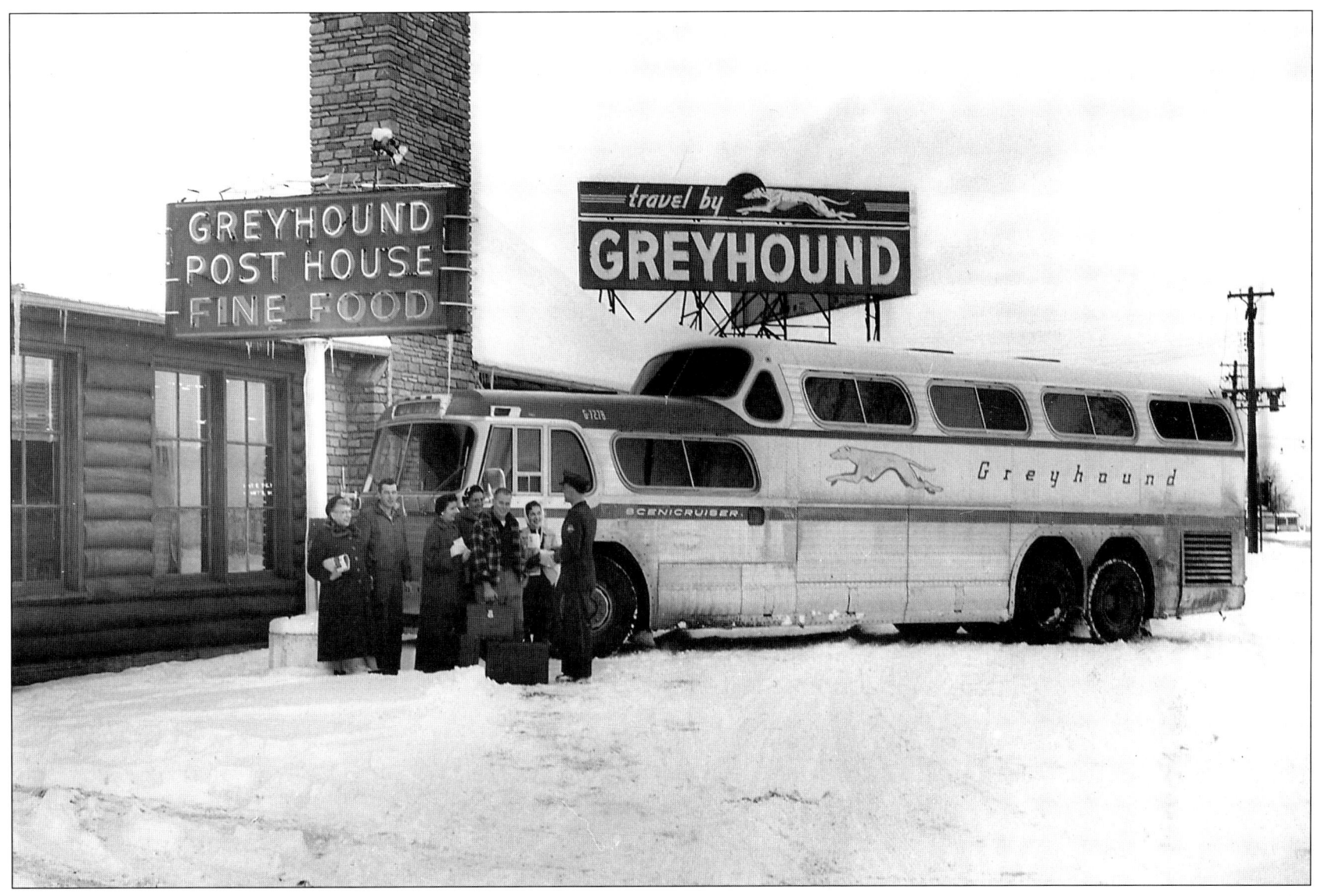

In the 1940s, Greyhound Lines introduced Post House restaurants. The Post Houses were located along Greyhound routes and served as convenient meal stops for passengers riding Greyhound buses. Some Post Houses also served as a ticket office and waiting room, as did this one at Mackinaw City, Michigan. A small service and storage area was provided here. A Great Lakes Greyhound Lines Scenicruiser is parked outside the Post House in this picture.

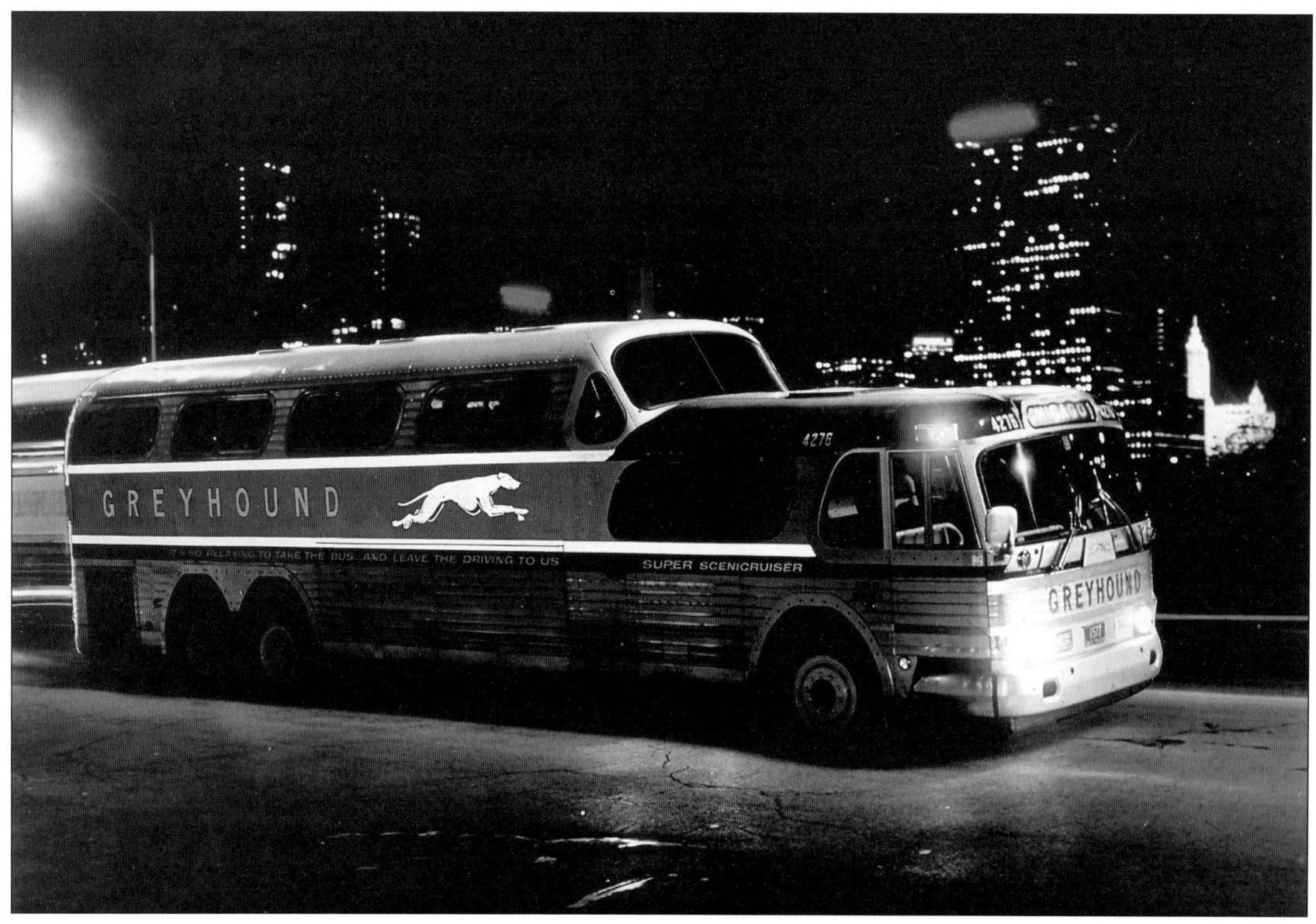

Greyhound revised the paint scheme on the Scenicruiser buses with larger Greyhound lettering in the 1960s. The lettering, Greyhound dog, and strips above and below were scotch light, considered a new safety feature. When this revision had been made, the Scenicruisers were equipped with a single Detroit Diesel 8V71 diesel engine.

Greyhound Buses Overseas

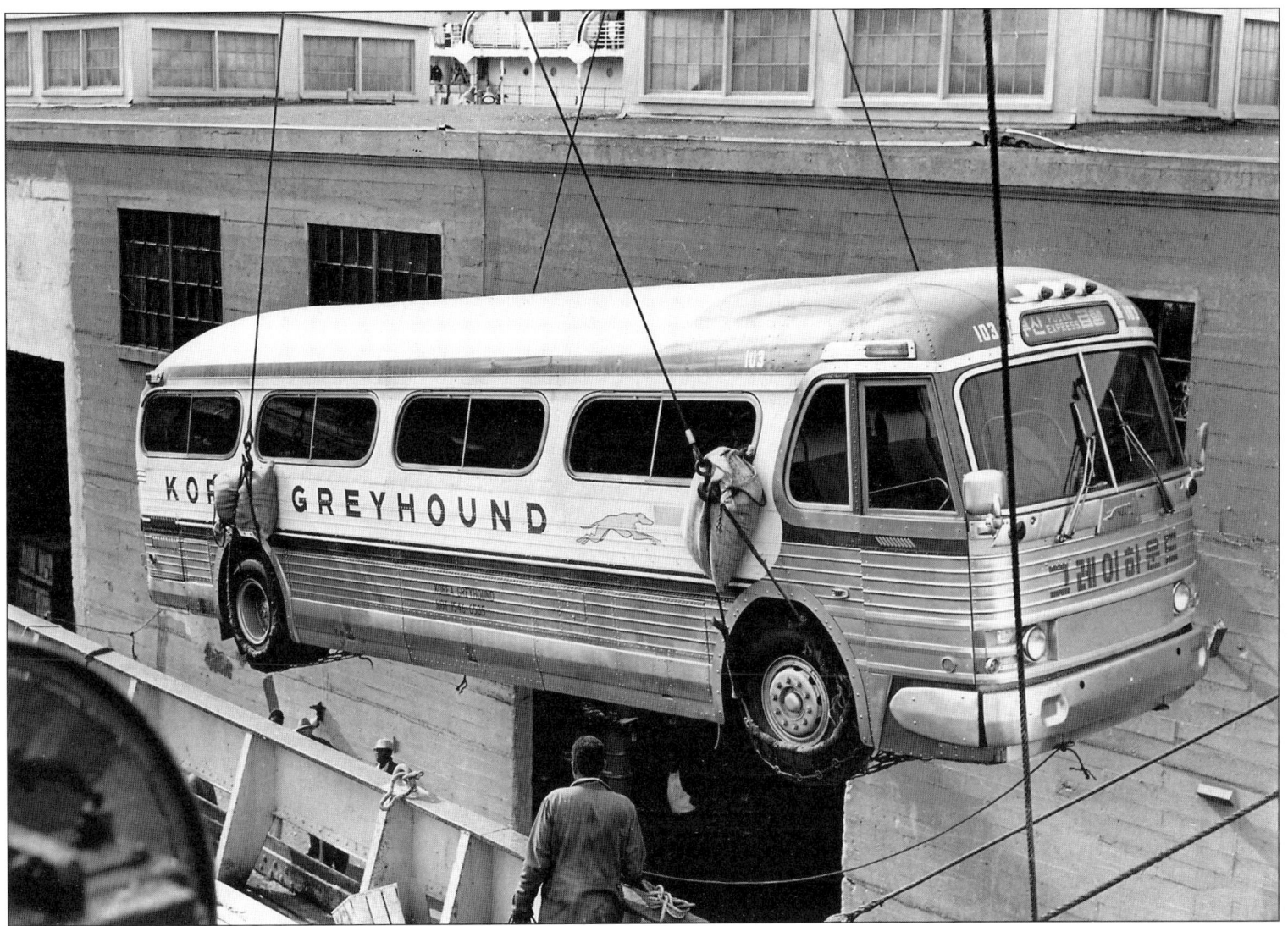

Greyhound entered into a joint venture in the early 1970s for bus service in Korea. Initially, 40 used buses, like this GM PD 4104-lettered Korea Greyhound, were shipped to Korea where they operated successfully. Some Scenicruiser buses were also in Korea Greyhound service. Eventually, Koreans assumed the service.

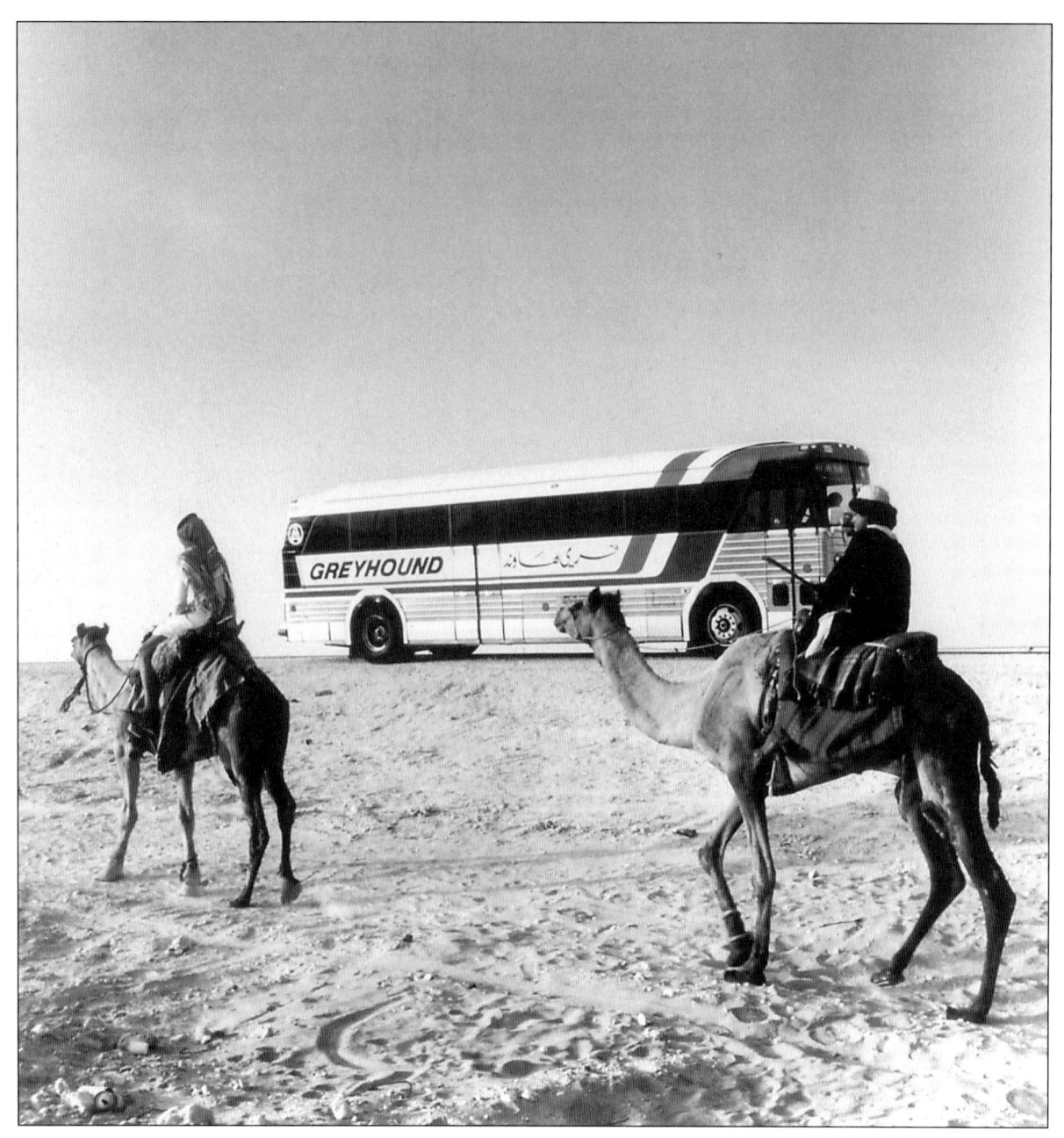

In 1980, Greyhound Lines entered into a joint venture with Aramco in Saudi Arabia for a bus operation in Al Khobar, where Aramco had a community especially for foreign workers. Greyhound provided 200 new MCI MC-5C buses in this community. In addition to a 40 percent interest in the joint venture, Greyhound had a management fee arrangement. Note the double roof, which was required for operation in the hot climate.

Final Greyhound General Motors Buses

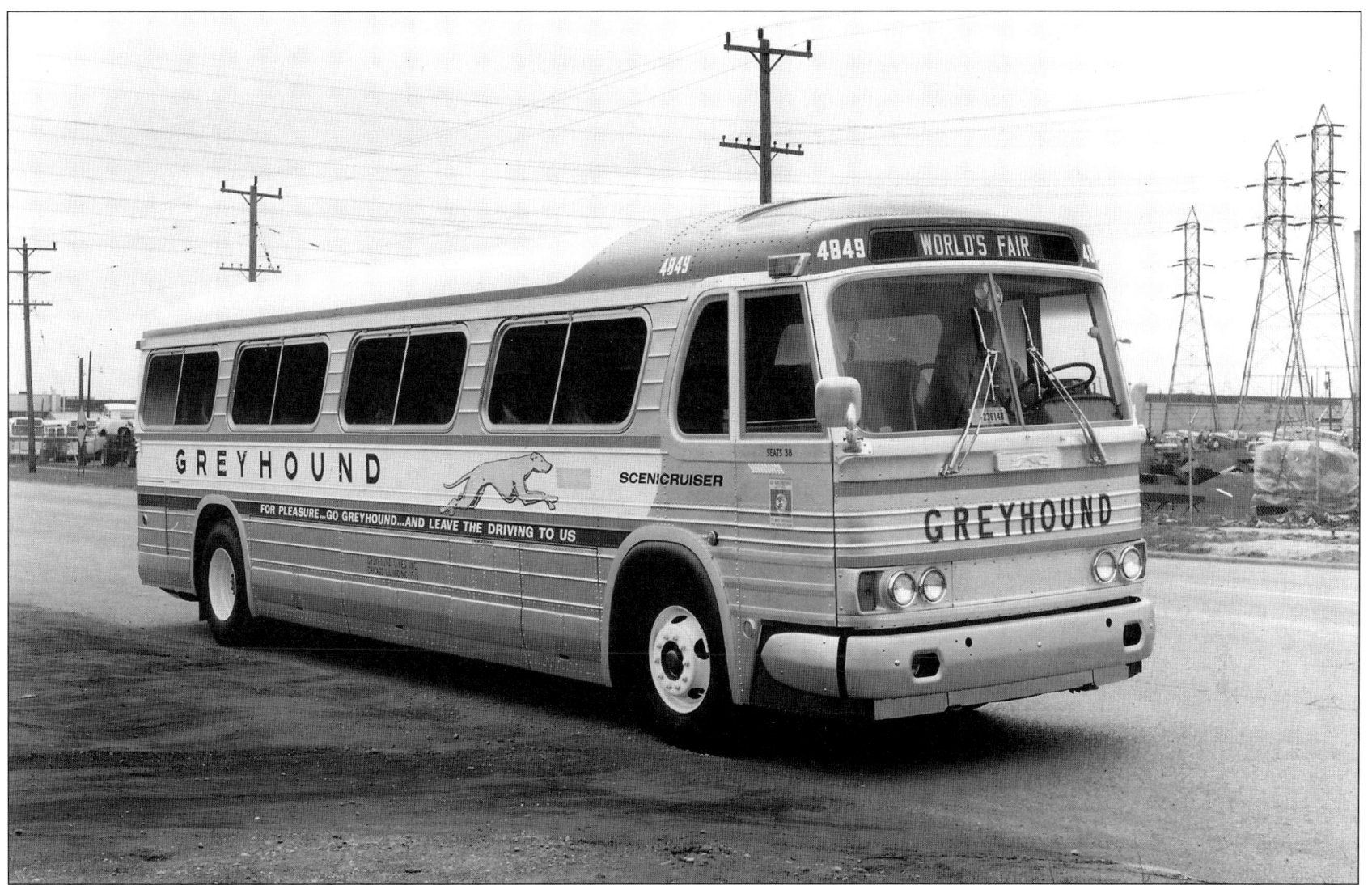

Greyhound purchased approximately 1,000 General Motors Model PD 4106 buses between 1960 and 1964. These buses had one of the popular Greyhound slogans, "For Pleasure...Go Greyhound...and Leave the Driving to Us." The Model 4106 had the first Detroit Diesel 8V71 diesel engines. The engines were large enough to also power the air-conditioning systems, whereas previous models had a separate gasoline engine for air-conditioning.

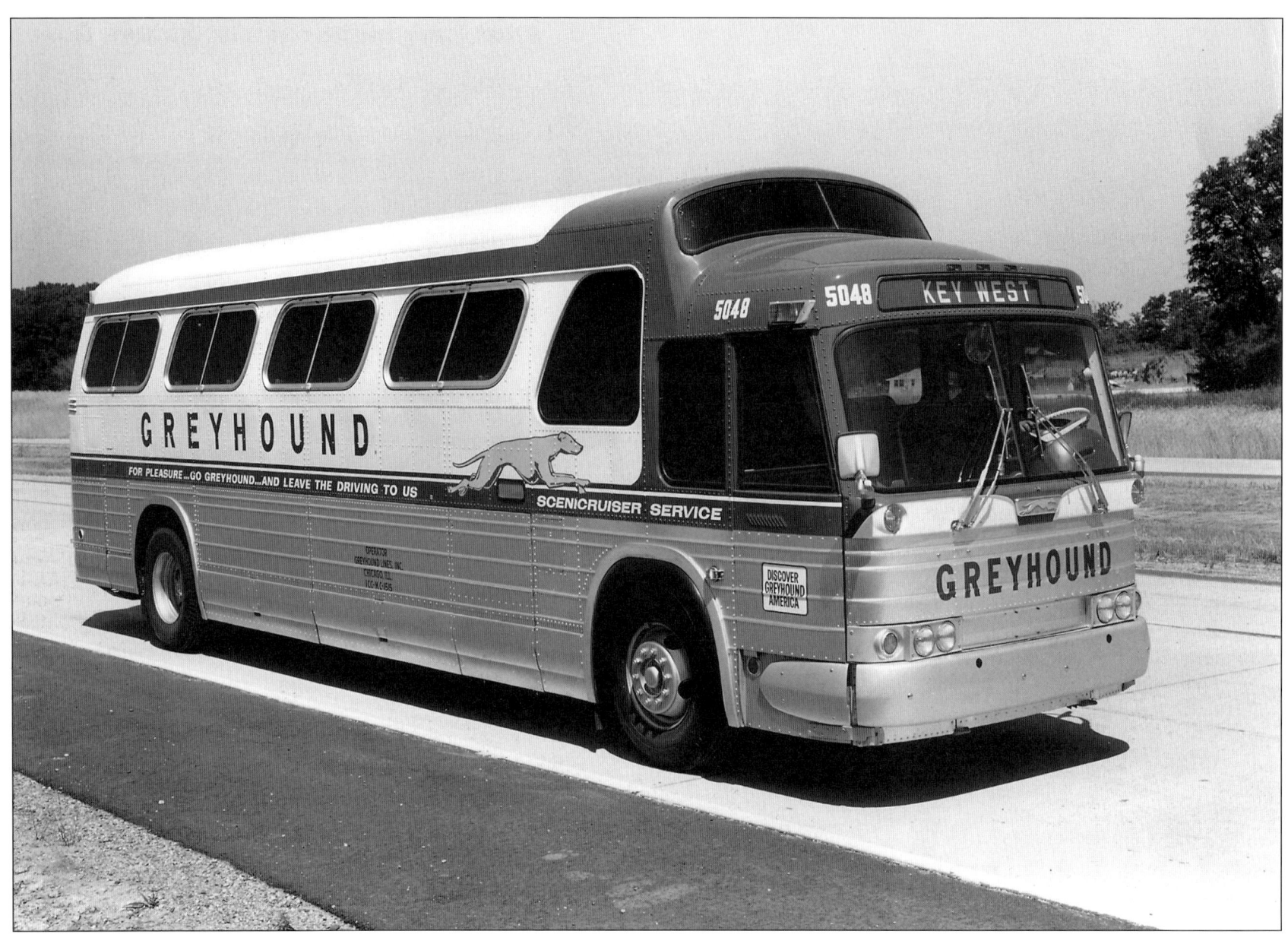

This General Motors Model PD 4107 bus and 161 others were delivered to Greyhound divisions in 1966. The following year, Greyhound divisions received 200 more PD 4107 buses. These were the last General Motors buses that were ordered by Greyhound.

Greyhound Motor Coach Industries Buses

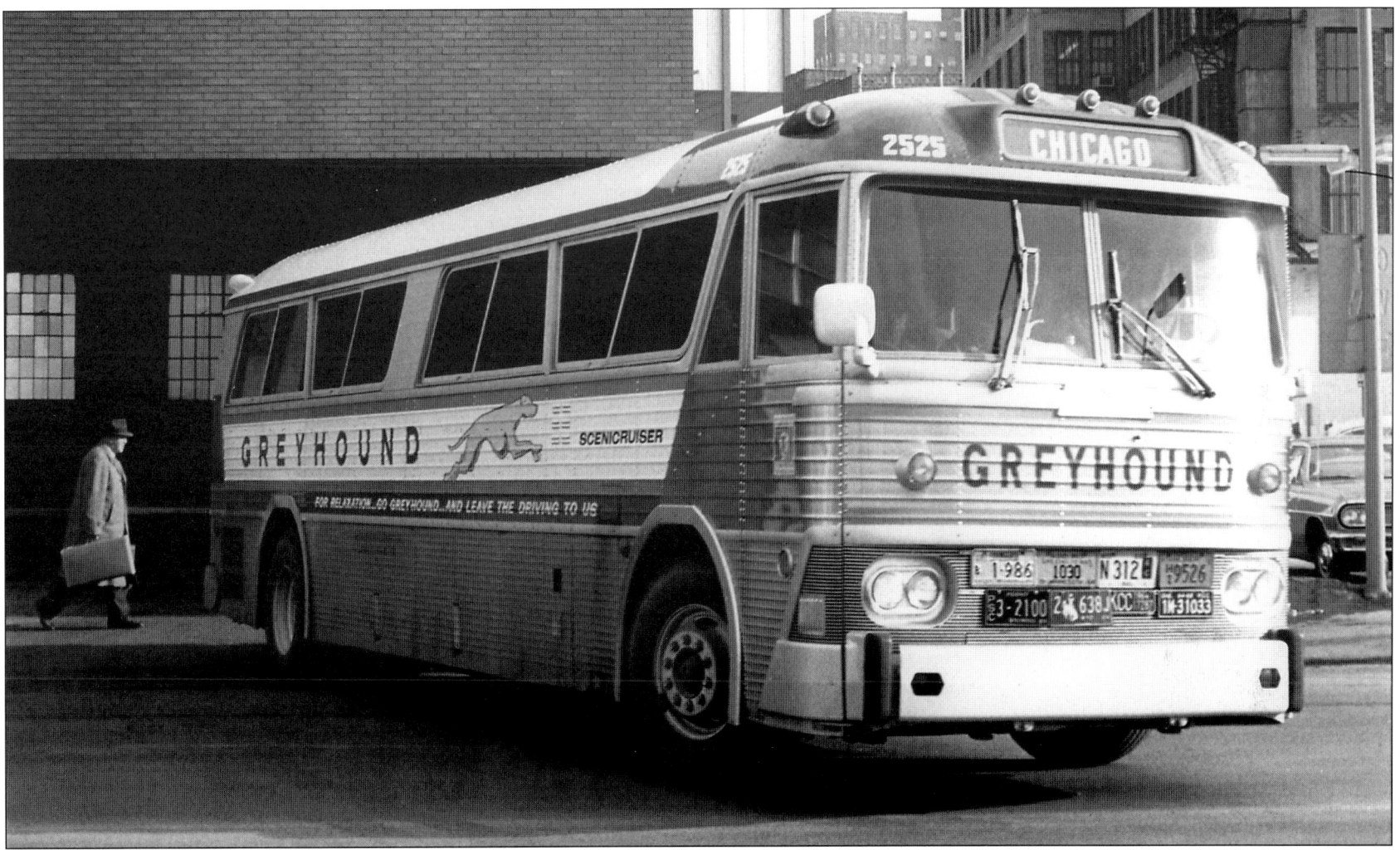

Motor Coach Industries (MCI) became fully owned by the Greyhound Corporation in 1961. Motor Coach Industries had been providing buses to Greyhound Lines of Canada for a number of years. In 1963, Greyhound began taking delivery of MCI MC-5 buses. Initial construction began in MCI's Winnipeg, Manitoba plant and finished in a new factory in Pembina, North Dakota. Pictured here is a Greyhound MCI MC-5 bus leaving the Minneapolis bus terminal on its way to Chicago. Note the multitude of license plates, representing several states. Eventually, a common plate with stickers for each state was used.

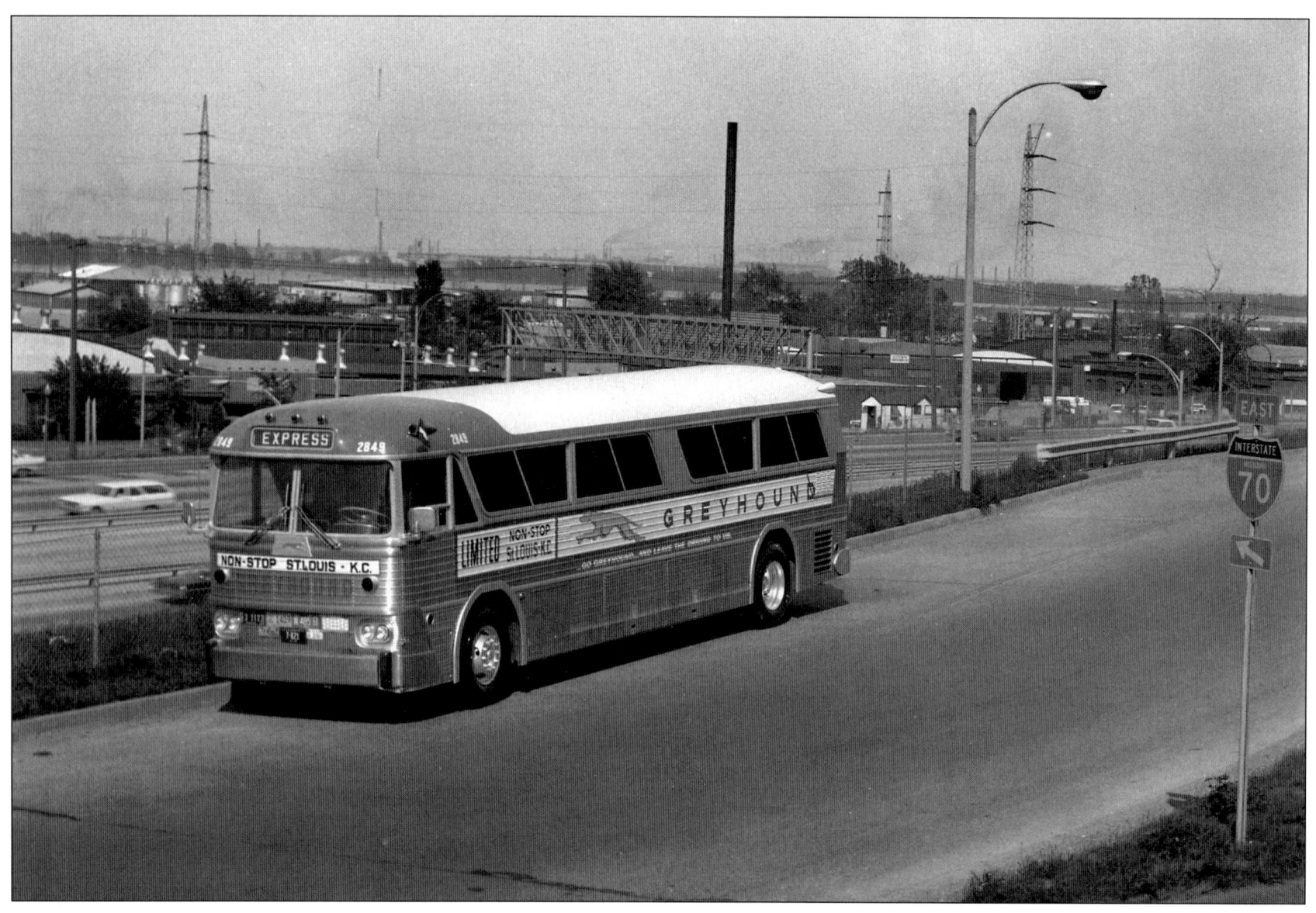

In the mid-1960s, new interstate highways opened possibilities of enhancing bus service. Greyhound operated non-stop express schedules between a number of metropolitan areas. The Motor Coach Industries MC-5A bus shown here was on a Greyhound non-stop service between Kansas City and St. Louis. Greater competition from private automobile travel created a need for improved bus service.

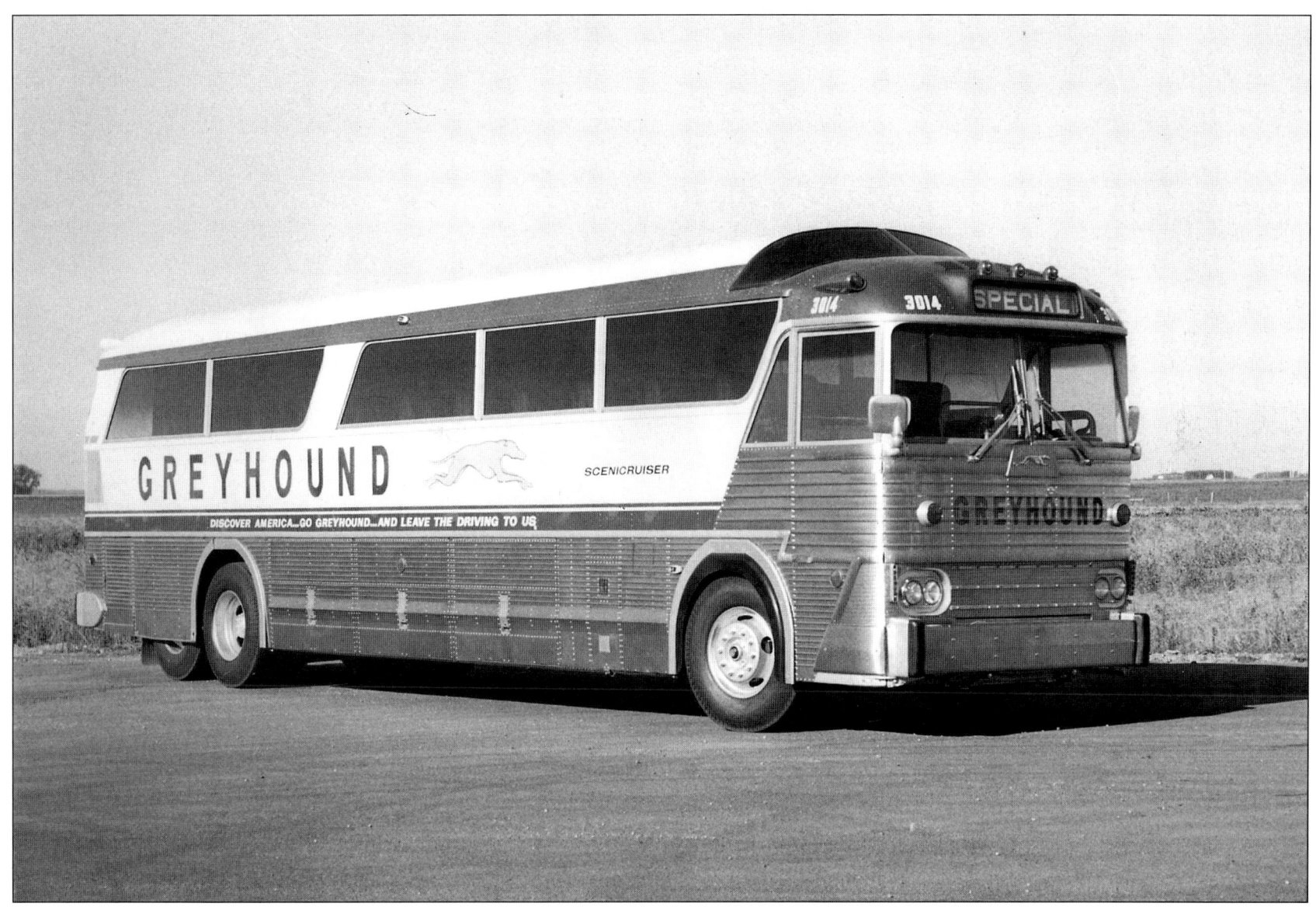

Motor Coach Industries (MCI) introduced the MC-7 model bus in 1968. It was 40 feet long and had an extra set of wheels following the driving axle to meet weight restrictions on 40-foot buses. The first MC-7 buses had the rearmost wheels mounted behind a body panel, as shown in this picture of one of the first MC-7 buses. Greyhound operated more than 1,300 MCI MC-7 buses.

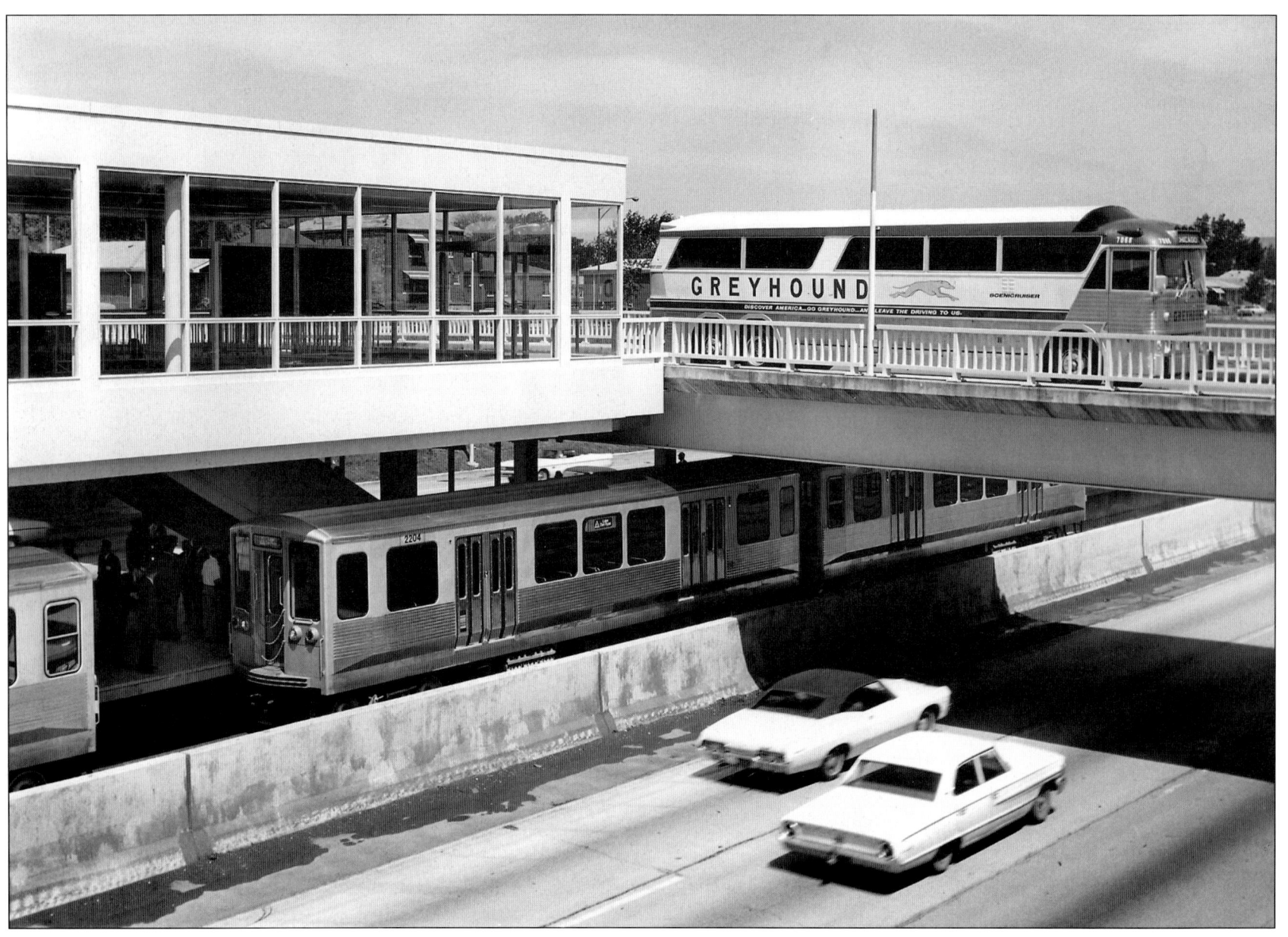

In June 1969, Greyhound established a satellite terminal at the 95th Street Station on the Dan Ryan Expressway in Chicago. This gave connections to Chicago Transit Authority's (CTA) Dan Ryan trains and CTA buses, as well as serving South Chicago. A Greyhound MCI MC-7 is shown at the station.

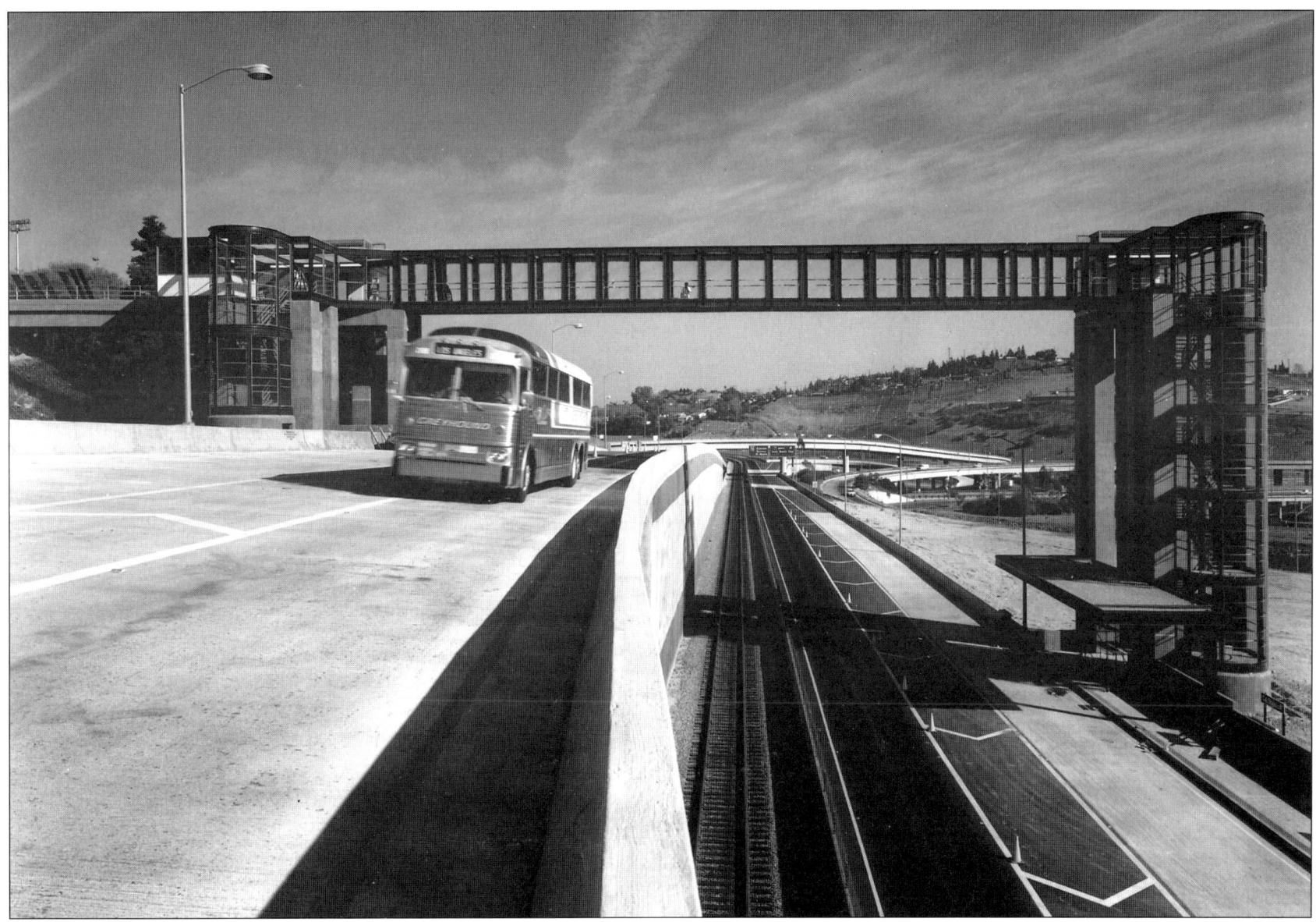

Busways were being built in various metropolitan areas in the 1970s to speed bus traffic and bypass congested streets and freeways. One of the early busways was the El Monte Busway in metropolitan Los Angeles. Pictured here is a Greyhound MCI MC-7 on the Busway. Busways are generally exclusive for buses, allowing passengers riding them to save considerable commuting time.

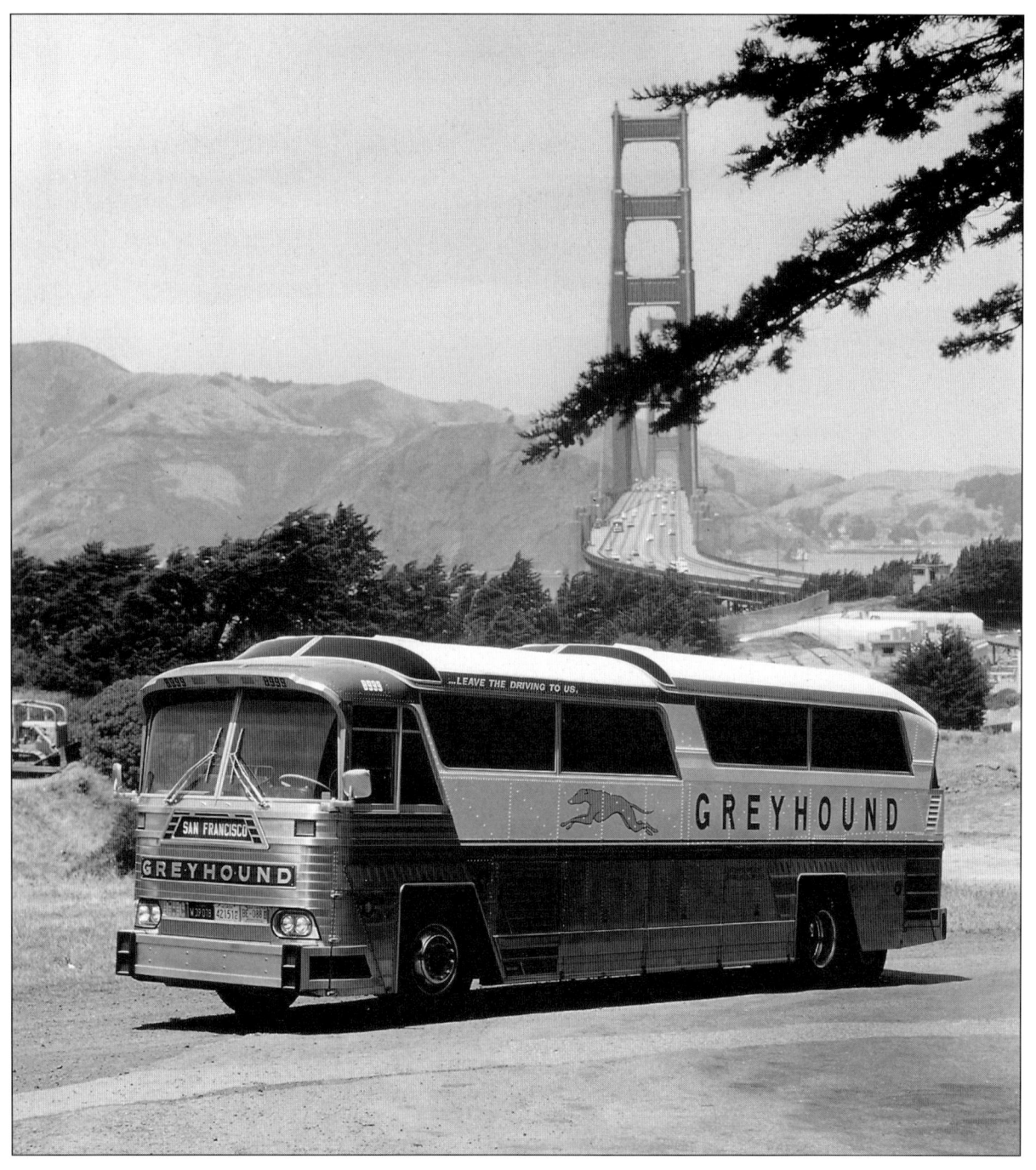

Greyhound and Motor Coach Industries developed the Motor Coach Industries MC-6 bus in 1968. It was to be the next generation Greyhound bus, presumably to replace the successful reign of the Greyhound Scenicruiser. However, it was ahead of its time. The MC-6 had a 102-inch width, which was not legal in most states. Also, the Detroit Diesel V-12 engine proved unsatisfactory due to poor fuel efficiency. In 1973 the V-12 engine was replaced by V-8 engines and an automatic transmission installed on most of the 100 MC-6 buses that were built. In Canada, 15 MC-6 buses continued to be operated with the V-12 engines.

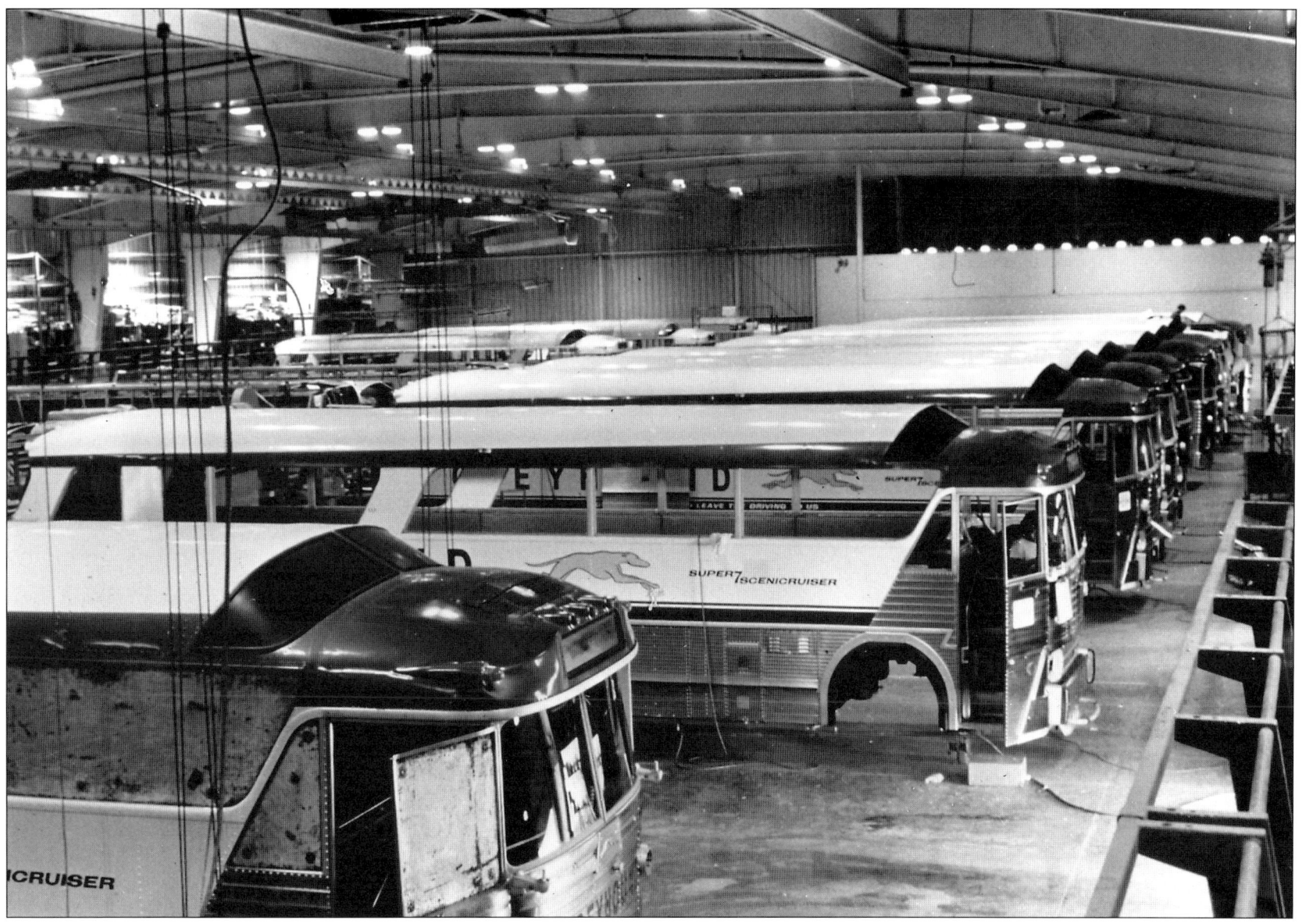

This picture shows Greyhound MC-7 buses under construction at the Motor Coach Industries factory in Winnipeg, Manitoba. The bodies were built in Winnipeg and then shipped on a trailer to Pembina, North Dakota, where engines, transmissions, and other components were installed. After other finishing work was completed the buses were ready for delivery.

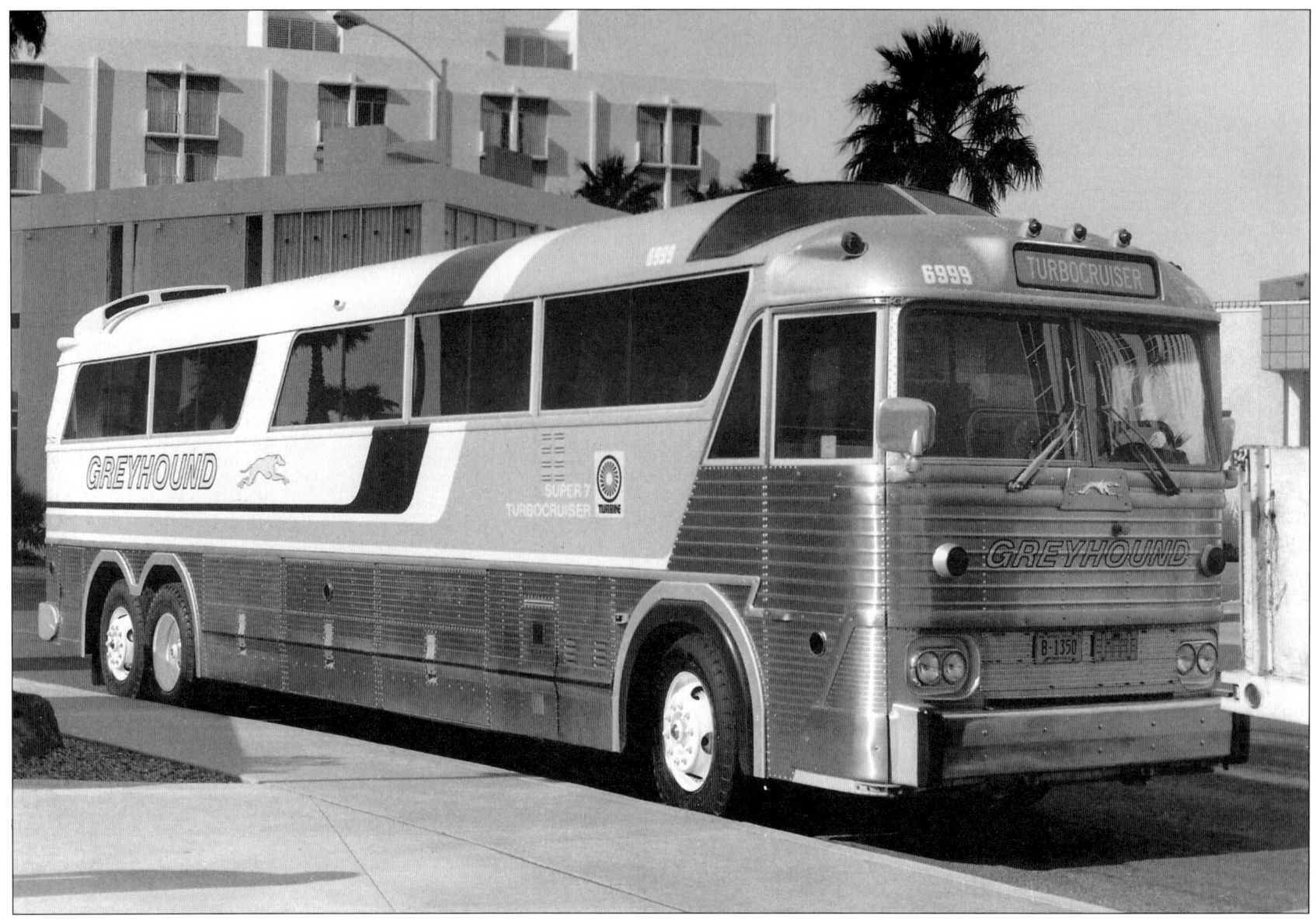

A fleet of four Greyhound "Turbocruiser" buses, which were Motor Coach Industries Model MC-7s, entered service September 6, 1972. These buses operated daily round trips between New York and Boston, and New York and Washington, D. C. The Turbocruisers offered a smooth, quiet ride, and the turbine engine in each bus emitted practically no waste particles in the air. Engine life was expected to be double that of the bus engines of the day.

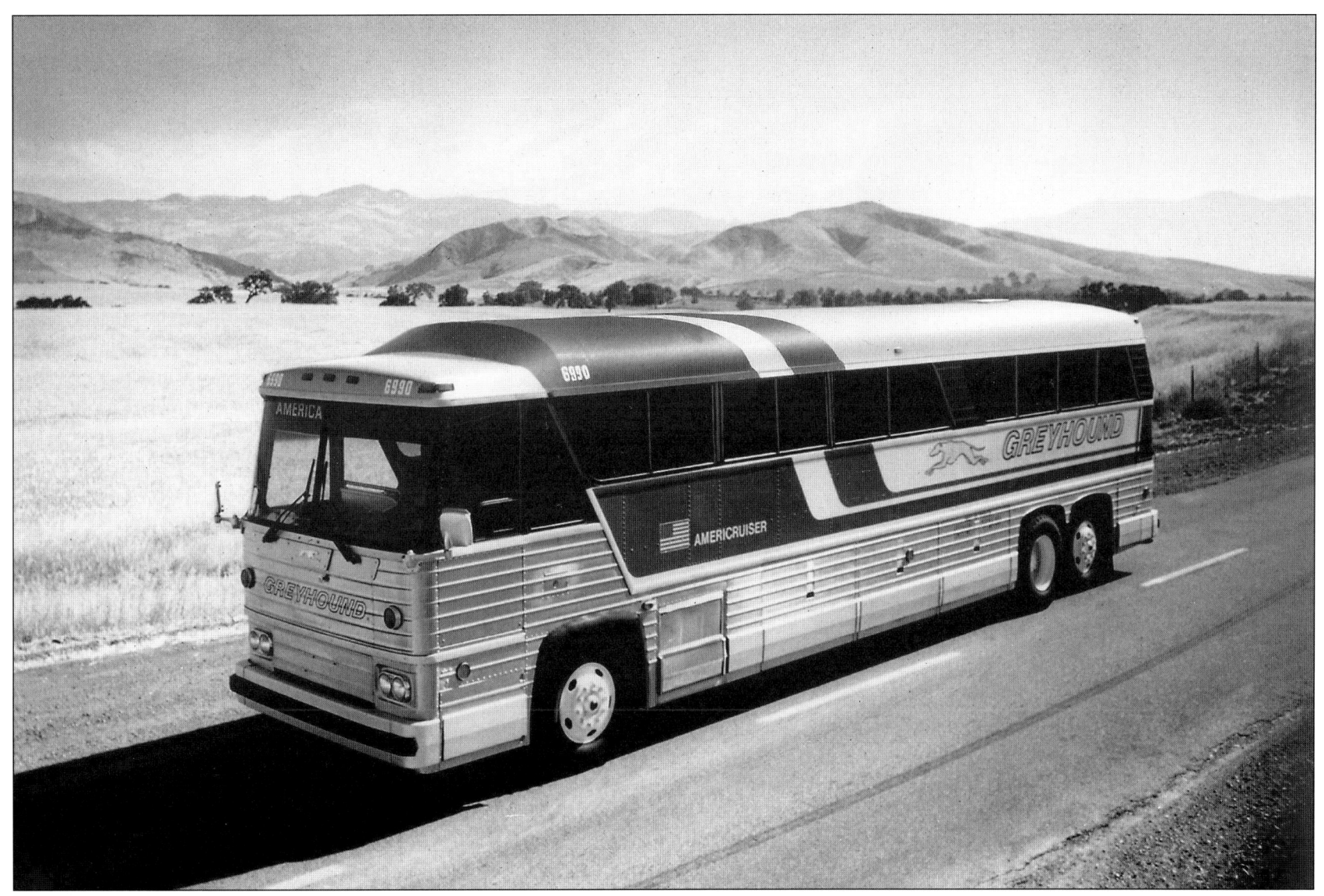

Greyhound Lines began taking delivery of Motor Coach Industries MC-8 buses in 1973. In preparation for the celebration of the United States' bicentennial, the MC-8 buses had a red stripe added along with a flag and were dubbed Americruisers by Greyhound. Some of the MC-8 buses in the Greyhound fleet were built at the new Transportation Manufacturing Corporation (TMC) plant in Roswell, New Mexico, which opened in 1976. Greyhound operated approximately 2,000 MC-8 buses.

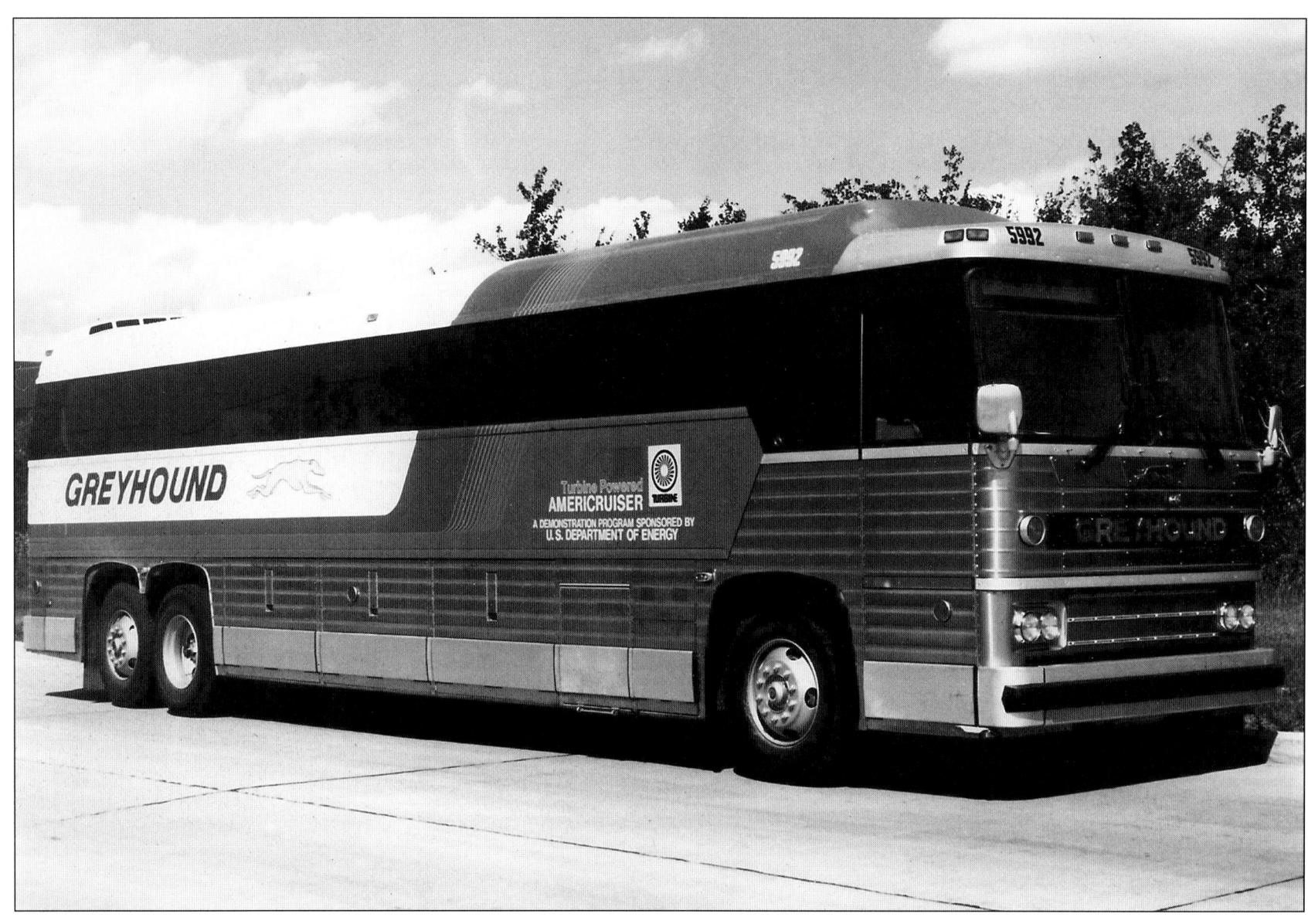

Four Motor Coach Industries MC-8 Greyhound buses were involved in a turbine engine demonstration program sponsored by the U.S. Department of Energy in 1980, replacing the MC-7 buses with turbines, which were tested by Greyhound earlier. The funding for further testing by the U.S. government was not available, and the program was dropped.

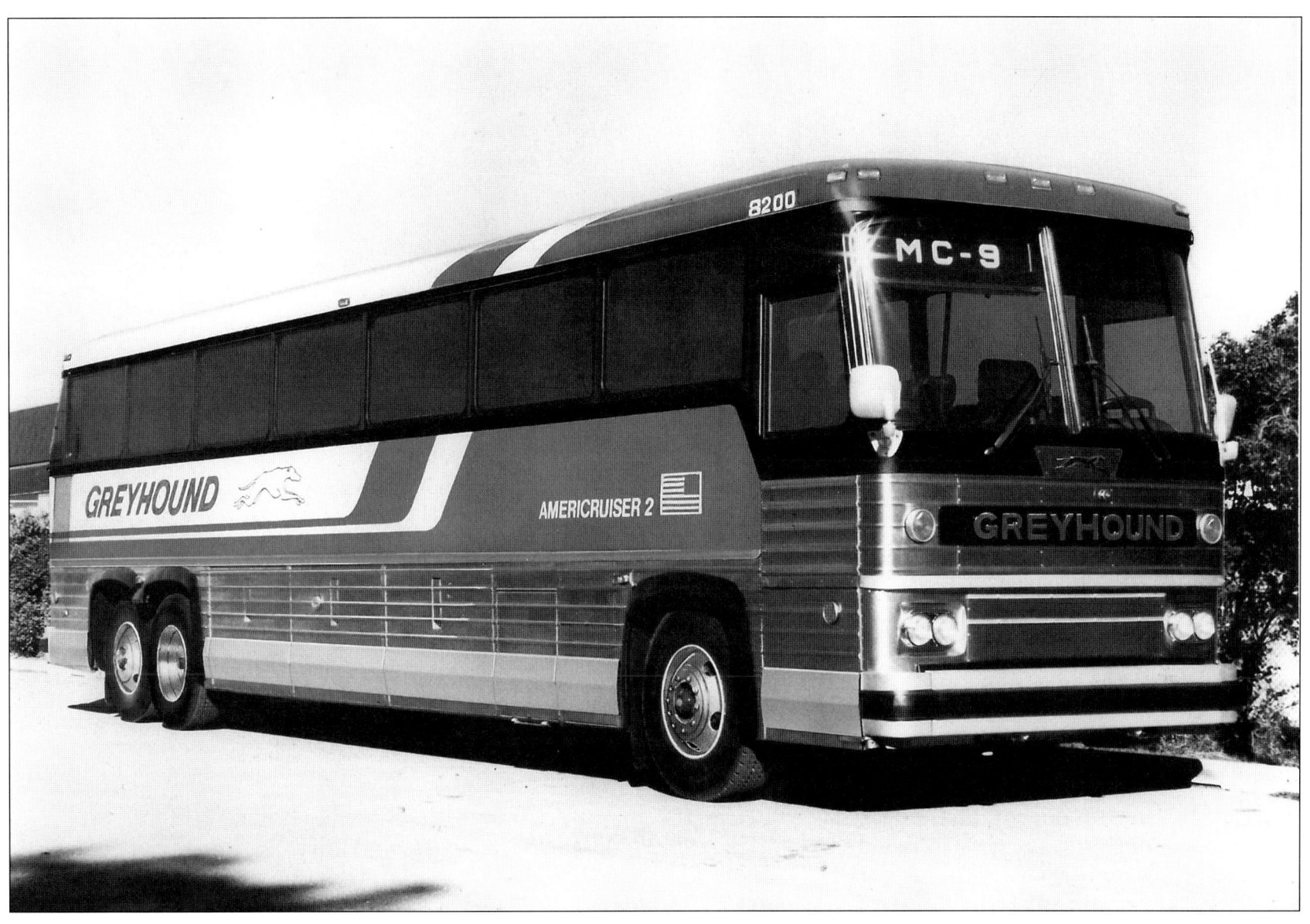

The Motor Coach Industries MC-9 bus was introduced in 1979 and production continued until 1985. Greyhound added the MC-9s to its fleet during the time. Americruiser 2 was the name Greyhound gave to these buses.

Greyhound Buses in the 1980s and 1990s

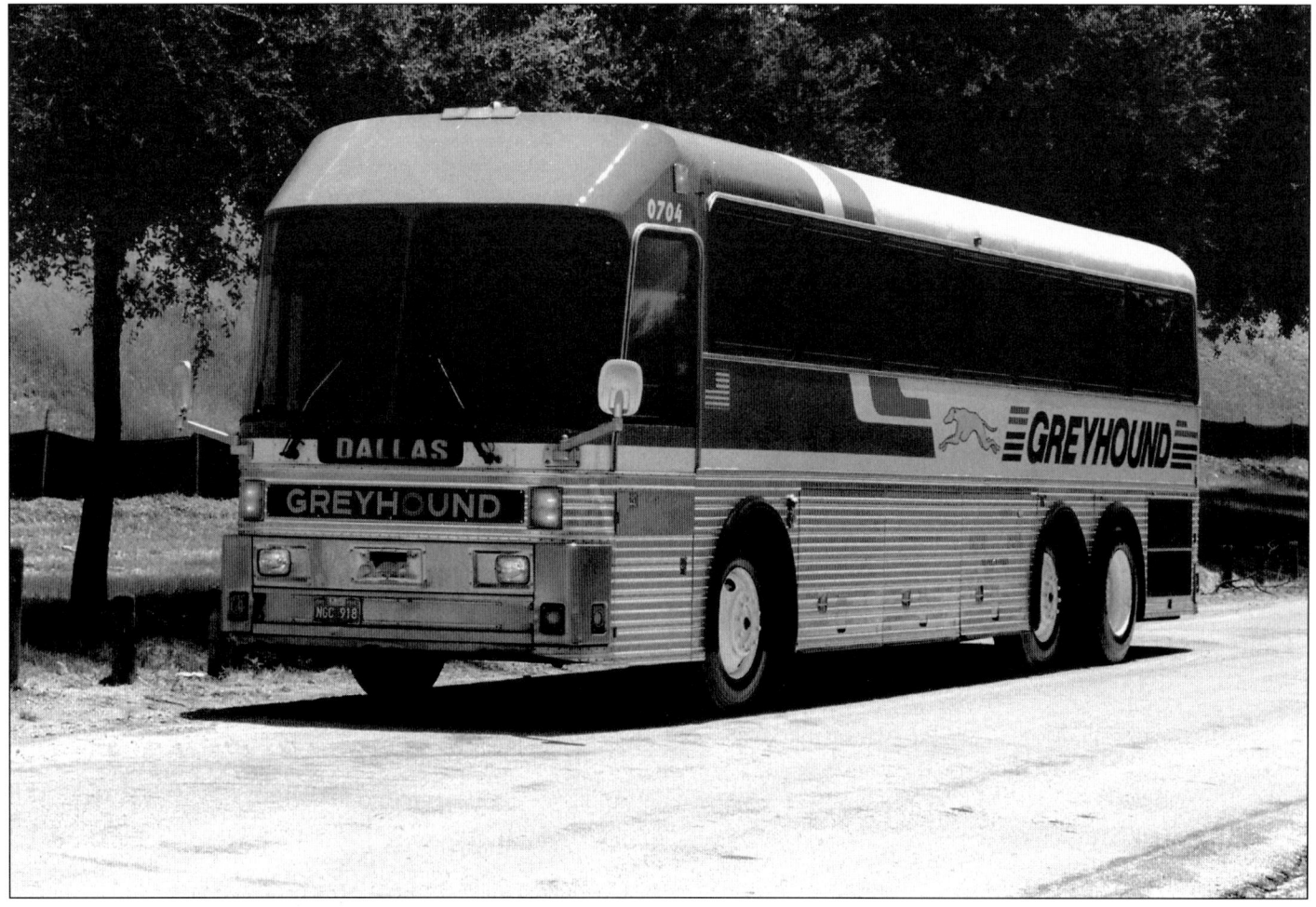

When Greyhound Lines acquired Trailways, Inc. in 1987, the Trailways-owned Eagle Manufacturing Company in Brownsville, Texas, was included. Many Eagle 10s were in Trailways service. For a time, they continued with the Greyhound running dog on the side. A number of Trailways Eagles were repainted in Greyhound colors. Pictured here is a Model 15 Eagle, which followed the Model 10 and was last used on Greyhound's Dallas-Houston service. All Eagle buses were eventually eliminated from the Greyhound fleet.

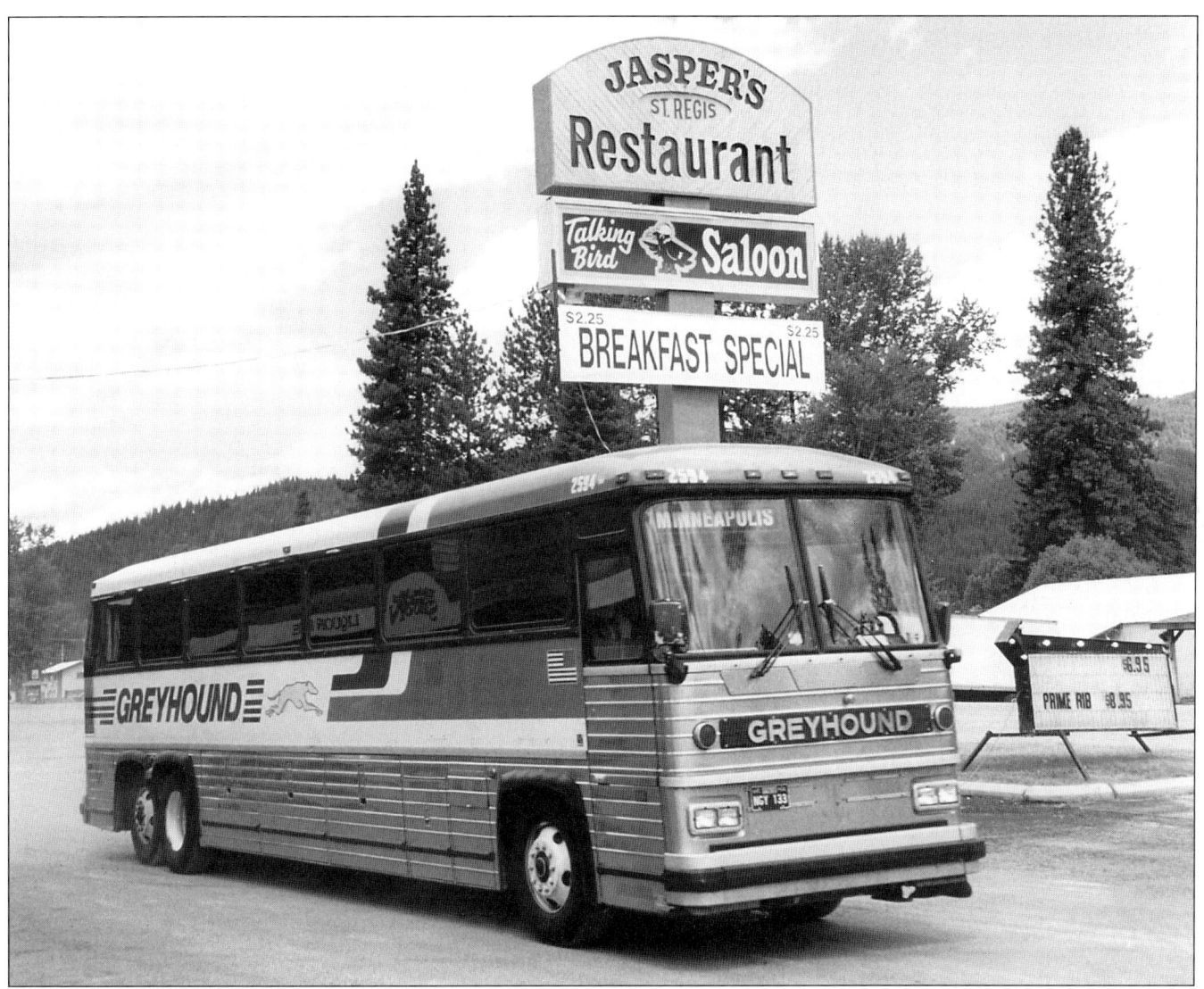

The Motor Coach Industries (MCI) Model MC-12 was the backbone of the Greyhound fleet between 1992 and 1998. More than 1,340 Model MC-12s were acquired by Greyhound. They were almost identical to the MCI Model MC-9 bus, popular in the 1980s. The MC-12 had a Detroit Diesel 6V92 TA engine and a HT740D Allison automatic transmission. Some MC-12s were tested using Detroit Diesel Series 50 diesel engines. The MC-12 pictured here was departing from a rest stop and driver change location at St. Regis, Montana, in 1998.

Modern Greyhound Buses

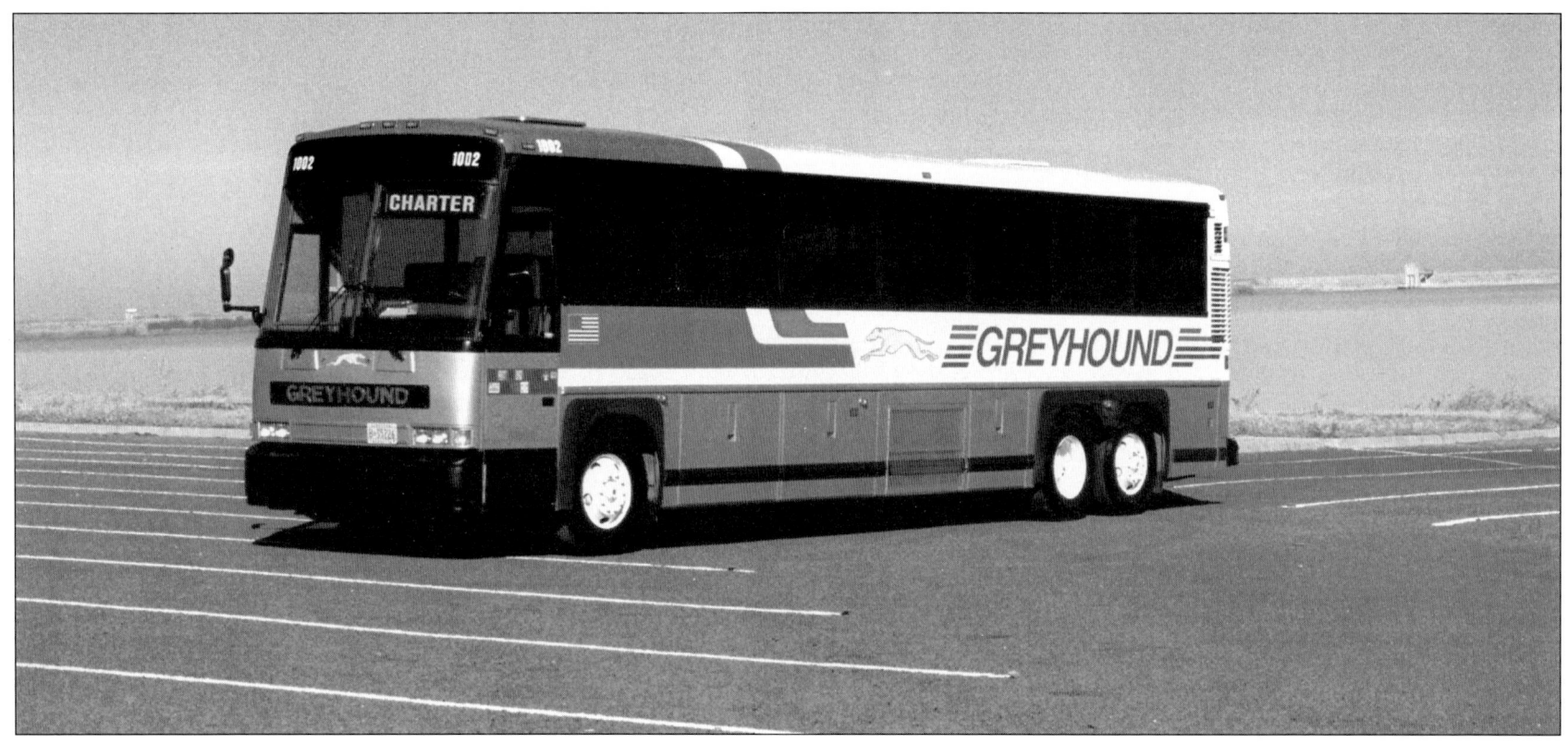

This bus, a Motor Coach Industries Model 102D3, was one of 10 received by Greyhound Lines in 1996. In the following year, 40 more MCI 102D3 buses were added to the Greyhound fleet. These buses were 40 feet long. Subsequent orders of the same type bus were for 45-foot models. This bus and the other Model 102D3 buses were assigned to Greyhound service out of the New York City area.

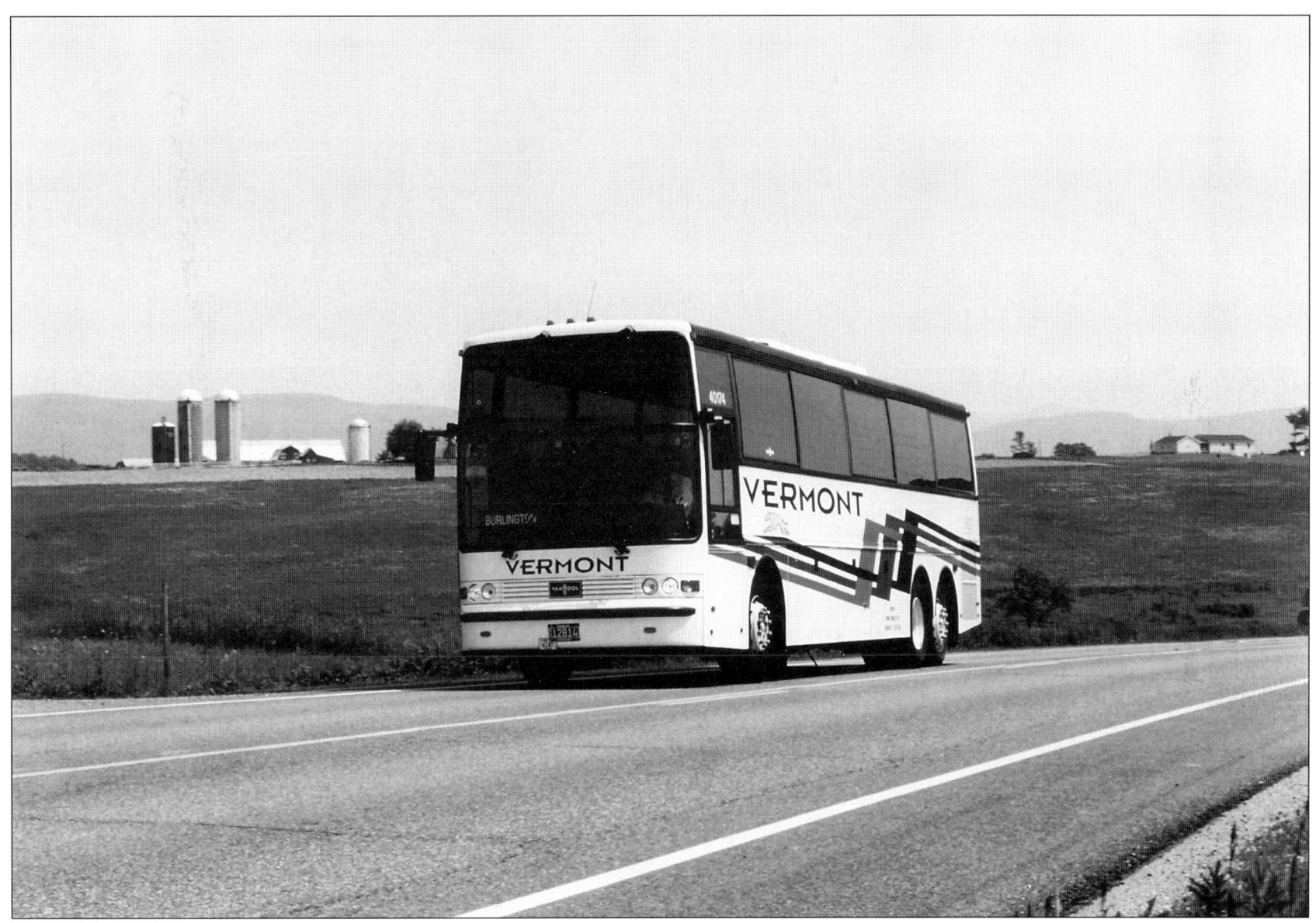

Greyhound has owned Vermont Transit Lines of Burlington, Vermont, since 1976. Vermont Transit's fleet is mostly comprised of Motor Coach Industries buses, but six Van Hool buses are also part of the fleet. Built in Belgium, the Van Hool buses are marketed in the United States by ABC Bus. The buses have mostly American mechanical components.

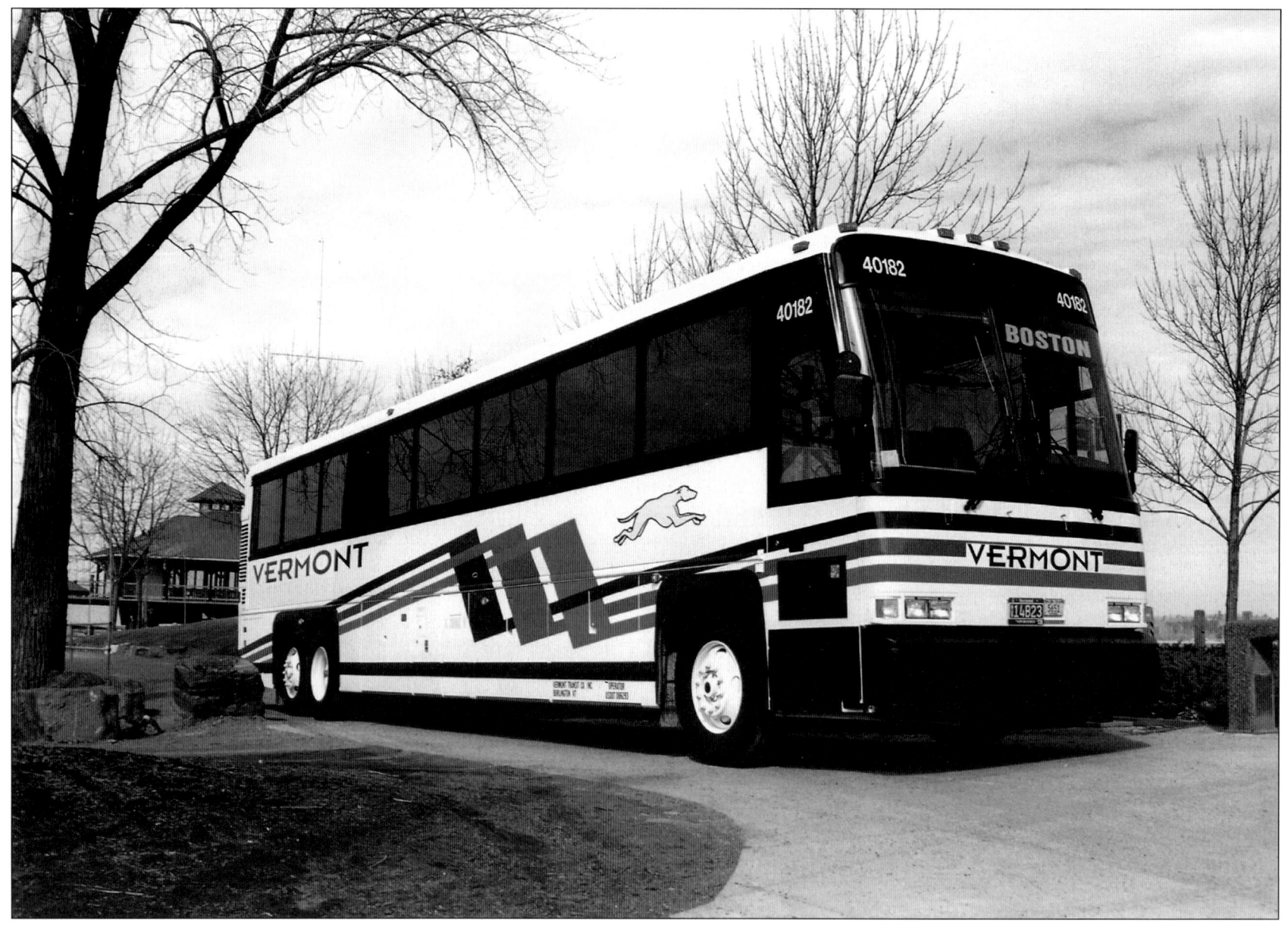

Greyhound-owned Vermont Transit Lines added three Motor Coach Industries 102DL3 buses to its fleet on March 5, 1999. These buses featured new green-and-black Vermont Transit graphics along with the Greyhound running dog emblem. The buses were equipped with wheelchair lifts.

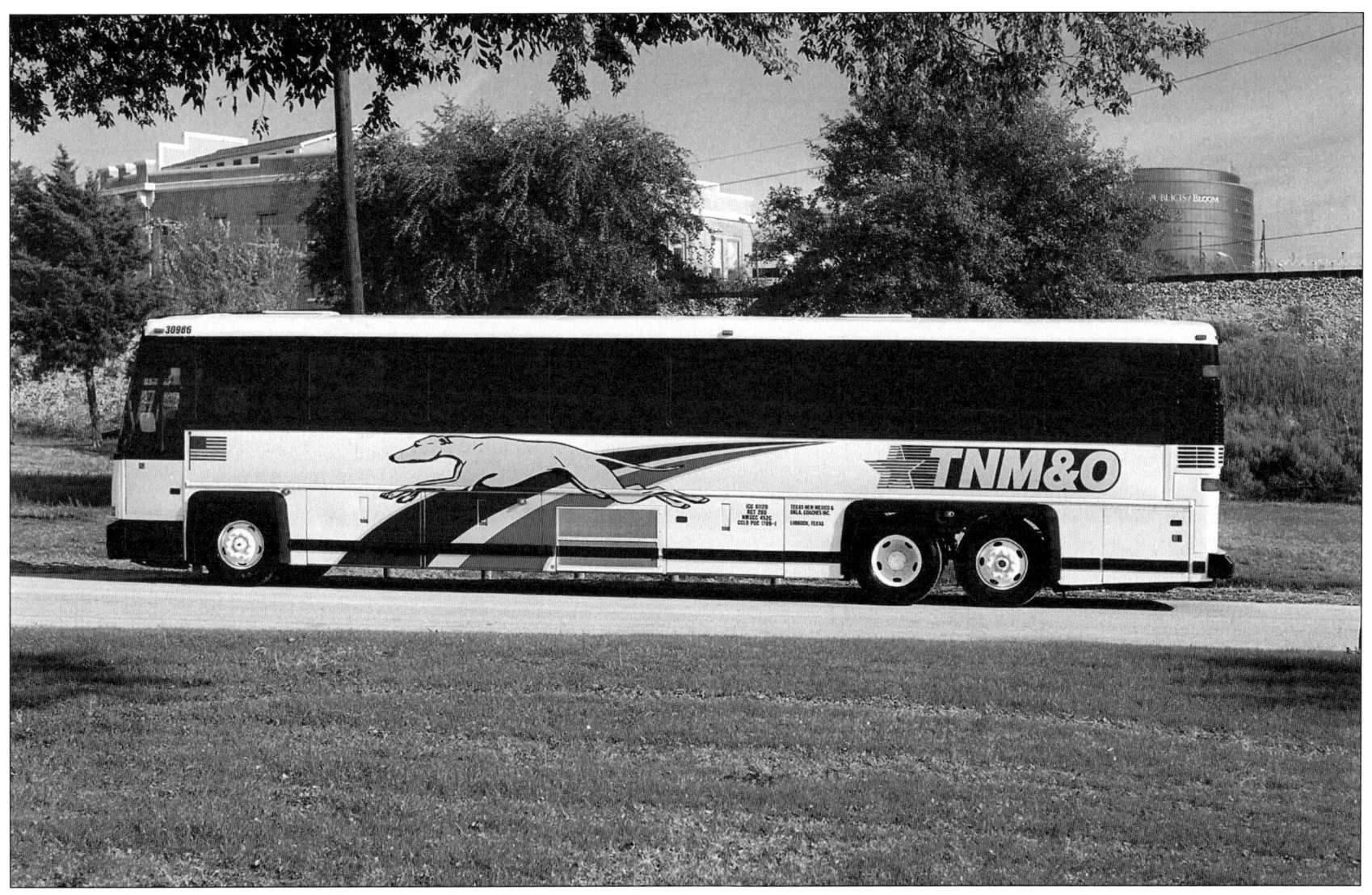

In September 1999, Greyhound-owned Texas, New Mexico and Oklahoma Coaches (TNM&O) added eight Motor Coach Industries 45-foot 102DL3 buses. These buses were equipped with wheelchair lifts and had new graphics featuring the larger Greyhound dog emblem and curved strips, along with the TNM&O logo. The buses were immediately assigned to TNM&O's Denver-Dallas service.

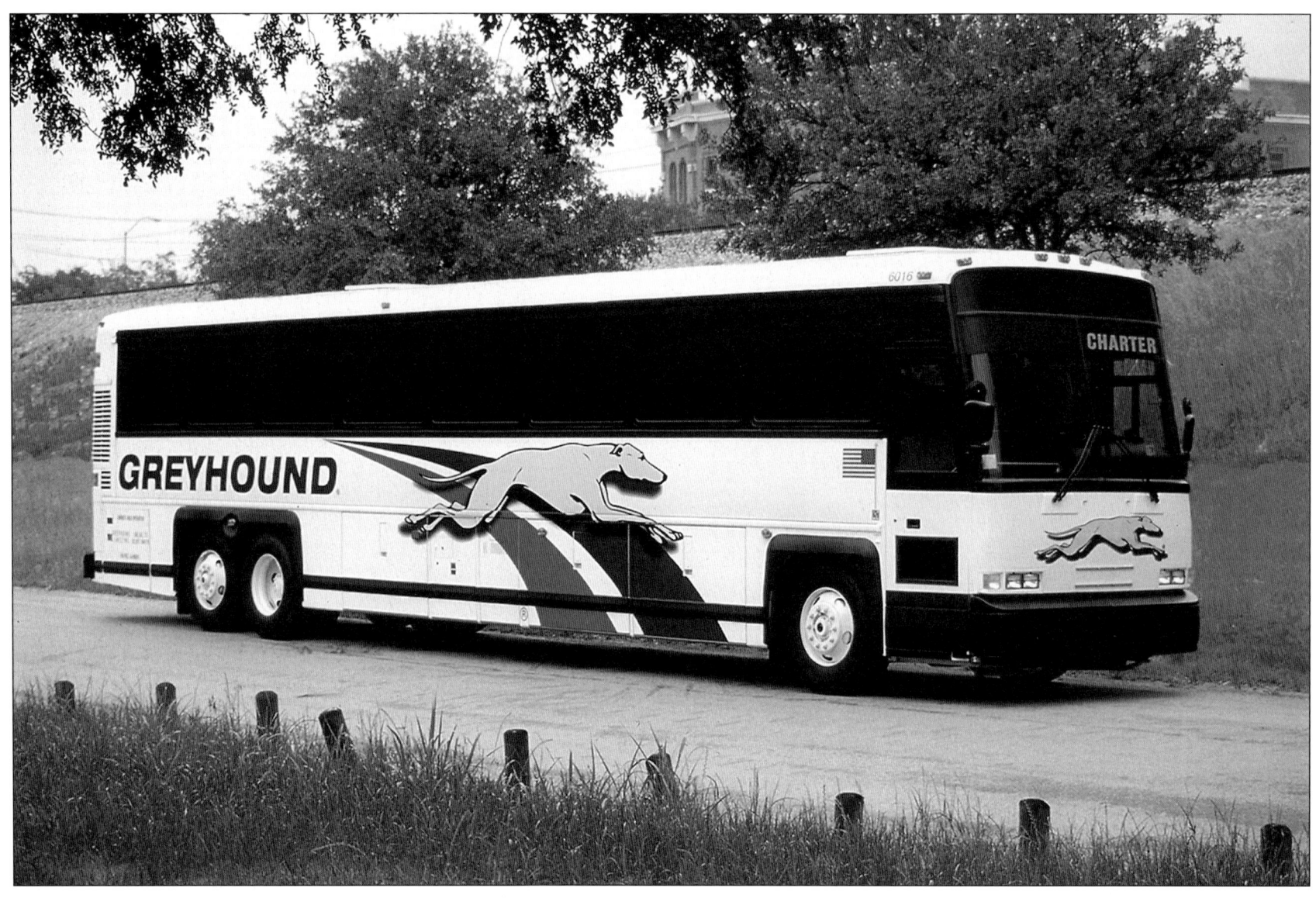
Greyhound began adding Motor Coach Industries 102DL3 buses to the fleet in 1998. At that time 70 were delivered, with 34 more following over the next two years. This bus type no longer had stainless-steel sides, which allowed opportunities for enhanced graphics. A larger Greyhound running dog is featured with a background of red, white, and blue curved strips. A running dog also appears on the front of the bus. These were the first 45-foot Greyhound buses.

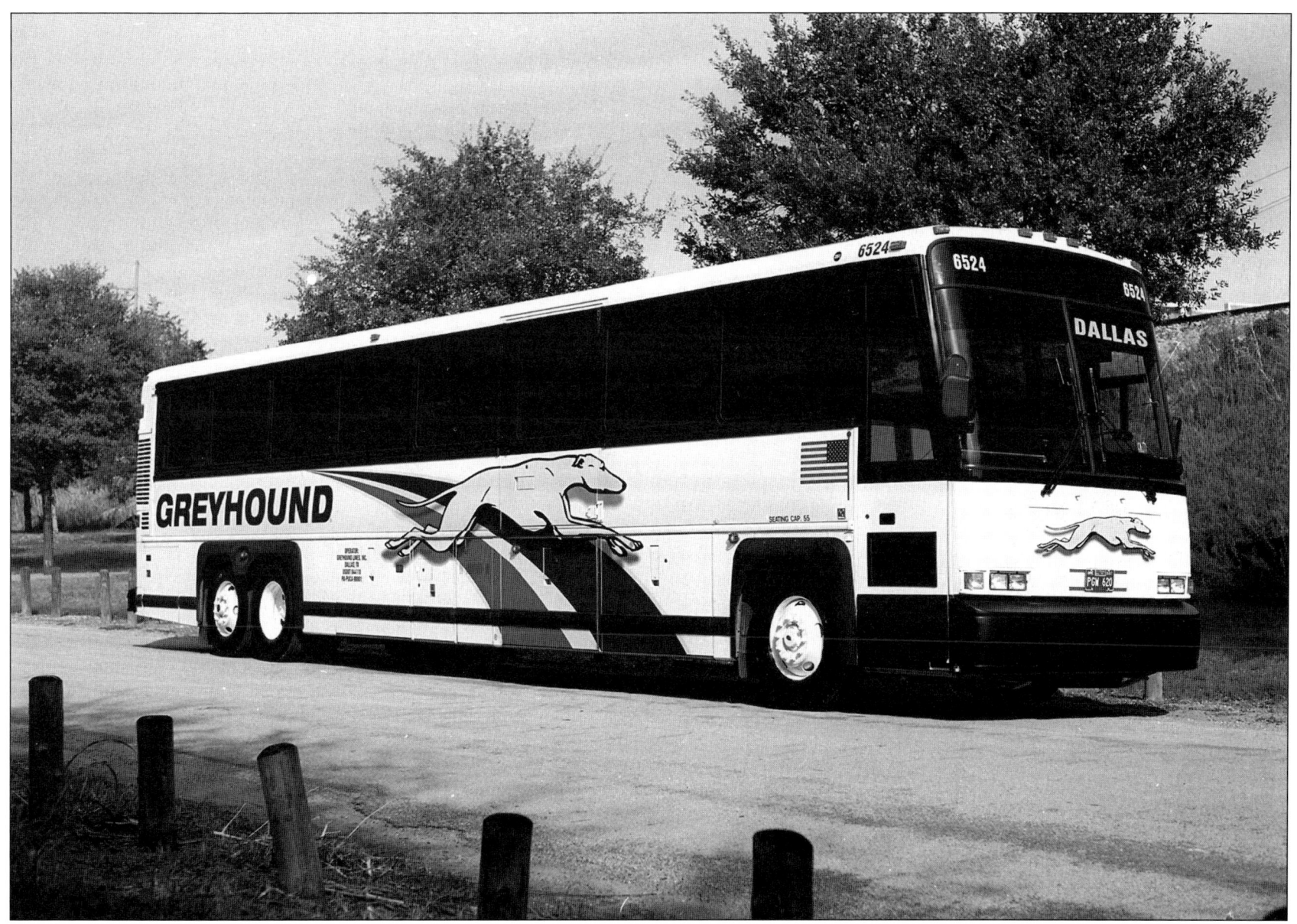

Beginning in 2000, all new Greyhound buses, like this Motor Coach Industries 45-foot 102DL3, use wheelchair lifts. The new buses also have the new Greyhound graphics, representing the first change in the popular red, white, and blue that was introduced in the 1970s.

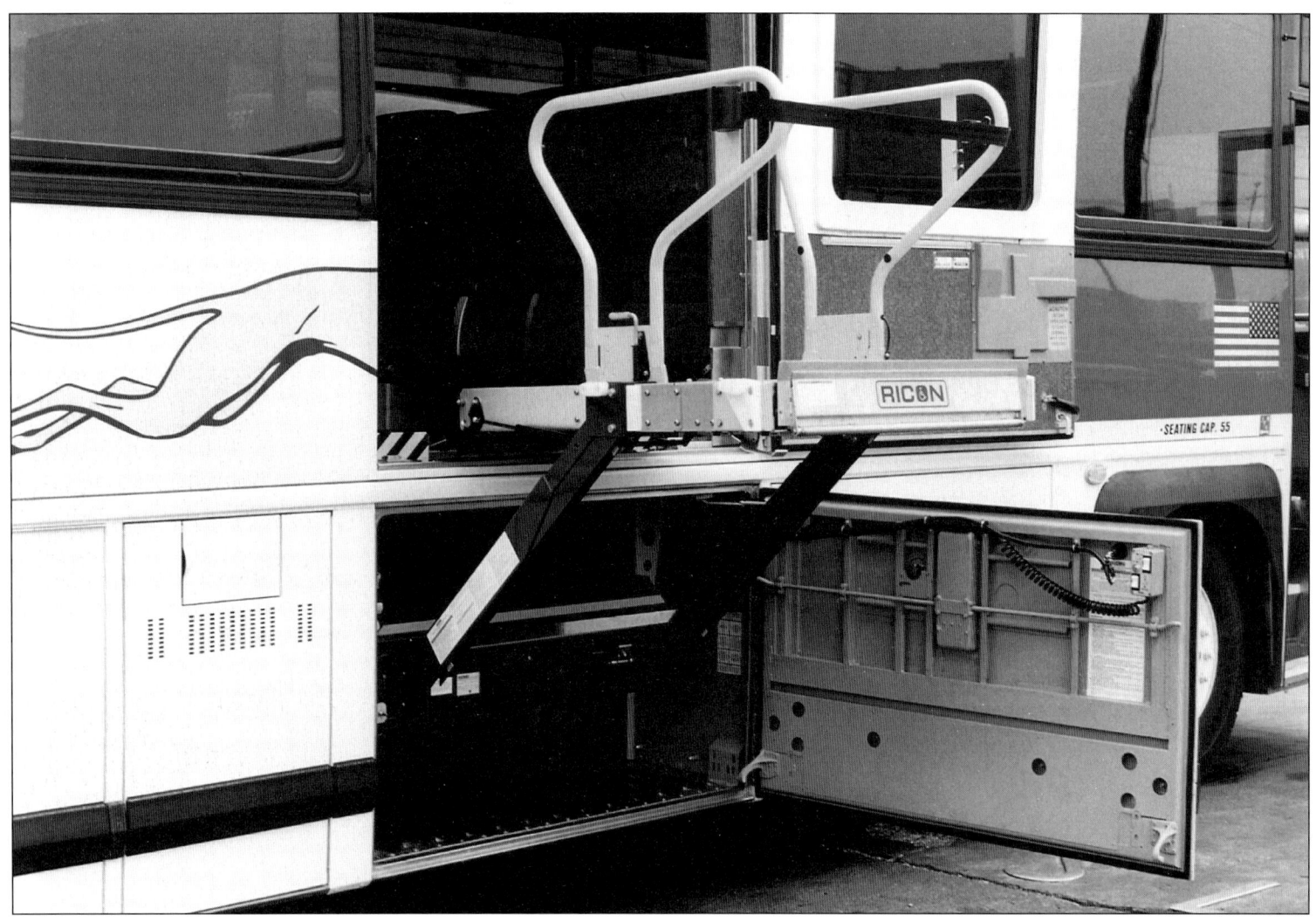

Wheelchair lifts became standard on all new Greyhound buses in 2000. With the introduction of the lifts, the company began its "Access Greyhound" program. The program, which initially involved 500 employees, presented the requirements of the Americans with Disabilities Act (ADA) and gave demonstrations of lift operation. The program has continued.

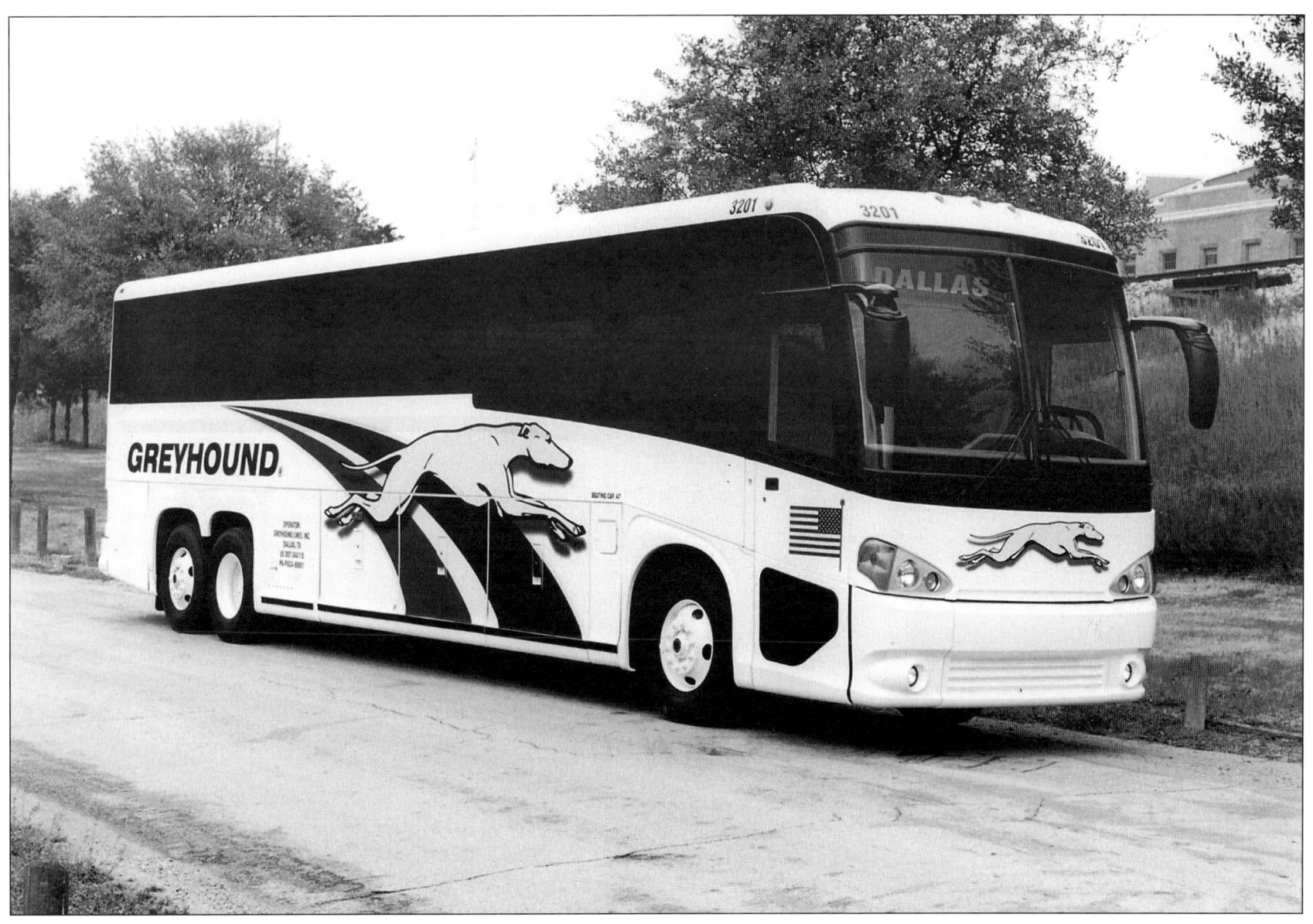

Greyhound began receiving the Motor Coach Industries 102G3 model in 2000. This bus had considerable styling changes, especially in the front with stylized light treatment. Also, a number of improvements in passenger comfort and mechanical performance were incorporated.

Greyhound Bus Origin Museum

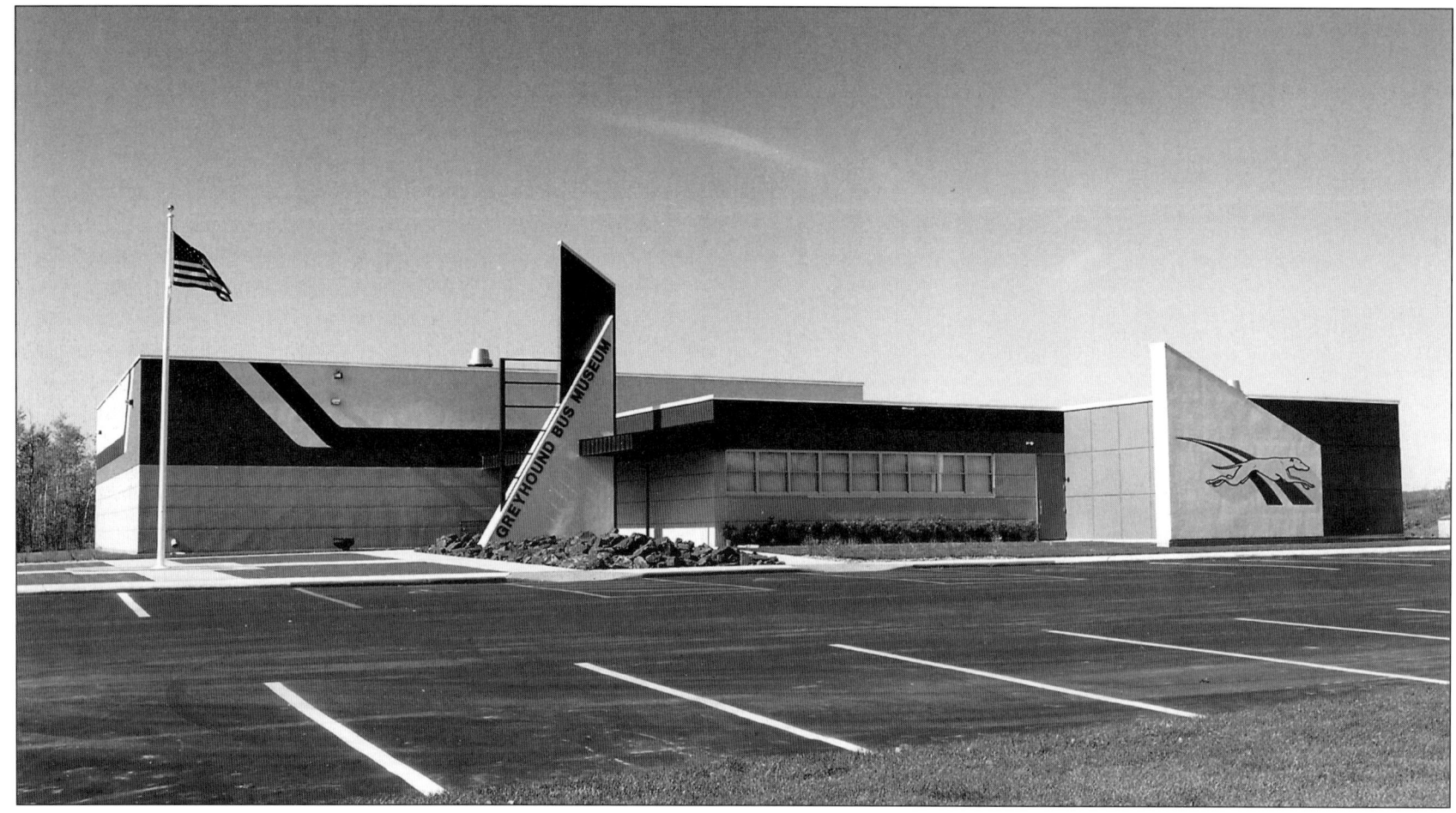

On July 10, 1999, the Greyhound Bus Origin Museum was opened in Hibbing, Minnesota, on Greyhound Boulevard. That was the bus route of the original bus line that eventually became the transcontinental Greyhound system. The Museum is a result of the enthusiasm and dedication of the Director, Gene Nicolelli, as well as the many volunteers in the Hibbing area. It is also the result of contributions of many companies and firms interested in preserving the history of Greyhound. The Museum houses several restored buses and many artifacts. *Greyhound Bus Origin Museum*

Restored Buses

Greyhound Lines, which has had a rich history for more than 80 years, has preserved some of the history by restoring several buses that operated Greyhound service over the years.

At present, there are seven buses in the Greyhound restored buses fleet. They are a 1914 Hupmobile touring car (reported to be Greyhound's first "bus" in 1914) a 1931 Mack, a 1937 Yellow Coach Model 743 Super Coach, a 1947 General Motors PD 3751 Silversides, a 1948 Greyhound ACF-Brill IC/41, a 1953 Greyhound General Motors PD 4501 Scenicruiser, and a 1968 Motor Coach Industries MC-7.

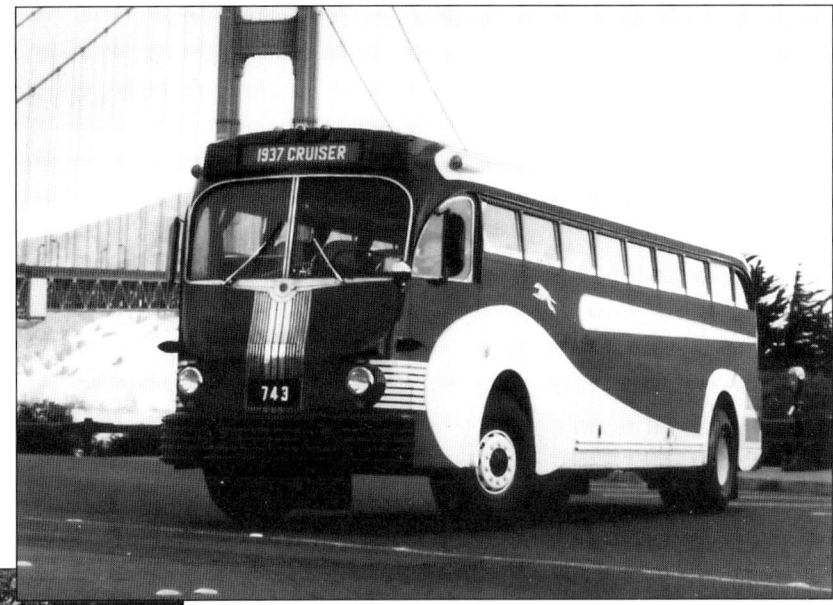

1937 Greyhound Super Coach

These buses have appeared in promotional events in various cities. The buses have also appeared in movies and television presentations. The restorations started in the 1970s.

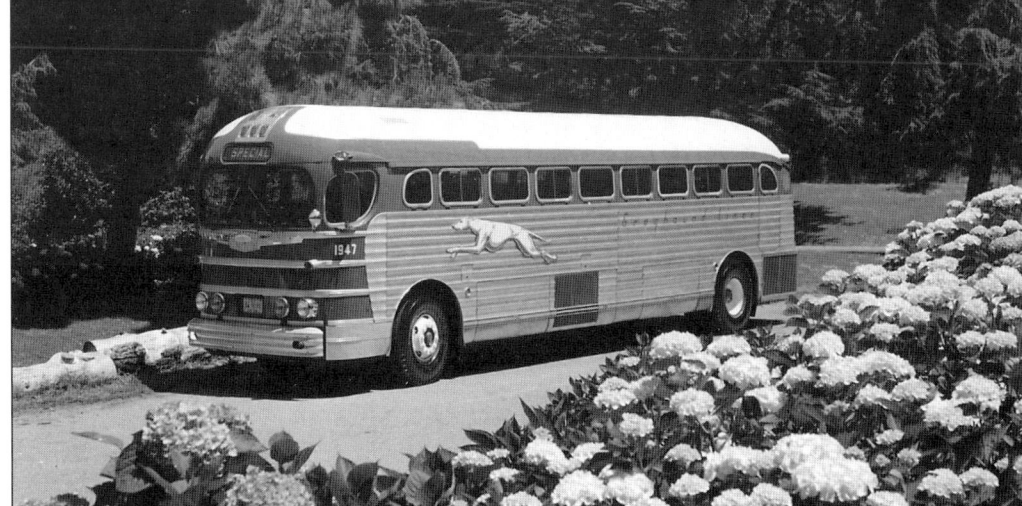

1947 Greyhound Silversides

1948 Greyhound ACF-Brill

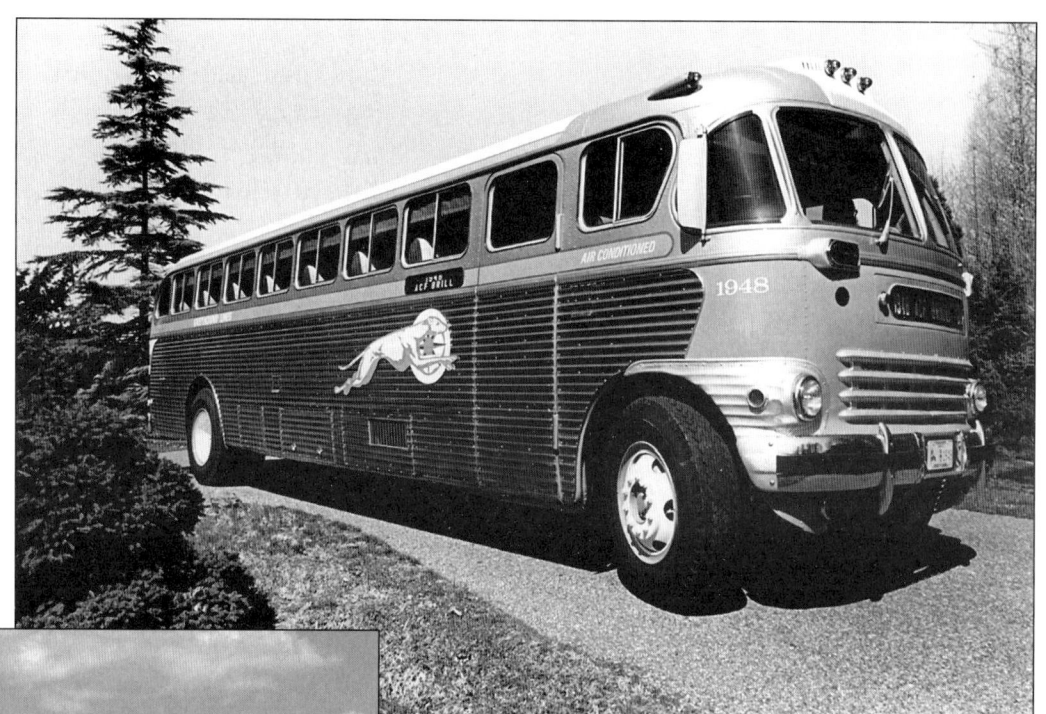

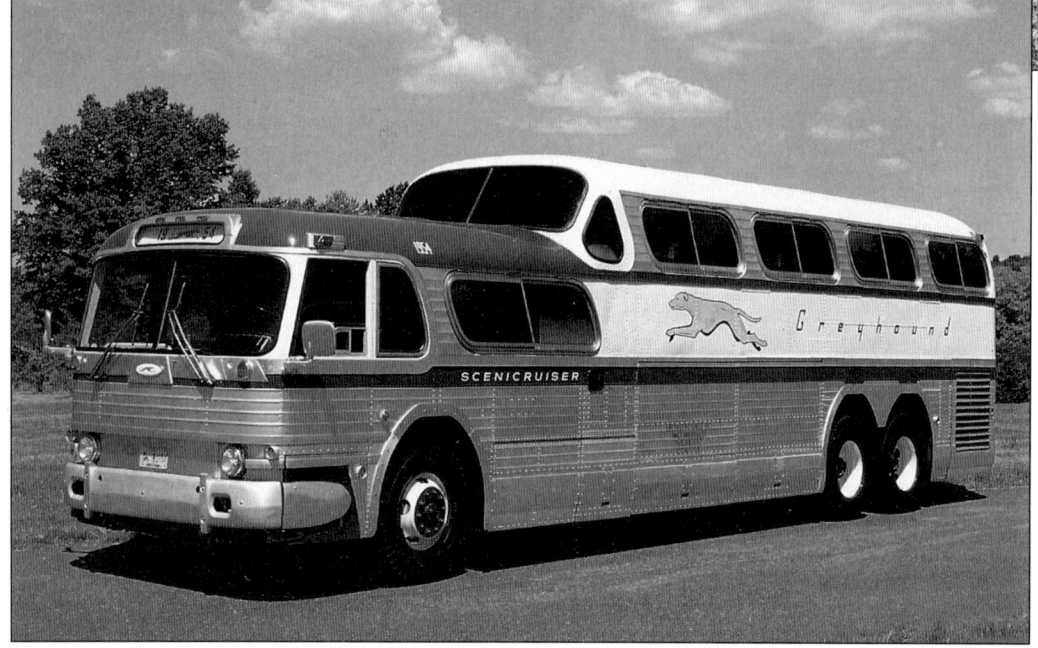

1953 Greyhound Scenicruiser

Tour Travel Brochures

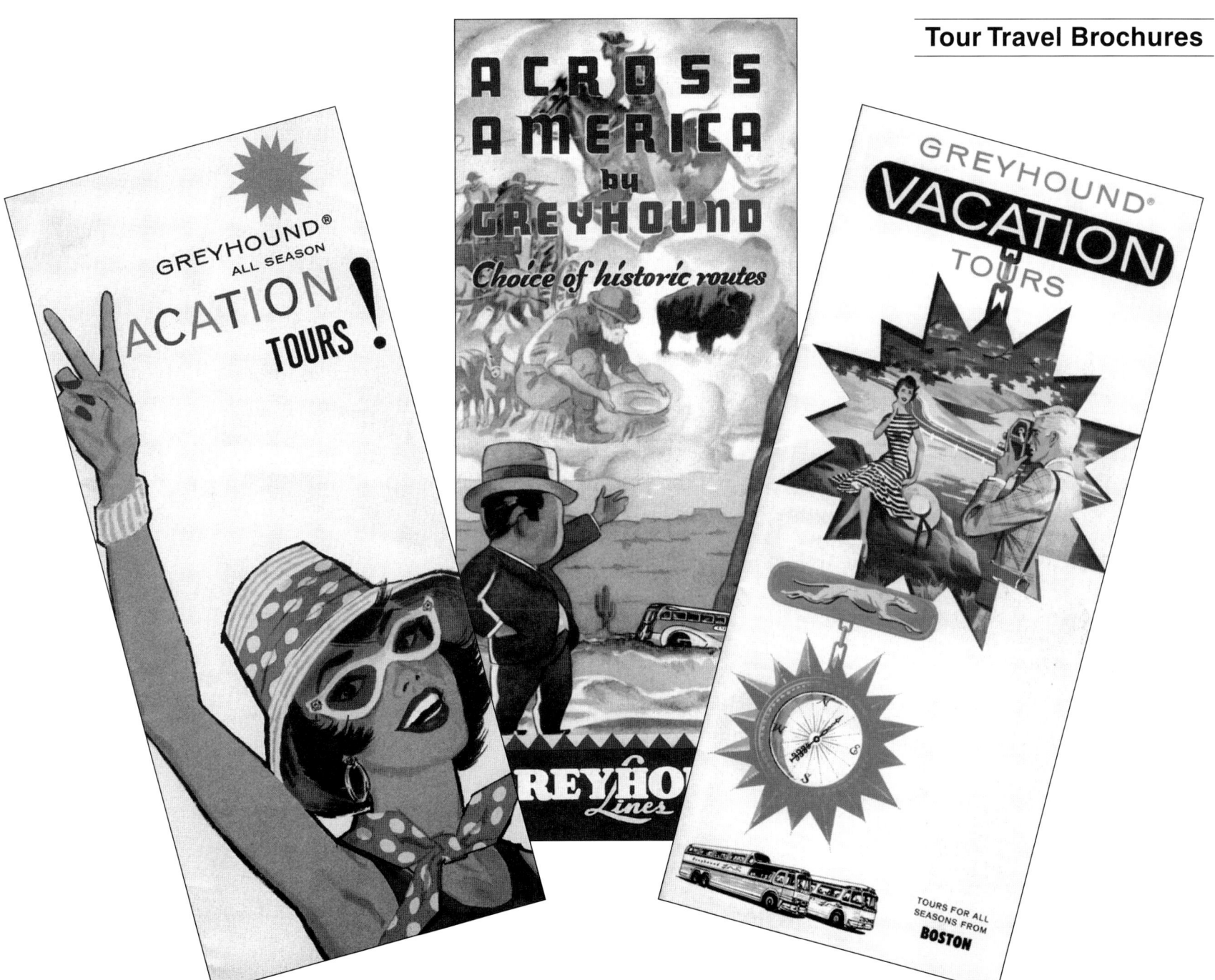

Time Tables

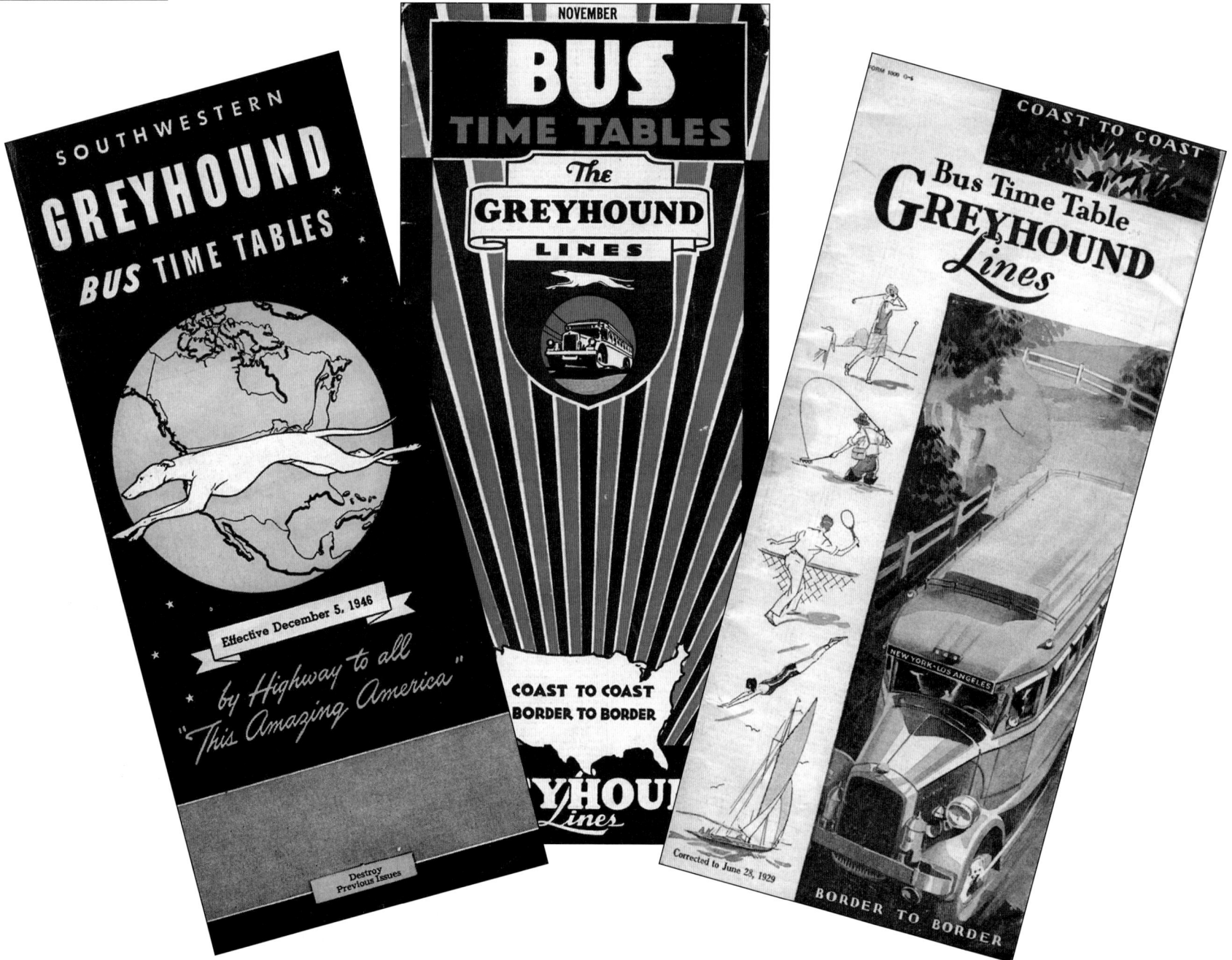

NORTHLAND TRANSPORTATION CO.

TWIN CITIES—FOREST LAKE—TAYLORS FALLS
FREDERIC—GRANTSBURG—SUPERIOR—DULUTH

READ DOWN — READ UP — **5**

Daily P.M.	Daily P.M.	Daily A.M.		Daily A.M.	Daily P.M.	Ex. Sun. P.M.	Sun. Only P.M.
5 30	1 00	9 30	Lv.**Minneapolis**†....Ar	11 20	5 50	8 40	9 40
6 10	1 40	10 05	Lv.**St. Paul**†....Ar	10 45	5 15	8 05	9 05
6 35	2 05	10 30	White Bear	10 17	4 47	7 37	8 37
			Collett				
6 45	2 15	10 40	Hugo	10 07	4 37	7 27	8 27
			Vet's Rest Lodge				
			Garen				
6 55	2 28	10 50	**Forest Lake** (1)	9 55	4 25	7 15	8 15
7 02	2 34	10 57	Wyoming Cor	9 47	4 17	7 07	8 07
			Bonnie Glen				
7 12	2 44	11 07	Chisago City	9 37	4 07	6 57	7 57
7 17	2 49	11 12	Lindstrom	9 32	4 02	6 52	7 52
7 22	2 53	11 16	Center City	9 28	3 58	6 48	7 48
7 27	2 59	11 22	Shafer Road	9 22	3 52	6 42	7 42
7 37	3 10	11 32	Ar.**Taylors Falls, Minn**Lv	9 10	3 40	6 30	7 30
7 45	3 15	11 37	Lv.**Taylors Falls**....Ar	9 03	3 40	6 30	7 23
7 48	3 17	11 40	St. Croix Falls, Wis.	9 00	3 35	6 25	7 20
8 06	3 35	11 58	Centuria	8 42	3 17	6 07	7 02
8 21	3 50	12 13	Milltown	8 27	3 02	5 52	6 47
8 31	4 00	12 33	Luck	8 17	2 52	5 42	6 37
8 43	4 12	*12 55	Lv.**Frederic**....Lv	8 05	*2 40	5 30	6 25
8 51	x4 20	1 03	Lewis	7 55	2 15		6 15
9 03	x4 31	1 15	**Siren**	7 43	2 03		6 03
			Mudhen Lake	7 34			5 54
9 12	x4 41		Falun	7 29			5 49
9 17	x4 46		Alpha	7 24			5 44
9 22	x4 51		Grantsburg	7 15			5 35
9 35	x5 00		Webster				
	1 24		Danbury		1 54		
	1 40		Green and White		1 38		
	1 57		Riverside Park		1 21		
	2 08		Cozy Corner		1 10		
	*2 23		**Dairyland**....Lv		*1 00		
	2 32		Moose Road		12 46		
	2 42		Chaffey		12 36		
	2 58		Manitou Falls		12 20		
	3 20		**Superior, Wis.** (11)		12 00		
	3 35		Ar.**Duluth, Minn.**†..Lv		11 45		

x—Sunday only.
*—Comfort stop.
f—Stop on signal.
†—See index for connecting schedules.

DULUTH, TWO HARBORS, GRAND MARAIS, FORT WILLIAM, PORT ARTHUR

READ DOWN — READ UP — **6**

Sun. only P.M.	Daily P.M.	Daily P.M.	Daily A.M.	Daily A.M.	(Central Time)	Daily A.M.	Daily A.M.	Daily P.M.	Daily P.M.	Daily P.M.	Sun. only P.M.
11 30	7 00	5 15	4 00	1 30	Lv.**Duluth**†....Ar	9 50	11 20	3 20	3 50	6 50	9 50
11 50	7 20	5 35	4 20	1 50	f Lakewood	9 30	11 00	3 00	3 30	6 30	9 30
11 55	7 25	5 40	4 25	1 55	French River	9 25	10 55	2 55	3 25	6 25	9 25
12 00	7 30	5 45	4 30	2 00	f Palmers	9 20	10 50	2 50	3 20	6 20	9 20
12 06	7 36	5 51	4 36	2 06	Knife River	9 14	10 44	2 44	3 14	6 14	9 14
12 09	7 39	5 54	4 39	2 09	Larsmont	9 11	10 43	2 41	3 11	6 11	9 11
12 20	7 50	6 05	4 50	2 20	Ar.**Two Harbors**...Lv	9 00	10 30	2 30	3 00	6 00	9 00
		6 05			Lv.**Two Harbors**...Ar		10 30		3 00		
		f			f Stewart River						
		f			f Encampment River						
		f			f Gooseberry River						
		f			f Split Rock						
		f			Kings Landing						
		6 50			Beaver Bay		9 30		2 10		
		f			f Baptism River						
		7 10			Ar.**Ilgen City**...Lv		9 10		1 55		
		7 15			Lv.**Ilgen City**...Ar		9 05		1 50		
		7 25			Little Marais		9 00		1 35		
		f			f Manitou River						
		f			f Caribou River						
		f			f Two Island River						
		7 50			Schroeder		8 32		1 10		
		7 55			Tofte		8 27		1 00		
		8 10			Lutsen		8 15		12 45		
		f			f Cascade						
		f			f Good Harbor Hill						
		8 40			Ar.**Grand Marais**..Lv		7 45		12 05		
		1 10			Lv.**Grand Marais**..Ar				11 45		
		f			f Five Mile Rock						
		1 35			Naniboujou				11 20		
		1 50			Hovland				11 05		
		f			f Big Bay						
		2 20			Mineral Center				10 45		
		2 35			Ar.**Pigeon River**...Lv				10 25		

(Eastern Standard Time)

		4 15			Lv.**U. S. Boundary**..Ar				11 00		
		f			Middle Falls, Ont.						
		f			Pine River						
		f			Jarvis Cor.						
		f			Hamilton Cor.						
		6 00			Fort William				9 20		
		6 15			Ar.**Port Arthur**...Lv				9 00		

f—Stop on signal.
†—See index for connecting schedules.

Why Northland-Greyhound Travel is Better

- Costs Less
- More Convenient
- Dependable Service
- Saves Time
- Nation-Wide System
- Careful, Courteous Drivers

Safe Reliable, Economical Transportation

Ask for Schedules, Fares and information.

ELLIOTT BROS. TRANSPORTATION CO.
WADENA, FERGUS FALLS, WAHPETON

READ DOWN — READ UP — **7**

Daily P.M.	Daily A.M.		Daily A.M.	Daily P.M.
5 50	7 30	Lv.**Wadena** (13-17)....Ar	10 20	7 20
6 10	7 55	Deer Creek	10 00	6 35
6 25	8 15	Henning	9 45	6 10
6 45	8 35	Vining	9 25	6 10
7 00	8 50	Clitherall	9 10	6 00
7 10	9 05	Battle Lake	9 00	5 45
7 25	9 20	Underwood	8 45	5 30
7 40	9 35	f Wall Lake	8 25	5 15
7 50	9 50	Ar.**Fergus Falls** (18)..Lv	8 15	5 00
	11 00	Lv.**Fergus Falls**....Ar		2 30
	11 30	f Foxhome		2 00
	11 45	f Everdell		1 45
	11 55	**Breckenridge**, Minn.		1 35
	12 00	Ar. **Wahpeton** (30), N.D. Lv.		1 30

f—Stop on signal.
Direct connections at Wadena to and from Duluth.

ST. CLOUD — MILACA — MORA — HINCKLEY

READ DOWN — READ UP — **8**

Daily A.M.		Daily P.M.
8 00	Lv.**St. Cloud** (15-16-17-18) ...Ar	2 42
8 20	f Parent	2 22
8 27	f Foley	2 14
8 32	Ronneby	2 08
8 38	Oak Park	2 02
8 48	Foreston	1 50
8 55	**Milaca** (9)	1 45
9 10	Bock	1 34
9 22	Ogilvie	1 22
9 37	**Mora** (9)	1 07
9 49	Quamba	12 55
9 58	Brook Park	12 46
	f Mission Creek	
10 14	Ar.**Hinckley** (1)....Lv	12 30
10 33	Lv.**Hinckley**....Ar	12 09
	f Friesland	
10 51	Sandstone	11 53
	f Finlayson Road	
11 05	Rutledge	11 39
11 12	Willow River	11 33
11 18	Sturgeon Lake	11 26
11 28	Moose Lake	11 16
11 34	Barnum	11 11
11 42	Mahtowa	11 01
11 47	Atkinson	10 54
11 55	**Carlton** (1-13)	10 40
12 00	Ar.**Cloquet Transfer**.Lv	10 30
12 20	Lv.**Cloquet Transfer**..Ar	10 10
	f Scanlon	
12 30	Cloquet	10 00
	f Esko's Corner	
	f Nopeming Rd.	
12 45	Ar.**Duluth** †....Lv	10 00
1 30	Lv.**Duluth** †....Ar	9 30	9 50
1 57	f Four Corners	9 00	9 20
	f Outlet		
2 05	f Twig	8 53	9 13
2 10	**N. E. Crossing** (14)	8 48	9 08
	f Independence		
2 23	f Canyon	8 37	8 57
	f Three Lakes Rd.		
2 40	Cotton	8 25	8 45
	f Ellsmere Road		
2 52	f Central Lakes	8 05	8 25
	f Town Line Road		
	f Half Moon Lake		
3 15	**Eveleth** (10)	7 45	
3 30	**Virginia** (4-10)	7 30	
3 43	Mountain Iron	7 14	
4 01	Buhl	6 58	
4 11	**Chisholm** (1)	6 48	7 44
4 25	Ar.**Hibbing** (9-10)..Lv	6 30	7 30

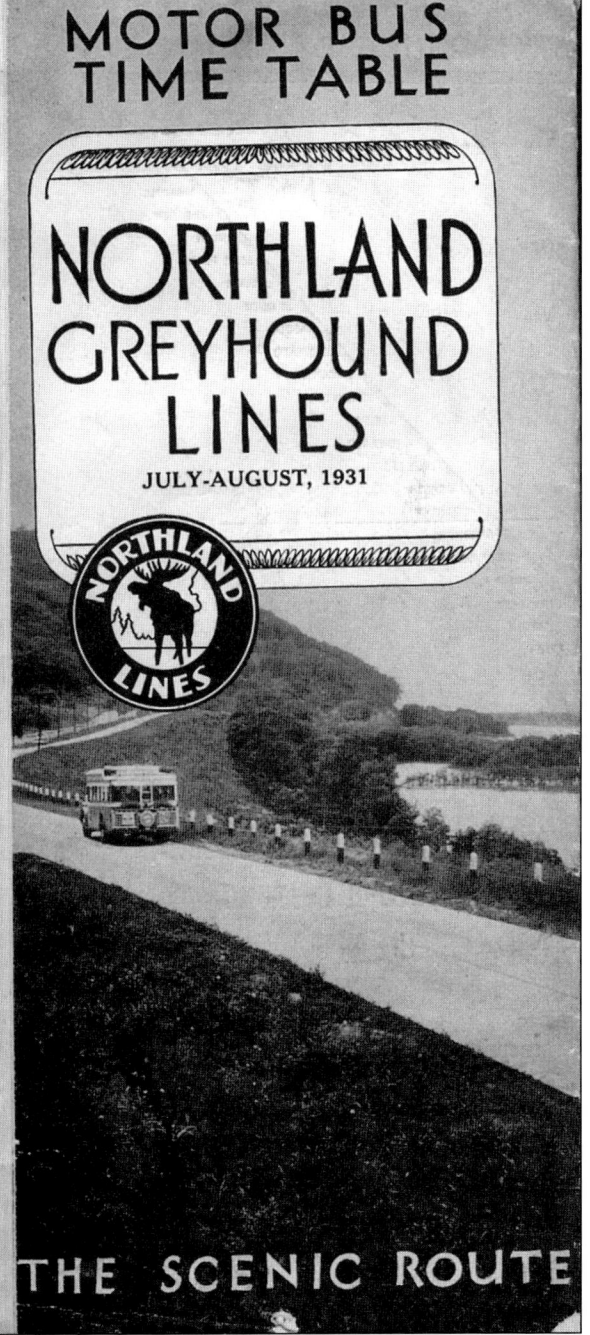

MOTOR BUS TIME TABLE

NORTHLAND GREYHOUND LINES

JULY-AUGUST, 1931

THE SCENIC ROUTE

A Word from the Author

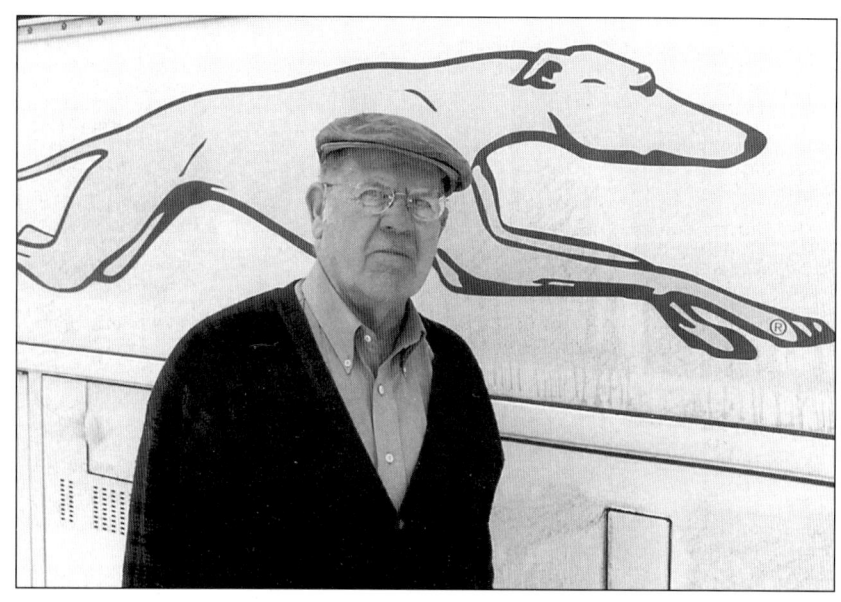

The bus industry has been my vocation and avocation for many years. I have enjoyed more than 50 years employed in the bus industry, 25 years in various positions with intercity bus companies, and more than 30 years owning a bus industry trade journal with my wife, Adelene.

Although I was never employed by Greyhound Lines, I have always had a special interest in Greyhound. I grew up in Virginia, Minnesota, just 26 miles from Hibbing, where Greyhound had its beginnings.

I spent considerable time during my school days visiting the bus depot in Virginia and selling newspapers in order to earn enough money to travel by Greyhound to Hibbing, Duluth and other nearby cities. My first long trip on Greyhound Lines was between Virginia and Minneapolis in 1936 aboard one of the new Greyhound Model 719 Super Coaches. I believe that trip and that bus convinced me to follow a career in bus transportation.

Since that time, I have traveled thousands of miles on Greyhound buses. I have been on most Greyhound model buses, including the Super Coach and even older models such as Will and Yellow Coach Z-250 buses.
I have also established friendships with bus industry people around the world. Many of these friends have been Greyhound people.

Some of the bus people I have met have been the pioneers of bus transportation. One was Andy Anderson, who with Carl Wickman and others began the Greyhound venture in Hibbing in 1914. Another pioneer with whom I had many enjoyable visits was Pete Eckland, whose company, Eckland Brothers, built many buses for Greyhound in the 1920s.

My library of bus transportation includes considerable bus history information. There are many books, trade journals, reports, timetables, and a large selection of bus photographs, many of which appear in this Photo Archive.

The bus industry has been a very enjoyable and rewarding life for my wife and myself.

William A. Luke
March, 2000

More Titles from Iconografix:

AMERICAN CULTURE
AMERICAN SERVICE STATIONS 1935-1943 PHOTO ARCHIVE	ISBN 1-882256-27-1
COCA-COLA: A HISTORY IN PHOTOGRAPHS 1930-1969	ISBN 1-882256-46-8
COCA-COLA: ITS VEHICLES IN PHOTOGRAPHS 1930-1969	ISBN 1-882256-47-6
PHILLIPS 66 1945-1954 PHOTO ARCHIVE	ISBN 1-882256-42-5

AUTOMOTIVE
CADILLAC 1948-1964 PHOTO ALBUM	ISBN 1-882256-83-2
CAMARO 1967-2000 PHOTO ARCHIVE	ISBN 1-58388-032-1
CORVETTE THE EXOTIC EXPERIMENTAL CARS, LUDVIGSEN LIBRARY SERIES	ISBN 1-58388-017-8
CORVETTE PROTOTYPES & SHOW CARS PHOTO ALBUM	ISBN 1-882256-77-8
EARLY FORD V-8S 1932-1942 PHOTO ALBUM	ISBN 1-882256-97-2
IMPERIAL 1955-1963 PHOTO ARCHIVE	ISBN 1-882256-22-0
IMPERIAL 1964-1968 PHOTO ARCHIVE	ISBN 1-882256-23-9
LINCOLN MOTOR CARS 1920-1942 PHOTO ARCHIVE	ISBN 1-882256-57-3
LINCOLN MOTOR CARS 1946-1960 PHOTO ARCHIVE	ISBN 1-882256-58-1
PACKARD MOTOR CARS 1935-1942 PHOTO ARCHIVE	ISBN 1-882256-44-1
PACKARD MOTOR CARS 1946-1958 PHOTO ARCHIVE	ISBN 1-882256-45-X
PONTIAC DREAM CARS, SHOW CARS & PROTOTYPES 1928-1998 PHOTO ALBUM	ISBN 1-882256-93-X
PONTIAC FIREBIRD TRANS-AM 1969-1999 PHOTO ALBUM	ISBN 1-882256-95-6
PONTIAC FIREBIRD 1967-2000 PHOTO HISTORY	ISBN 1-58388-028-3
STUDEBAKER 1933-1942 PHOTO ARCHIVE	ISBN 1-882256-24-7
STUDEBAKER 1946-1958 PHOTO ARCHIVE	ISBN 1-882256-25-5

BUSES
THE GENERAL MOTORS NEW LOOK BUS PHOTO ARCHIVE	ISBN 1-58388-007-0
GREYHOUND BUSES 1914-2000 PHOTO ARCHIVE	ISBN 1-58388-027-5
MACK® BUSES 1900-1960 PHOTO ARCHIVE*	ISBN 1-58388-020-8
TRAILWAYS BUSES 1936-2001 PHOTO ARCHIVE	ISBN 1-58388-029-1

EMERGENCY VEHICLES
AMERICAN LAFRANCE 700 SERIES 1945-1952 PHOTO ARCHIVE	ISBN 1-882256-90-5
AMERICAN LAFRANCE 700 SERIES 1945-1952 PHOTO ARCHIVE VOLUME 2	ISBN 1-58388-025-9
AMERICAN LAFRANCE 700 & 800 SERIES 1953-1958 PHOTO ARCHIVE	ISBN 1-882256-91-3
AMERICAN LAFRANCE 900 SERIES 1958-1964 PHOTO ARCHIVE	ISBN 1-58388-002-X
CLASSIC AMERICAN AMBULANCES 1900-1979 PHOTO ARCHIVE	ISBN 1-882256-94-8
CLASSIC AMERICAN FUNERAL VEHICLES 1900-1980 PHOTO ARCHIVE	ISBN 1-58388-016-X
CLASSIC SEAGRAVE 1935-1951 PHOTO ARCHIVE	ISBN 1-58388-034-8
FIRE CHIEF CARS 1900-1997 PHOTO ALBUM	ISBN 1-882256-87-5
LOS ANGELES CITY FIRE APPARATUS 1953 - 1999 PHOTO ARCHIVE	ISBN 1-58388-012-7
MACK MODEL B FIRE TRUCKS 1954-1966 PHOTO ARCHIVE*	ISBN 1-882256-62-X
MACK MODEL C FIRE TRUCKS 1957-1967 PHOTO ARCHIVE*	ISBN 1-58388-014-3
MACK MODEL CF FIRE TRUCKS 1967-1981 PHOTO ARCHIVE*	ISBN 1-882256-63-8
MACK MODEL L FIRE TRUCKS 1940-1954 PHOTO ARCHIVE*	ISBN 1-882256-86-7
NAVY & MARINE CORPS FIRE APPARATUS 1836 -2000 PHOTO GALLERY	ISBN 1-58388-031-3
PIERCE ARROW FIRE APPARATUS 1979-1998 PHOTO ARCHIVE	ISBN 1-58388-023-2
SEAGRAVE 70TH ANNIVERSARY SERIES PHOTO ARCHIVE	ISBN 1-58388-001-1
VOLUNTEER & RURAL FIRE APPARATUS PHOTO GALLERY	ISBN 1-58388-005-4
WARD LAFRANCE FIRE TRUCKS 1918-1978 PHOTO ARCHIVE	ISBN 1-58388-013-5
YOUNG FIRE EQUIPMENT 1932-1991 PHOTO ARCHIVE	ISBN 1-58388-015-1

RACING
GT40 PHOTO ARCHIVE	ISBN 1-882256-64-6
INDY CARS OF THE 1950s, LUDVIGSEN LIBRARY SERIES	ISBN 1-58388-018-6
INDIANAPOLIS RACING CARS OF FRANK KURTIS 1941-1963 PHOTO ARCHIVE	ISBN 1-58388-026-7
JUAN MANUEL FANGIO WORLD CHAMPION DRIVER SERIES PHOTO ALBUM	ISBN 1-58388-008-9
LE MANS 1950: THE BRIGGS CUNNINGHAM CAMPAIGN PHOTO ARCHIVE	ISBN 1-882256-21-2
MARIO ANDRETTI WORLD CHAMPION DRIVER SERIES PHOTO ALBUM	ISBN 1-58388-009-7
SEBRING 12-HOUR RACE 1970 PHOTO ARCHIVE	ISBN 1-882256-20-4
VANDERBILT CUP RACE 1936 & 1937 PHOTO ARCHIVE	ISBN 1-882256-66-2
WILLIAMS 1969-1998 30 YEARS OF GRAND PRIX RACING PHOTO ALBUM	ISBN 1-58388-000-3

RAILWAYS
CHICAGO, ST. PAUL, MINNEAPOLIS & OMAHA RAILWAY 1880-1940 PHOTO ARCHIVE	ISBN 1-882256-67-0
CHICAGO & NORTH WESTERN RAILWAY 1975-1995 PHOTO ARCHIVE	ISBN 1-882256-76-X
GREAT NORTHERN RAILWAY 1945-1970 PHOTO ARCHIVE	ISBN 1-882256-56-5
GREAT NORTHERN RAILWAY 1945-1970 VOL 2 PHOTO ARCHIVE	ISBN 1-882256-79-4
MILWAUKEE ROAD 1850-1960 PHOTO ARCHIVE	ISBN 1-882256-61-1
SHOW TRAINS OF THE 20TH CENTURY	ISBN 1-58388-030-5
SOO LINE 1975-1992 PHOTO ARCHIVE	ISBN 1-882256-68-9
TRAINS OF THE TWIN PORTS, DULUTH-SUPERIOR IN THE 1950s PHOTO ARCHIVE	ISBN 1-58388-003-8
TRAINS OF THE CIRCUS 1872-1956 PHOTO ARCHIVE	ISBN 1-58388-024-0
WISCONSIN CENTRAL LIMITED 1987-1996 PHOTO ARCHIVE	ISBN 1-882256-75-1
WISCONSIN CENTRAL RAILWAY 1871-1909 PHOTO ARCHIVE	ISBN 1-882256-78-6

TRUCKS
BEVERAGE TRUCKS 1910-1975 PHOTO ARCHIVE	ISBN 1-882256-60-3
BROCKWAY TRUCKS 1948-1961 PHOTO ARCHIVE*	ISBN 1-882256-55-7
DODGE PICKUPS 1939-1978 PHOTO ALBUM	ISBN 1-882256-82-4
DODGE POWER WAGONS 1940-1980 PHOTO ARCHIVE	ISBN 1-882256-89-1
DODGE POWER WAGON PHOTO HISTORY	ISBN 1-58388-019-4
DODGE TRUCKS 1929-1947 PHOTO ARCHIVE	ISBN 1-882256-36-0
DODGE TRUCKS 1948-1960 PHOTO ARCHIVE	ISBN 1-882256-37-9
JEEP 1941-2000 PHOTO ARCHIVE	ISBN 1-58388-021-6
JEEP PROTOTYPES & CONCEPT VEHICLES PHOTO ARCHIVE	ISBN 1-58388-033-X
LOGGING TRUCKS 1915-1970 PHOTO ARCHIVE	ISBN 1-882256-59-X
MACK MODEL AB PHOTO ARCHIVE*	ISBN 1-882256-18-2
MACK AP SUPER-DUTY TRUCKS 1926-1938 PHOTO ARCHIVE*	ISBN 1-882256-54-9
MACK MODEL B 1953-1966 VOL 1 PHOTO ARCHIVE*	ISBN 1-882256-19-0
MACK MODEL B 1953-1966 VOL 2 PHOTO ARCHIVE*	ISBN 1-882256-34-4
MACK EB-EC-ED-EE-EF-EG-DE 1936-1951 PHOTO ARCHIVE*	ISBN 1-882256-29-8
MACK EH-EJ-EM-EQ-ER-ES 1936-1950 PHOTO ARCHIVE*	ISBN 1-882256-39-5
MACK FC-FCSW-NW 1936-1947 PHOTO ARCHIVE*	ISBN 1-882256-28-X
MACK FG-FH-FJ-FK-FN-FP-FT-FW 1937-1950 PHOTO ARCHIVE*	ISBN 1-882256-35-2
MACK LF-LH-LJ-LM-LT 1940-1956 PHOTO ARCHIVE*	ISBN 1-882256-38-7
MACK TRUCKS PHOTO GALLERY*	ISBN 1-882256-88-3
NEW CAR CARRIERS 1910-1998 PHOTO ALBUM	ISBN 1-882256-98-0
PLYMOUTH COMMERCIAL VEHICLES PHOTO ARCHIVE	ISBN 1-58388-004-6
STUDEBAKER TRUCKS 1927-1940 PHOTO ARCHIVE	ISBN 1-882256-40-9
STUDEBAKER TRUCKS 1941-1964 PHOTO ARCHIVE	ISBN 1-882256-41-7
WHITE TRUCKS 1900-1937 PHOTO ARCHIVE	ISBN 1-882256-80-8

TRACTORS & CONSTRUCTION EQUIPMENT
CASE TRACTORS 1912-1959 PHOTO ARCHIVE	ISBN 1-882256-32-8
CATERPILLAR PHOTO GALLERY	ISBN 1-882256-70-0
CATERPILLAR POCKET GUIDE THE TRACK-TYPE TRACTORS 1925-1957	ISBN 1-58388-022-4
CATERPILLAR D-2 & R-2 PHOTO ARCHIVE	ISBN 1-882256-99-9
CATERPILLAR D-8 1933-1974 INCLUDING DIESEL 75 & RD-8 PHOTO ARCHIVE	ISBN 1-882256-96-4
CATERPILLAR MILITARY TRACTORS VOLUME 1 PHOTO ARCHIVE	ISBN 1-882256-16-6
CATERPILLAR MILITARY TRACTORS VOLUME 2 PHOTO ARCHIVE	ISBN 1-882256-17-4
CATERPILLAR SIXTY PHOTO ARCHIVE	ISBN 1-882256-05-0
CATERPILLAR TEN INCLUDING 7C FIFTEEN & HIGH FIFTEEN PHOTO ARCHIVE	ISBN 1-58388-011-9
CATERPILLAR THIRTY 2ND ED. INC. BEST THIRTY, 6G THIRTY & R-4 PHOTO ARCHIVE	ISBN 1-58388-006-2
CLETRAC AND OLIVER CRAWLERS PHOTO ARCHIVE	ISBN 1-882256-43-3
ERIE SHOVEL PHOTO ARCHIVE	ISBN 1-882256-69-7
FARMALL CUB PHOTO ARCHIVE	ISBN 1-882256-71-9
FARMALL F- SERIES PHOTO ARCHIVE	ISBN 1-882256-02-6
FARMALL MODEL H PHOTO ARCHIVE	ISBN 1-882256-03-4
FARMALL MODEL M PHOTO ARCHIVE	ISBN 1-882256-15-8
FARMALL REGULAR PHOTO ARCHIVE	ISBN 1-882256-14-X
FARMALL SUPER SERIES PHOTO ARCHIVE	ISBN 1-882256-49-2
FORDSON 1917-1928 PHOTO ARCHIVE	ISBN 1-882256-33-6
HART-PARR PHOTO ARCHIVE	ISBN 1-882256-08-5
HOLT TRACTORS PHOTO ARCHIVE	ISBN 1-882256-10-7
INTERNATIONAL TRACTRACTOR PHOTO ARCHIVE	ISBN 1-882256-48-4
INTERNATIONAL TD CRAWLERS 1933-1962 PHOTO ARCHIVE	ISBN 1-882256-72-7
JOHN DEERE MODEL A PHOTO ARCHIVE	ISBN 1-882256-12-3
JOHN DEERE MODEL B PHOTO ARCHIVE	ISBN 1-882256-01-8
JOHN DEERE MODEL D PHOTO ARCHIVE	ISBN 1-882256-00-X
JOHN DEERE 30 SERIES PHOTO ARCHIVE	ISBN 1-882256-13-1
MINNEAPOLIS-MOLINE U-SERIES PHOTO ARCHIVE	ISBN 1-882256-07-7
OLIVER TRACTORS PHOTO ARCHIVE	ISBN 1-882256-09-3
RUSSELL GRADERS PHOTO ARCHIVE	ISBN 1-882256-11-5
TWIN CITY TRACTOR PHOTO ARCHIVE	ISBN 1-882256-06-9

*This product is sold under license from Mack Trucks, Inc. Mack is a registered Trademark of Mack Trucks, Inc. All rigfhts reserved.

All Iconografix books are available from direct mail specialty book dealers and bookstores worldwide, or can be ordered from the publisher. For book trade and distribution information or to add your name to our mailing list and receive a **FREE CATALOG** contact:

Iconografix, PO Box 446, Hudson, Wisconsin, 54016   Telephone: (715) 381-9755, (800) 289-3504 (USA), Fax: (715) 381-9756

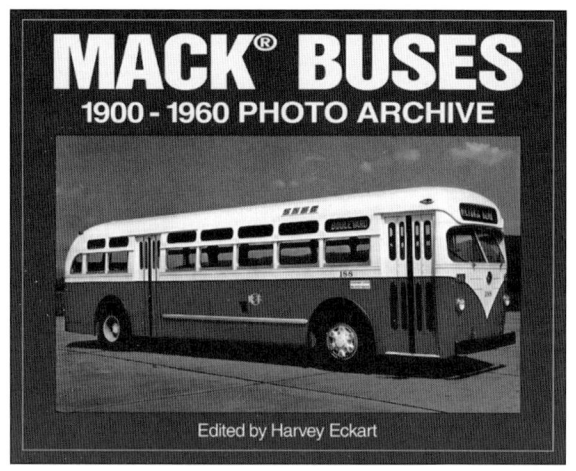

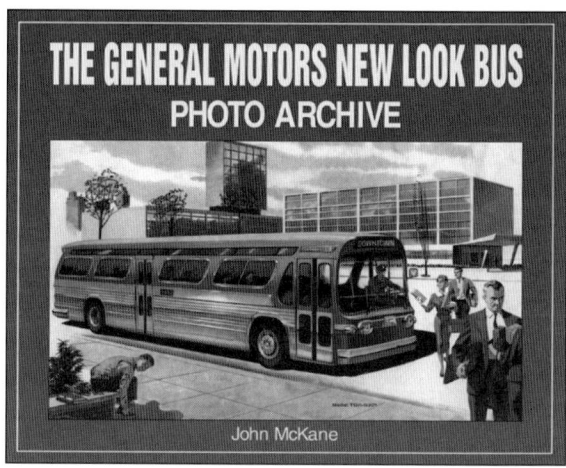

MORE GREAT BOOKS FROM ICONOGRAFIX

MACK® BUSES 1900-1960 PHOTO ARCHIVE*
ISBN 1-58388-020-8

THE GENERAL MOTORS NEW LOOK BUS PHOTO ARCHIVE
ISBN 1-58388-007-0

NEW CAR CARRIERS 1910-1998 PHOTO ALBUM
ISBN 1-882256-98-0

TRAILWAYS BUSES 1936-2001 PHOTO ARCHIVE
ISBN 1-58388-029-1

MACK TRUCKS PHOTO GALLERY*
ISBN 1-882256-88-3

VOLUNTEER & RURAL FIRE APPARATUS PHOTO GALLERY
ISBN 1-58388-005-4

NAVY & MARINE CORPS FIRE APPARATUS 1836 - 2000 PHOTO GALLERY
ISBN 1-58388-031-3

*This product is sold under license from Mack Trucks, Inc. Mack is a registered Trademark of Mack Trucks, Inc. All rigfhts reserved.

ICONOGRAFIX, INC. P.O. BOX 446, DEPT BK, HUDSON, WI 54016
FOR A FREE CATALOG CALL:
1-800-239-3504

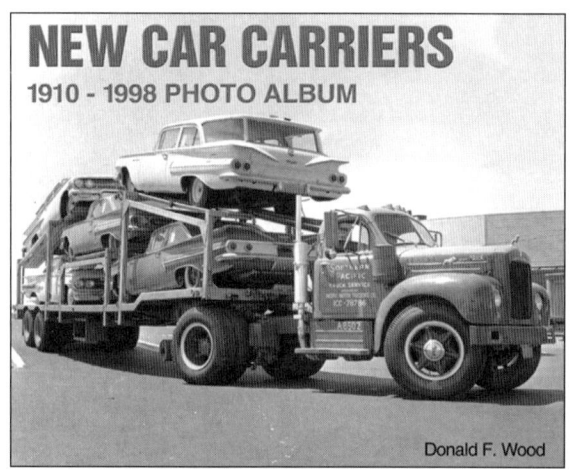

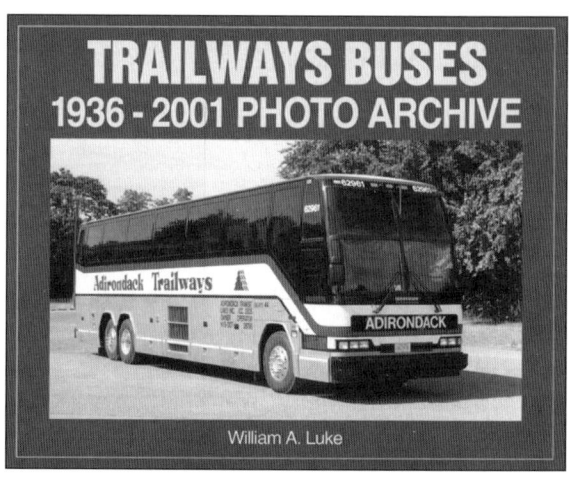

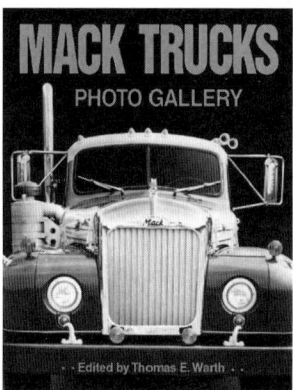

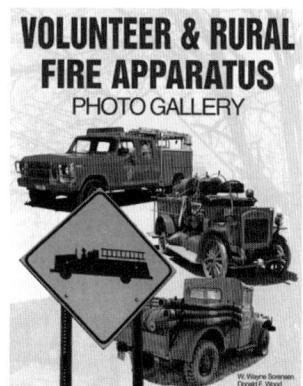

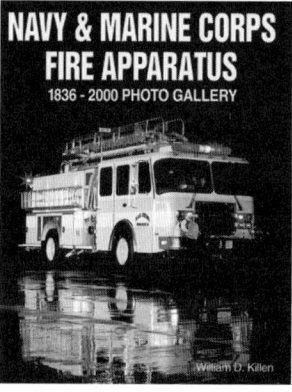